GW00738751

# Bullying in School

Lisa H. Rosen • Kathy DeOrnellas • Shannon R. Scott
Editors

# Bullying in School

## Perspectives from School Staff, Students, and Parents

*Editors*
Lisa H. Rosen
Texas Woman's University
Denton, Texas, USA

Shannon R. Scott
Texas Woman's University
Denton, Texas, USA

Kathy DeOrnellas
Texas Woman's University
Denton, Texas, USA

ISBN 978-1-137-59892-9 ISBN 978-1-137-59298-9 (eBook)
DOI 10.1057/978-1-137-59298-9

Library of Congress Control Number: 2016963364


Cover design by Fatima Jamadar

Printed on acid-free paper

This Palgrave Macmillan imprint is published by Springer Nature
The registered company is Nature America Inc.
The registered company address is: 1 New York Plaza, New York, NY 10004, U.S.A.

# Acknowledgment of Third Party Materials

We gratefully acknowledge Dr. Daniel Olweus for Fig. 2.1 depicting the spectrum of bystander roles. In addition, we gratefully acknowledge the National Association of School Nurses for the questions school nurses should ask about bullying and the responsibilities of school nurses in preventing bullying.

# Contents

# List of Contributors

***Cade Charlton*** received his doctorate from the Disability Disciplines program at Utah State University and his MBA from the Huntsman School of Business. Cade is currently a visiting Assistant Professor in the Counseling Psychology and Special Education department at Brigham Young University. His research focus is on the effects of feedback systems designed to improve outcomes for youth and adults in schools. This interest has been well served by Cade's work as a member of the Utah State Office of Education's School Support Team. As a member of the School Support Team, Cade has worked with struggling elementary and secondary schools throughout the Intermountain West. This work has included opportunities to assist in the implementation of Schoolwide Positive Behavior Support, Professional Learning Communities, and targeted interventions to reduce bullying and other antisocial behaviors.

***Kathy DeOrnellas*** earned her undergraduate degree from Stephen F. Austin State University and her doctoral degree in School Psychology from Texas Woman's University. She is currently an Associate Professor and Director of the Specialist Program in School Psychology at Texas Woman's University. Dr. DeOrnellas' research focuses on peer relationships, autism, and transition to post-secondary education for students with disabilities.

***Kenneth Jenks*** began a professional law enforcement career in 1981 when he was hired by the Killeen, TX Police Department. During his 21-year tenure in Killeen, he worked in nearly every area the Department had to offer including Patrol, Special Weapons And Tactics (SWAT), Detectives, Juvenile/Youth Services (SRO), Air Support, and Administrative Services. Kenny graduated from the FBI National Academy's 190th session in 1997. Currently, Kenny serves as the Chief of Police/ Deputy City Manager in the City of Anna, Texas. He is recognized by the State of

Texas as a Master Peace Officer and Instructor and is a certified teacher in Texas. He has received several awards for his instruction.

***Christopher Kowalski*** has an Ed.D. in Leisure, Youth and Human Services from the University of Northern Iowa. He holds a Master of Science in Recreation Management from the University of Idaho and a BA in Psychology, Sociology, and Criminal Justice from Creighton University (Nebraska). He has supervised community and youth recreation programs for over 20 years in Idaho, Iowa, Nebraska, and Texas, as well as abroad in Europe, Asia, and the Middle East. His research interests are coaching, youth leadership, and self-efficacy in the recreation field.

***Emily M. Lund*** MEd, is a current doctoral student in the Disability Disciplines program at Utah State University, where she is specializing in both special education and rehabilitation counseling. Her primary research interests include interpersonal violence, bullying, and peer victimization, especially in people with disabilities; suicide and non-suicidal self-injury, particularly as they relate trauma and disability; and the experience of psychology trainees with disabilities. She has published more than 35 peer-reviewed journal articles in outlets such as *School Psychology Quarterly*, *Psychology of Women Quarterly*, *Rehabilitation Psychology*, *Journal of Affective Disorders*, and *Trauma, Violence, and Abuse*.

***Ronald S. Palomares*** earned his Ph.D. in school psychology from Texas A&M University. He is currently the director of the school psychology doctoral program at Texas Woman's University. Previously, he served on staff at the American Psychological Association where he staffed the APA Task Force on Zero Tolerance Policies and was a coauthor on the Task Force's report (2008). His research focuses on military children and resilience. He was recently honored with the Outstanding Contribution to Public Service Award from the Texas Psychological Association.

***Lisa H. Rosen*** earned her undergraduate degree from Rice University and her doctoral degree in developmental psychology from the University of Texas at Austin. She is currently an Assistant Professor and Director of the Undergraduate Psychology Program at Texas Woman's University. Dr. Rosen's research focuses on adolescent social development, and she has previously coedited *Social Development: Relationships in Infancy, Childhood, and Adolescence*. Her current research examines risk factors for and consequences of peer victimization, and her work has been published in numerous scientific journals.

***Scott W. Ross*** Ph.D., BCBA-D, directs the Office of Learning Supports (OLS) for the Colorado Department of Education, which is responsible for advancing a Multi-Tiered System of Supports (MTSS) in the state. Previously, Dr. Ross was an Assistant Professor in the Department of Special Education and Rehabilitation at Utah State University where he taught coursework in direct instruction, curriculum development, classroom and behavior management, coaching, and systems change. Dr. Ross is also the author of the Bullying Prevention in Positive Behavior Support curriculum and corresponding empirical analyses, for which he received the Initial Research of the Year award in 2010 from the Association of Positive Behavior Support. Dr. Ross has published and reviewed extensively for education journals, including Journal of Applied Behavior Analysis, School Psychology Quarterly, Teaching Exceptional Children, and the Journal of Positive Behavior Support.

***Christian Sabey*** is a recent graduate of the Disability Disciplines doctoral program at Utah State University and currently works as an Assistant Professor at Brigham Young University in the Counseling Psychology and Special Education Department. There he teaches classes on behavior analysis and classroom management and conducts research on behavior management strategies. His research interests include school-based social skills training, implementation of multi-tiered systems of support, schoolwide positive behavior support, teacher training in behavior management, effective behavior management strategies, and the practice of applied behavior analysis in schools. Christian has worked in schools in a number of capacities including paraprofessional, dean of students, school psychologist, and behavior specialist.

***Shannon R. Scott*** earned her undergraduate degree from Stephen F Austin State University and her doctoral degree in cognitive psychology from Tufts University. She is currently the Chair of the Department of Psychology and Philosophy and a professor at Texas Woman's University. Dr. Scott's research focuses on body image, weight stigma, and anti-fat attitudes as well as examining development and consequences of peer victimization. Her work has been published in numerous scientific journals as well as encyclopedias and books.

***Angelia Spurgin*** is currently a Ph.D. candidate in the School Psychology Doctoral Program at Texas Woman's University in Denton, TX. Previously, she spent six years educating young minds at Eagle Mountain-Saginaw Independent School District in Fort Worth, TX, where she was inspired to serve and support the field of mental health. Additionally, she holds BA and MAT degrees from Texas Woman's University.

***Laura Trujillo-Jenks*** is a graduate of the University of Texas at Austin, receiving both her bachelor's and Ph.D. in educational administration and her master's degree from Austin Peay State University in Tennessee. She has been an educator in public education at the elementary, middle, and high school levels as a general and special education teacher and as a special education coordinator, assistant principal, and principal in school districts in Texas, Colorado, and Kentucky. In higher education, Laura has worked at the University of North

Texas at Dallas, teaching courses in the Educational Administration program where she also served on the Faculty Alliance/Senate as both secretary and chair-elect. Currently, Laura is an Assistant Professor in the Department of Teacher Education at Texas Woman's University, where she teaches courses in the Educational Leadership program and she also is an instructor for Capella University teaching doctoral courses for the School of Education. Laura is an associate editor for the *Journal of Cases in Educational Leadership*. Books Laura has authored and coauthored are *Survival Guide for New Teachers: How to become a Professional, Effective, and Successful Teacher*; *The Survival Guide for New Campus Administrators: How to Become a Professional, Effective, and Successful Administrator* with Minerva Trujillo; and *Case Studies on Safety, Bullying, and Social Media in Schools* with Kenneth Jenks.

***Nora Zinan*** is Assistant Professor at the University of Saint Joseph in West Hartford, Connecticut. Dr. Zinan's expertise encompasses the public health arena and includes helping underserved populations manage issues like asthma and heart disease. She is most proud, though, of her advocacy to advance the role school nurses play in the fight against bullying. She also is an advocate for holistic nursing and alternative therapies. She received her Doctorate of Nursing Science in Public Health Nursing Leadership, and Masters of Science in Public Health degree from the University of Massachusetts Amherst, and her Bachelor of Science in Nursing from Syracuse University.

# List of Figures

# List of Tables

CHAPTER 1

# An Overview of School Bullying

*Lisa H. Rosen, Shannon R. Scott, and Kathy DeOrnellas*

Experiences of peer maltreatment like those depicted in the opening vignettes are far too common an occurrence in schools worldwide. Being bullied can be tremendously painful, and victimization has been associated with a myriad of adjustment problems (McDougall & Vaillancourt, 2015). Not only do victimized youth suffer, but aggressive youth are also at increased risk for maladjustment (Coyne, Nelson, & Underwood, 2011). Fortunately, bullying has become an issue of growing concern for

"For two years, Johnny, a quiet 13-year-old, was a human plaything for some of his classmates. The teenagers badgered Johnny for money,... beat him up in the rest room and tied a string around his neck, leading him around as a 'pet'. When Johnny's torturers were interrogated about the bullying, they said they pursued their victim because it was fun" (Olweus, 1995, p. 196 drawing from a newspaper clipping).

"In conclusion, there is no conclusion to what children who are bullied live with. They take it home with them at night. It lives inside them and eats away at them. It never ends. So neither should our struggle to end it" (Sarah, age 16, sharing her reflections on the bullying she has endured, Hymel & Swearer, 2015, p. 296).

L.H. Rosen (✉) • S.R. Scott • K. DeOrnellas
Texas Woman's University, Denton, TX, USA





L.H. Rosen et al. (eds.), *Bullying in School*,
DOI 10.1057/978-1-137-59298-9_1

educators as there is increasing awareness that bullying has the potential to negatively impact all members of the school community.

The overarching theme of this book is that the multiple perspectives of key school staff (i.e., teachers, principals, school resource officers, school psychologists/counselors, nurses, and coaches) and students can provide a more complete understanding of bullying, which can in turn lead to the development of more effective prevention and intervention programs. This introductory chapter sets the stage by defining bullying, discussing prevalence rates, reviewing the research on gender and bullying, and identifying risk factors for bullying involvement. The association between bullying and well-being is also examined with attention to the physical health, mental health, and school outcomes that have been identified in the literature.

## Definition and Forms of Bullying

Bullying can be defined as "a specific type of aggression in which (1) the behavior is intended to harm or disturb, (2) the behavior occurs repeatedly over time, and (3) there is an imbalance of power, with a more powerful person or group attacking a less powerful one" (Nansel et al., 2001, p. 2094). This widely agreed upon definition stems from the pioneering work of Dr. Daniel Olweus (1993) who identified intentionality, repetitive nature, and imbalance of power as three key features that differentiate bullying from other forms of aggression. These defining features of bullying are also evident in the definitions of bullying put forth by the American Psychological Association and the National Association of School Psychologists (Hymel & Swearer, 2015).

Recently, the Centers for Disease Control and Prevention (CDC) organized a panel to develop a uniform definition of bullying. This initiative stemmed from recognition of the importance of researchers and policymakers adopting a uniform definition of bullying to better understand prevalence rates and trends over time. The development of a uniform definition was also believed to be critical for guiding prevention and intervention efforts. The uniform definition outlined by the CDC panel described bullying as "any unwanted aggressive behavior(s) by another youth or group of youths who are not siblings or current dating partners that involves an observed or perceived power imbalance and is repeated multiple times or is highly likely to be repeated. Bullying may inflict harm or distress on the targeted youth including physical, psychological, social, or educational harm" (Gladden, Vivolo-Kantor, Hamburger, & Lumpkin, 2014, p. 7). This definition drew upon the three essential characteristics of bullying described in Olweus' earlier and frequently cited work but made several, important distinctions between bullying and other forms of violence. First, the CDC definition distinguishes bullying from child maltreatment by noting that the behavior must occur between peers and does not include adult aggression directed toward children. Further, the CDC definition differentiates bullying from sibling violence by noting that the term bullying is not appropriate to describe conflict between siblings. An additional important distinction in the CDC definition is highlighting a separation between bullying and teen dating violence/intimate partner violence.

The definitions outlined above indicate that bullying behaviors are intended to inflict harm, but these definitions do not indicate specific types of behaviors in order to acknowledge that there are many different forms of bullying (Gladden et al., 2014). The most commonly identified forms of bullying are physical bullying, verbal bullying, property damage, social bullying, and cyber bullying. Physical bullying refers to use of force by the bully/bullies and includes behaviors such as hitting, kicking, or punching the victim. Verbal bullying refers to disdainful oral or written communication directed toward the victim and includes taunting, name-calling, and sending mean notes. Property damage refers to the bully/bullies taking or destroying the victim's possessions (Gladden et al., 2014).

Social bullying is aimed at harming another's social status or relationships (Underwood, 2003). Common examples of socially aggressive behavior include social exclusion, malicious gossip, and friendship manipulation. Relational bullying and indirect bullying are terms that have been used to refer to similar constructs. Of all the terms put forth, social bullying is the broadest by acknowledging aggressive behaviors that are verbal as well as nonverbal and direct as well as indirect in nature (Underwood, 2003).

Bullying others through electronic channels is a relatively new phenomenon, and many terms have been used to refer to this type of behavior including cyber bullying, electronic bullying, online harassment, Internet bullying, and online social cruelty (Hinduja & Patchin, 2009). The term cyber bullying is becoming widely adopted and has been defined as "willful and repeated harm inflicted through the use of computers, cell phones, and other electronic devices" (Hinduja & Patchin,

2009, p. 5). Researchers and educators are beginning to pay a great deal of attention to this type of behavior given the proliferation of mobile devices, which means cyber attacks can be shared with a large audience in a matter of minutes. Cyber bullying is also distinct from other forms of bullying in that victims may experience cyber bullying 24 hours a day, regardless of where they are. Thus, cyber bullying has the potential to be omnipresent, which may lead to increased feelings of vulnerability among victims. Cyber bullies may feel less inhibited than traditional bullies given that they can potentially remain anonymous through the use of pseudonyms and do not have face-to-face contact with their victims (Hinduja & Patchin, 2009).

## Prevalence of Bullying and Victimization

Nansel et al. (2001) conducted one of the most widely cited investigations into the prevalence of bullying behavior among U.S. youth. They drew upon a nationally representative sample of 15,686 students and focused on those reporting moderate or frequent involvement in bullying. Approximately 30% of students reported moderate to frequent involvement in bullying with 13% identified as bullies, 11% identified as victims, and 6% identified as bullies/victims. Males reported more frequent involvement in bullying than girls both as perpetrators and as victims; however, this is a more complex issue to which we return in the next section on gender and bullying.

Although the findings of Nansel and colleagues are frequently cited, it is important to note that there is wide variability in reported prevalence rates of bullying (Hymel & Swearer, 2015). Estimates of prevalence for bullying perpetration have ranged from 10% to 90% of youth, and estimates of prevalence for bullying victimization have ranged from 9% to 98% of youth (Modecki, Minchin, Harbaugh, Guerra, & Runions, 2014). There are a number of reasons that have been posed to explain this substantial variability in prevalence rates. Many suggest that these differences are likely a function of using different measurement tools (e.g., Hymel & Swearer, 2015; Modecki et al., 2014). Bullying victimization and perpetration have been assessed using parent, teacher, and peer reports as well as observational assessments; however, self-report remains the most common way to assess bullying involvement. Each reporter (e.g., teacher or student) provides a unique perspective, and thus there is often low to moderate correspondence between raters

(Leff, Kupersmidt, Patterson, & Power, 1999). Important differences in measurement tools exist even when limiting focus to self-reports of bullying involvement; for example, some measures require participants to indicate whether they carried out or experienced specific forms of bullying behaviors (e.g., *have you hit or shoved other kids, has anyone tried to turn people against you for revenge or exclusion*; Rosen, Beron, & Underwood, 2013), whereas other measures ask participants the extent to which they have bullied others and have been bullied by others without differentiating forms of bullying behaviors. Sampling issues may also contribute to this variability with many researchers relying on community samples that are convenience-based and may differ in important ways such as gender composition (Hymel & Swearer, 2015; Modecki et al., 2014).

Given this wide variability, Modecki et al. (2014) conducted a meta-analysis to further examine bullying prevalence. This meta-analysis included 80 studies and examined traditional as well as cyber bullying. Drawing across the 80 studies, Modecki and colleagues found the mean prevalence rate of traditional bullying perpetration to be 35% and the mean prevalence rate of traditional bullying victimization to be 36%. The mean prevalence rates of cyber bullying perpetration and cyber victimization were considerably lower at 16% and 15%, respectively. Pulling across these 80 studies, there was a moderately strong degree of overlap between perpetration of traditional bullying and cyber bullying and victimization by traditional bullying and cyber bullying (mean correlations of 0.47 and 0.40, respectively). These results suggest that there is great similarity in youth's behavior and vulnerability across online and offline settings. Interestingly, 33% of cyber victims believed the perpetrator was someone they considered to be a friend, and 28% believed the perpetrator was someone from school (Waasdorp & Bradshaw, 2015). Based on these findings, it would appear that what happens in school spills over to cyber space and vice versa.

We now turn our attention to how bullying prevalence rates differ based on culture, grade level, and disability status. Researchers examining bullying prevalence rates across countries have found notable variability (Due et al., 2005); of the countries examined, the lowest levels of bullying were reported in Sweden with 5.1% of girls and 6.3% of boys reporting being bullied, and the highest levels of bullying were reported in Lithuania with 38.2% of girls and 41.4% of boys reporting being bullied. This variability in prevalence rates may be due to cultural differences in willingness to report bullying. Researchers and policymakers also ascribe this variability in prevalence rates to differing legislation; some countries like Sweden have strong laws in place to protect children in the school environment from bullying. Further analysis suggests that bullying may be more common in countries characterized by significant income inequality as this may lead to decreased sense of community and greater class competition (Elgar, Craig, Boyce, Morgan, &Vella-Zarb, 2009).

In addition, bullying prevalence rates may vary as a function of grade level. Bullying is believed to reach its peak in sixth grade (around 11 years of age) and then decrease. A report from the National Center for Education Statistics indicated that 24% of sixth graders reported being bullied, whereas only 7% of twelfth graders reported being bullied (DeVoe & Kaffenberger, 2005). The transition to middle school, which usually occurs at sixth grade, may be especially challenging. As students enter middle school, they may resort to bullying in an attempt to gain dominance in the social hierarchy; however, bullying may decrease over time as dominance hierarchies become more established. An alternative explanation is that older students may bully younger students, and there are fewer potential older bullies at higher grade levels.

Important differences in prevalence of bullying also exist between students in general and special education. Rose, Espelage, and Monda-Adams (2009) found the rate of bullying perpetration to be 10% for students without disabilities, 16% for students with disabilities in inclusive settings, and 21% for students with disabilities in self-contained settings. Similar differences were found for victimization with the rate of 12% for students without disabilities, 19% for students with disabilities in inclusive settings, and 22% for students with disabilities in self-contained settings. Bullying of students with a disability often takes the form of name-calling or mimicking aspects of the disability (Swearer, Espelage, Vaillancourt, & Hymel, 2010). Students with disabilities may be at increased risk for involvement in bullying as a result of limited social and communication skills (Rose, Simpson, & Moss, 2015). Those students with disabilities who are in an inclusive classroom setting may be less at risk as they may be more likely to develop their social skills by learning from their classmates without disabilities. Additionally, students with disabilities in inclusive settings may be more accepted and less likely to be subject to stereotypes than those in self-contained settings (Rose et al., 2009).

## Gender and Bullying

Boys are often believed to be involved in bullying at higher rates than girls as both perpetrators and victims (Underwood & Rosen, 2011). As outlined in the previous section, Nansel et al. (2001) drew upon a large, nationally representative sample of U.S. youth and found that boys were more likely to report being both victims and perpetrators. Participants in this study were provided with a definition of bullying that did not differentiate between subtypes of bullying (i.e., "We say a student is BEING BULLIED when another student, or a group of students, say or do nasty and unpleasant things to him or her. It is also bullying when a student is teased repeatedly in a way he or she doesn't like", p. 2095) and were then asked to indicate whether they had bullied others or had been bullied by others. Many studies utilize similar measures that fail to differentiate between physical and social forms of bullying, and this may explain why boys are found to be both bullies and victims at higher rates than girls (Underwood & Rosen, 2011).

Gender differences seem to be contingent on the type of bullying examined. Boys are more physically aggressive than girls, and this appears to be a robust finding that is supported by a recent meta-analysis (Card, Stucky, Sawalani, & Little, 2008). A number of reasons have been put forth to explain boys' greater physical aggression including their typically stronger physique than girls. Parental socialization may also be an important contributor as parents may deem it more acceptable for boys to use physical aggression as they see them as more tough and dominant than girls (Rosen & Rubin, 2016).

Stereotypically girls and women are thought to be more socially aggressive than are boys and men. This is commonly reflected in media portrayals such as the film "Mean Girls" (Rosen & Rubin, 2015). The propensity to view social aggression as the realm of girls and women has been termed *gender oversimplification of aggression* (Swearer, 2008) and is evident as early as the preschool years. Giles and Heyman (2005) presented children with examples of socially aggressive behavior such as "I know a kid who told someone, 'You can't be my friend' just to be mean to them" (p. 112). When asked to guess the gender of the perpetrator, both preschoolers and elementary school-aged children tended to infer that the socially aggressive character had been a girl. However, not all research has been consistent with this commonly held belief that females are more socially aggressive; although some studies have found girls are higher on social aggression, other studies have found no gender differences or even that boys are higher on social aggression (Rosen & Rubin, 2016). Drawing across 148 studies, Card et al. (2008) meta-analysis found girls were significantly higher on social aggression than were boys; however, this difference was so small that these researchers deemed it trivial.

Researchers have turned to examine gender differences in cyber bullying. Although cyber bullying behavior can be direct or indirect in nature (Chibbaro, 2007), many forms of cyber bullying resemble social aggression (e.g., spreading rumors online, posting content to embarrass a peer). Similar to investigations of social aggression, findings from research examining gender differences in cyber bullying have been mixed (Berkman Center for Internet & Society at Harvard University, 2008; Hertz & David-Ferdon, 2008; Kowalski, Limber, & Agatston, 2008). Some studies have found that boys are involved in cyber bullying at higher rates than girls (Finkelhor, Mitchell, & Wolak, 2000; Mitchell, Finkelhor, & Wolak, 2003). However, the majority of the research suggests that girls are involved in cyber bullying at equivalent or greater rates than are boys (Hertz & David-Ferdon, 2008; Hinduja & Patchin, 2009; Kowalski et al., 2008; Lenhart, Madden, Macgill, & Smith, 2007; Williams & Guerra, 2007). Researchers are starting to note that girls and boys may engage in different types of cyber bullying behaviors (Underwood & Rosen, 2011). Boys' online social cruelty may be more likely to take the form of calling others mean names online or hacking into another's system. For girls, electronic aggression may be more likely to take the form of spreading rumors online.

Moving beyond mean differences in the rates of different forms of bullying, it is important to consider whether girls and boys play different roles in the bullying process. In the school setting, bullying is often a group process, in which students take different roles (Salmivalli, Lagerspetz, Björkqvist, Österman, & Kaukiainen, 1996). Boys are more likely to take the role of assistant than are girls, joining in on the bullying behavior in a role subordinate to the bully (e.g., may hold the victim). Likewise, boys are also more likely to serve as reinforcers, encouraging the bully through verbal comments or laughter. Conversely, girls are more likely to serve as defenders than are boys, supporting the victim and trying to intervene to stop the bullying. In addition to being defenders, girls are more likely than boys to take the role of outsider, remaining uninvolved and possibly trying to ignore the situation.

## Risk Factors for Bullying Involvement

Given that negative adjustment outcomes accrue for both bullies and victims, a great deal of research has attempted to identify risk factors for bullying involvement. Being aware of this literature may help teachers and other school officials identify those who are at risk for bullying perpetration and victimization. There is low to moderate agreement between peer and teacher reports of bullying perpetration and victimization (Leff et al., 1999), and teachers and other school officials may fail to identify those students involved with bullying who do not pose immediate behavior management difficulties or fail to fit their preconceived notions of the typical bully or victim. Although we review the most commonly identified risk factors, it is important to realize that bullies and victims can display diverse profiles, and teachers and other school officials may overlook at-risk students who do not match commonly held stereotypes of the bully or victim (Rosen, Scott, & DeOrnellas, 2016).

There are a number of family factors that have been associated with aggressive behavior (Coyne et al., 2011; Griffin & Gross, 2004; Underwood, 2011). Being subject to harsh child rearing and disciplinary techniques coupled with little parental warmth may place youth at risk for aggressive behavior (Griffin & Gross, 2004). Researchers have hypothesized that parental hostility may be associated with lower child self-regulatory behaviors or that social modeling is occurring as children learn by observing how their parents treat them as well as others (Coyne et al., 2011). Interestingly, permissive parenting, which is characterized by high parental warmth and low parental demands and control, has also been identified as a risk factor for aggressive behavior (Underwood, 2011).

In addition to family factors, peer and media influences may place children at risk for aggressive behavior (Underwood, 2011). As there could be tendencies to associate with similar peers and nonaggressive peers may avoid them, aggressive children often affiliate with aggressive peers. Affiliation with deviant peers has been associated with greater antisocial behavior (Underwood, 2011). Just as association with violent peers is a risk factor, so too is consumption of violent media. Viewing violent television programs and films predicts both concurrent and future aggressive behavior (Coyne et al., 2011; Huesmann, Moise-Titus, Podolski, & Eron, 2003). Similar to social modeling that may take place within families, observational learning may occur with violent shows and movies, and children may imitate the behaviors displayed in the media they watch. Further, listening to songs with violent lyrics or playing violent video games may be associated with aggressive thoughts and behaviors (Anderson, Carnagey, & Eubanks, 2003; Anderson & Dill, 2000).

Although a number of external influences have been discussed, there are also temperamental and psychological risk factors for aggression. Bullies may be impulsive and lack self-regulatory skills (Carrera, DePalma, & Lameiras, 2011; Griffin & Gross, 2004). Further, bullies may display a lack of guilt or empathy (Carrera et al., 2011; Griffin & Gross, 2004). Researchers have suggested that bullies may have low self-esteem, but this association is supported by only some studies (Griffin & Gross, 2004).

Bullies are often believed to lack social skills; however, some children use aggression to gain social status (Coyne et al., 2011; Hymel & Swearer, 2015). Some aggressive children may possess peer-valued characteristics (e.g., attractiveness, humor) that moderate the association between aggression and popularity. Although these youth may be disliked by peers, they may still be seen as popular. Rodkin, Farmer, Pearl, and Van Acker (2006) proposed four categories of students: popular-aggressive, popular-nonaggressive, nonpopular-aggressive, and nonpopular-nonaggresive. Popular-aggressive students may go undetected as teachers and other school officials overlook them (Hymel & Swearer, 2015).

Just as a number of risk factors have been identified for bullying perpetration, there are many factors believed to put youth at risk for victimization. Some victims may be viewed as passive and display submissive behavior and low self-esteem (Griffin & Gross, 2004; Schwartz, Dodge, & Coie, 1993). Conversely, some victims may be considered provocative as aggressive behavior is also a risk factor for victimization (Griffin & Gross, 2004; Hanish& Guerra, 2000).

A number of temperamental and social risk factors have been identified for victimization. Those youth who are victimized may be highly sensitive and lack regulatory skills, which in turn is associated with easily displaying their emotions (Carrera et al., 2011; Herts, McLaughlin, & Hatzenbuehler, 2012). In addition, victims are often socially isolated; they may lack strong friendships (Hodges, Malone, & Perry, 1997) and may have low-quality relationships with their parents (Beran & Violato, 2004).

Furthermore, appearance-based risk factors for victimization have been identified. Youth who are physically weak may be at increased risk for victimization (Hodges & Perry, 1999). Children and adolescents who are overweight are more likely to be victimized than their counterparts who are of average weight (Neumark-Sztainer, Story, & Faibisch, 1998). Low ratings of facial attractiveness have also been associated with increased victimization (Rosen, Underwood, & Beron, 2011). However, the findings have been mixed as to whether craniofacial anomalies are a risk factor for victimization (Carroll & Shute, 2005; Shavel-Jessop, Shearer, McDowell, & Hearst, 2012).

## Associations with Adjustment

Both bullying perpetration and victimization are associated with myriad forms of adjustment difficulties (Sigurdson, Wallander, & Sund, 2014). Children who are aggressive may have early difficulties regulating their emotions. These youth may be at risk for developing later adjustment problems that are associated with deficits in regulatory abilities (Underwood, Beron, & Rosen, 2011).

Aggressive behavior has been associated with internalizing problems as well as other forms of externalizing problems (Coyne et al., 2011; Underwood et al., 2011). Ratings of aggressive behavior predict internalizing problems including withdrawn depression, anxious depression, and somatic complaints (Crick, Ostrov, & Werner, 2006; Underwood et al., 2011). Many explanations have been put forth to explain this relationship including that aggressive children may experience difficulties with peers and school that place them at increased risk for internalizing problems. Further, aggressive behavior may predict delinquency and rule-breaking behaviors (Coyne et al., 2011; Underwood et al., 2011). Students identified as bullies are rated higher on teacher ratings of conduct disorder (Smith, Polenik, Nakasita, & Jones, 2012). Aggressive children may be impulsive, which puts them at risk for these other forms of externalizing problems.

Additionally, aggressive students are at risk for academic and peer problems at school (Coyne et al., 2011; Smith et al., 2012). Bullying behavior is associated with lower academic achievement as well as poor school attendance (Feldman et al., 2014). Some researchers caution that some academic achievement measures, such as GPA, could possibly reflect behavioral difficulties and not solely academic ability. Moreover, bullying is associated with peer rejection in school (Coyne et al., 2011). Youth who bully others may be isolated, which in turn may lead to lower self-esteem (Smith et al., 2012); however, findings regarding the association between bullying and self-esteem have been mixed (Griffin & Gross, 2004).

Longitudinal work suggests that bullying involvement in adolescence can predict maladjustment in adulthood (Sigurdson et al., 2014). Being identified as a bully at ages 14 and 15 was associated with lower educational attainment and higher rates of unemployment at ages 26 and 27. Of those who were employed, bullying in adolescence predicted poorer quality relationships at work. Further, those identified as bullies in adolescence also used more tobacco and illegal drugs than non-involved youth. Researchers believe that these longitudinal associations suggest "a continuation of early problem behavior" (Sigurdson et al., 2014, p. 1614).

The association between victimization and negative adjustment outcomes is also well documented in the literature with longitudinal investigations finding that being bullied in childhood can predict maladjustment in adulthood (McDougall & Vaillancourt, 2015). A great deal of concurrent and longitudinal research has shown that victimization experiences are linked to internalizing symptoms. Victimized youth report elevated levels of loneliness and social anxiety (Storch, Brassard, & Masia-Warner, 2003; Storch & Masia-Warner, 2004). Victims are also found to have lower self-esteem than their non-victimized counterparts (Prinstein, Boergers, & Vernberg, 2001). Furthermore, victimization is associated with increased risk for depression, suicidal thoughts, and suicide attempts (Klomek, Marrocco, Kleinman, Schonfeld, & Gould, 2007).

Likewise, victimization is associated with externalizing problems. Victimization is associated with both physical and relational aggression (Sullivan, Farrell, & Kliewer, 2006). In addition, victimization experiences predict delinquency, substance use, and increased sexual activity (Gallup, O'Brien, White, & Wilson, 2009; Sullivan et al., 2006). Victimization may also be related to onset of sexual activity for girls; female college students who reported being frequently victimized across adolescence reported having had more sexual partners and engaging in first intercourse at an earlier age (Gallup et al., 2009).

Victimization experiences have been associated with physical health. Those who had been victimized have higher levels of somatic complaints (Nishina, Juvonen, & Witkow, 2005). Two potential explanations were posed to account for this finding: the chronic stress of victimization could suppress the immune system leading to illness and victims may report being ill in order to miss school and escape their tormentors. In addition, the extant literature suggests that peer victimization is associated with poor quality sleep and disturbed eating patterns (Hatzinger et al., 2008;

van den Berg, Wertheim, Thompson, & Paxton, 2002). Self-reported experiences of peer victimization are negatively related to sleep efficiency as assessed with electroencephalographic sleep profiles (Hatzinger et al., 2008). For adolescent girls, a history of teasing is positively related to body dissatisfaction and, in turn, eating disturbances (van den Berg et al., 2002).

Experts have called for additional research examining the relation between peer victimization and educational outcomes (Schwartz, Gorman, Nakamoto, & Toblin, 2005). Victimization is associated with poorer school adjustment outcomes including decreased school liking (Kochenderfer & Ladd, 1996). Similarly, victimization is linked to lower GPA and standardized test scores in some studies (Schwartz et al., 2005). Experiencing bullying predicts school avoidance; some victims report missing school due to feeling unsafe (Hughes, Gaines, & Pryor, 2015).

Interestingly, not all bullied youth are affected to the same extent (McDougall & Vaillancourt, 2015). Some youth suffer more when faced with victimization whereas others appear to escape lasting maladjustment. These differing outcomes may be dependent on a number of risk and protective factors. Victimized youth seem to fare better when a large number of their classmates are bullied; given a sense of "shared plight", victims may be less apt to blame themselves for their experiences of peer maltreatment and rather make attributions to external factors. Additionally, the extent to which victimization is chronic or fleeting may make an important difference. Youth experiencing incessant bullying demonstrate the worst adjustment outcomes (Kochenderfer-Ladd & Wardrop, 2001; Rosen et al., 2009). Social support may be a significant protective function, and this support can come from multiple sources including friends, family members, and teachers (McDougall & Vaillancourt, 2015).

Moving beyond focusing on bullies and victims, research has begun to examine the association between simply witnessing bullying and maladjustment. In a daily diary study, 42% of middle school students reported witnessing at least one incident of peer harassment at school (Nishina & Juvonen, 2005). These bystanders may be at risk just as bullies and victims are as findings suggest that witnessing bullying is associated with multiple forms of maladjustment including substance use, anxiety, somatic complaints, and depressive symptoms (Rivers, Poteat, Noret, & Ashurst, 2009). A number of theories have been put forth to explain this association between witnessing bullying and negative adjustment outcomes.

Bystanders may experience maladjustment as they may worry that they could soon become victims themselves. In addition, bystanders may undergo “indirect covictimization through their empathic understanding of the suffering of the victim they observe” (Rivers et al., 2009, p. 220). Another possibility is that bystanders who do not intervene may experience extreme stress as they feel compelled to assist but do not do so (Rivers et al., 2009). Some have hypothesized that bystanders who themselves have been victimized at some point may be at greater risk for negative adjustment outcomes associated with witnessing bullying (Werth, Nickerson, Aloe, & Swearer, 2015).

## Bullying in the School Context

The majority of bullying episodes take place in the school setting. It is reported that 82% of incidents of emotional bullying and 59% of peer assaults occur at school (Turner, Finkelhor, Hamby, Shattuck, & Ormrod, 2011). Students were asked to identify places where bullying frequently occurred; 18.9% reported bullying was often experienced in the class setting, and 30.2% reported bullying was often experienced in the cafeteria or at recess (Seals & Young, 2003). Even if bullying takes place off school premises, there is often spillover to the school environment. For instance, teachers report that episodes of cyberbullying can influence what occurs in their classrooms (Rosen et al., 2016).

Scholars point to the importance of preventing bullying in schools as this is an issue of human rights (Smith, 2011). Students have the right not to be bullied, and school officials are devoting increasing efforts to address bullying on their campuses. Unfortunately, these bullying prevention efforts are not always effective (Espelage, 2013). Some researchers suggest that bullying can be best addressed by fostering a positive school climate stating that “bullying is most effectively prevented by the creation of an environment that nurtures and promotes prosocial and ethical norms and behaviors, more so than by simply targeting the eradication of bullying and related undesirable behaviors” (Cohen, Espelge, Twemlow, Berkowitz, & Comer, 2015, p. 7).

Given the importance of school climate, it is important to look more in depth at influencing factors. Researchers have posited that “school climate is based on patterns of people’s experience of school life and reflects norms, goals, values, interpersonal relationships, teaching, learning, leadership practices, and organizational structures” (Cohen et al., 2015, p. 8).

Some schools are believed to foster a "culture of bullying" (Espelage, Low, & Jimerson, 2014, p. 234) in which aggressive behavior is common and unlikely to elicit a response from teachers and school officials. In fact, school staff at these schools often hold passive or dismissive attitudes toward student aggression, and failure to intervene can reinforce bullying as there are no consequences for this form of misbehavior.

Conversely, a positive school climate can reduce problematic behaviors such as bullying by enforcing norms of a safe environment and fostering strong relationships (Espelage et al., 2014). Konold et al. (2014) identified the two main components of school climate as disciplinary structure and support of students. Fair enforcement of rules and policies coupled with a sense of perceived support and respect create a balanced environment, which has been termed an authoritative school climate. In these environments, students believe that teachers and school staff care about them, yet are aware that they will receive appropriate punishment if they break school rules. This type of school environment is often characterized by lower rates of bullying, higher levels of school liking, and greater completion of academic work.

Fostering a positive school climate to best address bullying requires all key players in the school to come together. It is important to recognize that "school-based aggression is a reflection of the complex, nested ecologies that constitute a 'schools' culture' and thus, is best understood through an ecological framework" (Espelage et al., 2014, p. 234). Too often researchers and policymakers limit their focus to only one perspective and by doing so are missing the utility of considering multiple perspectives. In fact, the failure to engage all key players in the school may be one of the main reasons that bullying prevention programs fail (Cohen et al., 2015). Programs that are school-wide and multidisciplinary are more likely to succeed (Swearer et al., 2010). When schools create teams to address bullying that draw across different professions, members are able to bring their unique expertise and have access to different resources, which in turn contributes to program success (Kub & Feldman, 2015).

Drawing on this work, the underlying premise of this book is that we can best understand and address bullying by considering multiple perspectives within the school. The second chapter examines bullying from the student point of view including that of the aggressor, victim, and bystander. Chapter 3 focuses on bullying from the teacher's perspective and highlights effective interventions for teachers to use in handling bullying in their classrooms. Chapter 4 addresses bullying from the perspectives of principals and school resource officers and discusses ways in which the two can effectively work together in order to best prevent and intervene in different forms of bullying. Chapter 5 describes the roles of school psychologists and school counselors in planning and implementing bullying prevention programs and their effect on schools. Chapter 6 explains how school nurses are important as members of teams to prevent and address bullying in schools. Chapter 7 incorporates the perspective of coaches and offers examples of bullying activities that occur in athletics and positive steps coaches may take to encourage athletes' success and growth in lieu of bullying. The eighth and final chapter integrates the different perspectives of key school staff and provides common themes. Based on the recommendations provided in each of the chapters, we discuss possible school-wide bullying prevention and intervention efforts. In so doing, we highlight the importance of whole school programs and offer recommendations for how these programs can best be implemented by drawing upon resources across the school.

## References


Anderson, C. A., Carnagey, N. L., & Eubanks, J. (2003). Exposure to violent media: The effects of songs with violent lyrics on aggressive thoughts and feelings. *Journal of Personality and Social Psychology, 84*, 960–971. doi:10.1037/0022-3514.84.5.960.

Anderson, C. A., & Dill, K. E. (2000). Video games and aggressive thoughts, feelings, and behavior in the laboratory and in life. *Journal of Personality and Social Psychology, 78*, 772–790. doi:10.1037/0022-3514.78.4.772.

Beran, T. N., & Violato, C. (2004). A model of childhood perceived peer harassment: Analyses of the Canadian national longitudinal survey of children and youth data. *The Journal of Psychology: Interdisciplinary and Applied, 138*, 129–147. doi:10.3200/JRLP.138.2.129-148.

Berkman Center for Internet & Society at Harvard University. (2008). *Enhancing child safety & online technologies: Final report of the Internet Safety Technical Task Force to the Multi-State Working Group on Social Networking of State Attorneys General of the United States.* Retrieved from https://cyber.harvard.edu/sites/cyber.law.harvard.edu/%20files/ISTTF_Final_Report.pdf

Card, N. A., Stucky, B. D., Sawalani, G. M., & Little, T. D. (2008). Direct and indirect aggression during childhood and adolescence: A meta-analytic review of gender differences, intercorrelations, and relations to maladjustment. *Child Development, 79*, 1185–1229. doi:10.1111/j.1467-8624.2008.01184.x.

Carrera, M. V., DePalma, R., & Lameiras, M. (2011). Toward a more comprehensive understanding of bullying in school settings. *Educational Psychology Review*, *23*, 479–499. doi:10.1007/s10648-011-9171-x.

Carroll, P., & Shute, R. (2005). School peer victimization of young people with craniofacial conditions: A comparative study. *Psychology, Health & Medicine*, *10*, 291–304. doi:10.1080/13548500500093753.

Chibbaro, J. S. (2007). School counselors and the cyberbully: Interventions and implications. *Professional School Counseling*, *11*, 65–68. doi:10.5330/PSC.n.2010-11.65.

Cohen, J., Espelage, D. L., Berkowitz, M., Twemlow, S., & Comer, J. (2015). Rethinking effective bully and violence prevention efforts: Promoting healthy school climates, positive youth development, and preventing bully-victim-bystander behavior. *International Journal of Violence and Schools*, *15*, 2–40.

Coyne, S. M., Nelson, D. A., & Underwood, M. K. (2011). Aggression in childhood. In P. K. Smith & C. H. Hart (Eds.), *The Wiley-Blackwell handbook of childhood social development* (pp. 491–509). West Sussex, UK: Wiley-Blackwell.

Crick, N. R., Ostrov, J. M., & Werner, N. E. (2006). A longitudinal study of relational aggression, physical aggression, and children's social-psychological adjustment. *Journal of Abnormal Child Psychology*, *34*, 131–142. doi:10.1007/s10802-005-9009-4.

DeVoe, J. F., & Kaffenberger, S. (2005). *Student reports of bullying: Results from the 2001 school crime supplement to the National Crime Victimization Survey* (NCES 2005–310). U.S. Department of Education, National Center for Education Statistics. Washington, DC: U.S. Government Printing Office.

Due, P., Holstein, B. E., Lynch, J., Diderichsen, F., Gabhain, S. N., Scheidt, P., & Currie, C. (2005). Bullying and symptoms among school-aged children: International comparative cross sectional study in 28 countries. *European Journal of Public Health*, *15*, 128–132. doi:10.1093/eurpub/cki105.

Elgar, F. J., Craig, W., Boyce, W., Morgan, A., & Vella-Zarb, R. (2009). Income inequality and school bullying: Multilevel study of adolescents in 37 countries. *Journal of Adolescent Health*, *45*, 351–359. doi:10.1016/j.jadohealth.2009.04.004.

Espelage, D. L. (2013). Why are bully prevention programs failing in U.S. schools? *Journal of Curriculum and Pedagogy*, *10*, 121–123. doi:10.1080/15505170.2013.849629.

Espelage, D. L., Low, S. K., & Jimerson, S. R. (2014). Understanding school climate, aggression, peer victimization, and bully perpetration: Contemporary science, practice, and policy. *School Psychology Quarterly*, *29*, 233–237. doi:10.1037/spq0000090.

Feldman, M. A., Ojanen, T., Gesten, E. L., Smith-Schrandt, H., Brannick, M., Totura, C. M. W., ... Brown, K. (2014). The effects of middle school bullying and victimization on adjustment through high school: Growth modeling of achievement, school attendance, and disciplinary trajectories. *Psychology in the Schools*, *51*, 1046–1062.

Finkelhor, D., Mitchell, K. J., & Wolak, J. (2000). Online victimization: A report on the nation's youth. Retrieved from http://www.missingkids.com/en_US/publications/NC62.pdf

Gallup, A. C., O'Brien, D. T., White, D. D., & Wilson, D. S. (2009). Peer victimization in adolescence has different effects on the sexual behavior of male and female college students. *Personality and Individual Differences*, *46*, 611–615. doi:10.1016/j.paid.2008.12.018.

Gladden, R. M., Vivolo-Kantor, A. M., Hamburger, M. E., & Lumpkin, C. D. (2014). *Bullying surveillance among youths: Uniform definitions for public health and recommended data elements, version 1.0.* Atlanta, GA; National Center for Injury Prevention and Control, Centers for Disease Control and Prevention and U.S. Department of Education.

Giles, J. W., & Heyman, G. D. (2005). Young children's beliefs about the relationship between gender and aggressive behavior. *Child Development*, *76*(1), 107–121. doi:10.1111/j.1467-8624.2005.00833.x.

Griffin, R. S., & Gross, A. M. (2004). Childhood bullying: Current empirical findings and future directions for research. *Aggression and Violent Behavior*, *9*, 379–400. doi:10.1016/S1359-1789(03)00033-8.

Hanish, L. D., & Guerra, N. G. (2000). Predictors of peer victimization among urban youth. *Social Development*, *9*, 521–543. doi:10.1111/1467-9507.00141.

Hatzinger, M., Brand, S., Perren, S., Stadelmann, S., von Wyl, A., von Klitzing, K., & Holsboer-Trachsler, E. (2008). Electroencephalographic sleep profiles and hypothalamic-pituitary-adrenocortical (HPA)-activity in kindergarten children: Early indication of poor sleep quality associated with increased cortisol secretion. *Journal of Psychiatric Research*, *42*, 532–543. doi:10.1016/j.jpsychires.2007.05.010.

Herts, K. L., McLaughlin, K. A., & Hatzenbuehler, M. L. (2012). Emotion dysregulation as a mechanism linking stress exposure to adolescent aggressive behavior. *Journal of Abnormal Child Psychology*, *40*, 1111–1122. doi:10.1007/s10802-012-9629-4.

Hertz, M. F., & David-Ferdon, C. (2008). Electronic media and youth violence: A CDC issue brief for educators and caregivers. Retrieved from http://www.cdc.gov/violenceprevention/%20pdf/EA-brief-a.pdf

Hinduja, S., & Patchin, J. W. (2009). *Bullying beyond the schoolyard: Preventing and responding to cyberbullying.* Thousand Oaks, CA: Sage Publications.

Hodges, E. V. E., Malone, M. J., & Perry, D. G. (1997). Individual risk and social risk as interacting determinants of victimization in the peer group. *Developmental Psychology*, *33*, 1032–1039. doi:10.1037/0012-1649.33.6.1032.

Hodges, E. V. E., & Perry, D. G. (1999). Personal and interpersonal antecedents and consequences of victimization by peers. *Journal of Personality and Social Psychology*, *76*, 677–685. doi:10.1037/0022-3514.76.4.677.

Huesmann, L. R., Moise-Titus, J., Podolski, C., & Eron, L. D. (2003). Longitudinal relations between children's exposure to TV violence and their aggressive and violent behavior in young adulthood: 1977–1992. *Developmental Psychology, 39*, 201–221. doi:10.1037/0012-1649.39.2.201.

Hughes, M. R., Gaines, J. S., & Pryor, D. W. (2015). Staying away from school: Adolescents who miss school due to feeling unsafe. *Youth Violence and Juvenile Justice, 13*, 270–290. doi:10.1177/1541204014538067.

Hymel, S., & Swearer, S. M. (2015). Four decades of research on school bullying: An introduction. *American Psychologist, 70*, 293–299. doi:10.1037/a0038928.

Klomek, A. B., Marrocco, F., Kleinman, M., Schonfeld, I. S., & Gould, M. S. (2007). Bullying, depression, and suicidality in adolescents. *Journal of the American Academy of Child & Adolescent Psychiatry, 46*, 40–49. doi:10.1097/01.chi.0000242237.84925.18.

Kochenderfer, B. J., & Ladd, G. W. (1996). Peer victimization: Manifestations and relations to school adjustment in kindergarten. *Journal of School Psychology, 34*, 267–283. doi:10.1016/0022-4405(96)00015-5.

Kochenderfer-Ladd, B., & Wardrop, J. L. (2001). Chronicity and instability of children's peer victimization experiences as predictors of loneliness and social satisfaction trajectories. *Child Development, 72*, 134–151. doi:10.1111/1467-8624.00270.

Konold, T., Cornell, D., Huang, F., Meyer, P., Lacey, A., Nekvasil, E., ... Shukla, K. (2014). Multilevel multi-informant structure of the authoritative school climate survey. *School Psychology Quarterly, 29*, 238–255. doi:10.1037/spq0000062; 10.1037/spq0000062.supp.

Kowalski, R. M., Limber, S. P., & Agatston, P. W. (2008). *Cyber bullying: Bullying in the digital age*. Malden, MA: Blackwell Publishing.

Kub, J., & Feldman, M. A. (2015). Bullying prevention: A call for collaborative efforts between school nurses and school psychologists. *Psychology in the Schools, 52*, 658–671. doi:10.1002/pits.21853.

Leff, S. S., Kupersmidt, J. B., Patterson, C. J., & Power, T. J. (1999). Factors influencing teacher identification of peer bullies and victims. *School Psychology Review, 28*, 505–517.

Lenhart, A., Madden, M., Macgill, A. R., & Smith, A. (2007). *Teens and social media* (Pew Internet & American Life Project Report). Retrieved from http://www.pewinternet.org

McDougall, P., & Vaillancourt, T. (2015). Long-term adult outcomes of peer victimization in childhood and adolescence: Pathways to adjustment and maladjustment. *American Psychologist, 70*, 300–310. doi:10.1037/a0039174.

Mitchell, K. J., Finkelhor, D., & Wolak, J. (2003). Victimization of youths on the Internet. *Journal of Aggression, Maltreatment, and Trauma, 8*, 1–39.

Modecki, K. L., Minchin, J., Harbaugh, A. G., Guerra, N. G., & Runions, K. C. (2014). Bullying prevalence across contexts: A meta-analysis measuring cyber and traditional bullying. *Journal of Adolescent Health, 55*, 602–611. doi:10.1016/j.jadohealth.2014.06.007.

Nansel, T. R., Overpeck, M., Pilla, R. S., Ruan, W. J., Simons-Morton, B., & Scheidt, P. (2001). Bullying behaviors among US youth: Prevalence and association with psychosocial adjustment. *JAMA: Journal of the American Medical Association*, *285*, 2094–2100. doi:10.1001/jama.285.16.2094.

Neumark-Sztainer, D., Story, M., & Faibisch, L. (1998). Perceived stigmatization among overweight African-American and Caucasian adolescent girls. *Journal of Adolescent Health*, *23*, 264–270. doi:10.1016/S1054-139X(98)00044-5.

Nishina, A., & Juvonen, J. (2005). Daily reports of witnessing and experiencing peer harassment in middle school. *Child Development*, *76*, 435–450. doi:10.1111/j.1467-8624.2005.00855.x.

Nishina, A., Juvonen, J., & Witkow, M. R. (2005). Sticks and stones may break my bones, but names will make me feel sick: The psychosocial, somatic, and scholastic consequences of peer harassment. *Journal of Clinical Child and Adolescent Psychology*, *34*(1), 37–48. doi:10.1207/s15374424jccp3401_4.

Olweus, D. (1993). *Bullying at school: What we know and what we can do*. Malden, MA: Blackwell Publishing.

Olweus, D. (1995). Bullying or peer abuse at school: Facts and interventions. *Current Directions in Psychological Science*, *4*, 196–200. doi:10.1111/1467-8721.ep10772640.

Prinstein, M. J., Boergers, J., & Vernberg, E. M. (2001). Overt and relational aggression in adolescents: Social-psychological adjustment of aggressors and victims. *Journal of Clinical Child Psychology*, *30*, 479–491. doi:10.1207/S15374424JCCP3004_05.

Rivers, I., Poteat, V. P., Noret, N., & Ashurst, N. (2009). Observing bullying at school: The mental health implications of witness status. *School Psychology Quarterly*, *24*, 211–223. doi:10.1037/a0018164.

Rodkin, P. C., Farmer, T. W., Pearl, R., & Van Acker, R. (2006). They're cool: Social status and peer group supports for aggressive boys and girls. *Social Development*, *15*, 175–204. doi:10.1111/j.1467-9507.2006.00336.x.

Rose, C. A., Espelage, D. L., & Monda-Amaya, L. (2009). Bullying and victimisation rates among students in general and special education: A comparative analysis. *Educational Psychology*, *29*, 761–776. doi:10.1080/01443410903254864.

Rose, C. A., Simpson, C. G., & Moss, A. (2015). The bullying dynamic: Prevalence of involvement among a large-scale sample of middle and high school youth with and without disabilities. *Psychology in the Schools*, *52*, 515–531. doi:10.1002/pits.21840.

Rosen, L. H., Beron, K. J., & Underwood, M. K. (2013). Assessing peer victimization across adolescence: Measurement invariance and developmental change. *Psychological Assessment*, *25*, 1–11. doi:10.1037/a0028985.

Rosen, L. H., & Rubin, L. J. (2015). Beyond Mean Girls: Identifying and intervening in episodes of relational aggression. *Teachers College Record*, http://www.tcrecord.org, ID Number 17959.

Rosen, L. H., &Rubin, L. J. (2016). Bullying. In N. Naples (Ed.), *Encyclopedia of Gender and Sexuality Studies*, Malden, MA: Wiley Blackwell.

Rosen, L. H., Scott, S., &DeOrnellas, K. (2016). Teachers' perceptions of student aggression: A focus group approach. *Journal of School Violence, 16*(1), 119–139. doi: 10.1080/15388220.2015.1124340.

Rosen, L. H., Underwood, M. K., & Beron, K. J. (2011). Peer victimization as a mediator of the relation between facial attractiveness and internalizing problems. *Merrill-Palmer Quarterly, 57*, 319–347. doi:10.1353/mpq.2011.0016.

Rosen, L. H., Underwood, M. K., Beron, K. J., Gentsch, J. K., Wharton, M. E., & Rahdar, A. (2009). Persistent versus periodic experiences of social victimization: Predictors of adjustment. *Journal of Abnormal Child Psychology, 37*, 693–704. doi:10.1007/s10802-009-9311-7.

Salmivalli, C., Lagerspetz, K., Björkqvist, K., Österman, K., & Kaukiainen, A. (1996). Bullying as a group process: Participant roles and their relations to social status within the group. *Aggressive Behavior, 22*, 1–15. doi:10.1002/(SICI)1098-2337(1996)22:1<1::AID-AB1>3.0.CO;2-T.

Schwartz, D., Dodge, K. A., & Coie, J. D. (1993). The emergence of chronic peer victimization in boys' play groups. *Child Development, 64*, 1755–1772. doi:10.2307/1131467.

Schwartz, D., Gorman, A. H., Nakamoto, J., & Toblin, R. L. (2005). Victimization in the peer group and children's academic functioning. *Journal of Educational Psychology, 97*, 425–435. doi:10.1037/0022-0663.97.3.425.

Seals, D., & Young, J. (2003). Bullying and victimization: Prevalence and relationship to gender, grade level, ethnicity, self-esteem, and depression. *Adolescence, 38*, 735–747.

Shavel-Jessop, S., Shearer, J., McDowell, E., & Hearst, D. (2012). Managing teasing and bullying. In S. Berkowitz (Ed.), *Cleft lip and palate* (pp. 917–926). New York: Springer. doi:10.1007/978-3-642-30770-6_46.

Sigurdson, J. F., Wallander, J., & Sund, A. M. (2014). Is involvement in school bullying associated with general health and psychosocial adjustment outcomes in adulthood? *Child Abuse & Neglect, 38*, 1607–1617. doi:10.1016/j.chiabu.2014.06.001.

Smith, H., Polenik, K., Nakasita, S., & Jones, A. P. (2012). Profiling social, emotional and behavioural difficulties of children involved in direct and indirect bullying behaviours. *Emotional & Behavioural Difficulties, 17*, 243–257. doi:10.1080/13632752.2012.704315.

Smith, P. K. (2011). Why interventions to reduce bullying and violence in schools may (or may not) succeed: Comments on this special section. *International Journal of Behavioral Development, 35*, 419–423. doi:10.1177/0165025411407459.

Storch, E. A., Brassard, M. R., & Masia-Warner, C. (2003). The relationship of peer victimization to social anxiety and loneliness in adolescence. *Child Study Journal, 33*, 1–18.

Storch, E. A., & Masia-Warner, C. (2004). The relationship of peer victimization to social anxiety and loneliness in adolescent females. *Journal of Adolescence, 27*, 351–362. doi:10.1016/j.adolescence.2004.03.003.

Sullivan, T. N., Farrell, A. D., & Kliewer, W. (2006). Peer victimization in early adolescence: Association between physical and relational victimization and drug use, aggression, and delinquent behaviors among urban middle school students. *Development and Psychopathology, 18*, 119–137. doi:10.1017/S095457940606007X.

Swearer, S. M. (2008). Relational aggression: Not just a female issue. *Journal of School Psychology, 46*, 611–616. doi:10.1016/j.jsp.2008.08.001.

Swearer, S. M., Espelage, D. L., Vaillancourt, T., & Hymel, S. (2010). What can be done about school bullying? Linking research to educational practice. *Educational Researcher, 39*, 38–47. doi:10.3102/0013189X09357622.

Turner, H. A., Finkelhor, D., Hamby, S. L., Shattuck, A., & Ormrod, R. K. (2011). Specifying type and location of peer victimization in a national sample of children and youth. *Journal of Youth and Adolescence, 40*, 1052–1067. doi:10.1007/s10964-011-9639-5.

Underwood, M. K. (2003). *Social aggression among girls*. New York: Guilford Press.

Underwood, M. K. (2011). Aggression. In M. K. Underwood & L. H. Rosen (Eds.), *Social development* (pp. 207–234). New York: Guilford.

Underwood, M. K., Beron, K. J., & Rosen, L. H. (2011). Joint trajectories for social and physical aggression as predictors of adolescent maladjustment: Internalizing symptoms, rule-breaking behaviors, and borderline and narcissistic personality features. *Development and Psychopathology, 23*, 659–678. doi:10.1017/S095457941100023X.

Underwood, M. K., & Rosen, L. H. (2011). Gender and bullying: Moving beyond mean differences to consider conceptions of bullying, processes by which bullying unfolds, and cyber bullying. In D. Espelage & S. Swearer (Eds.), *Bullying in American schools: An update* (pp. 13–22). New York: Lawrence Erlbaum.

van den Berg, P., Wertheim, E. H., Thompson, J. K., & Paxton, S. J. (2002). Development of body image, eating disturbance, and general psychological functioning in adolescent females: A replication using covariance structure modeling in an Australian sample. *International Journal of Eating Disorders, 32*, 46–51. doi:10.1002/eat.10030.

Waasdorp, T. E., & Bradshaw, C. P. (2015). The overlap between cyberbullying and traditional bullying. *Journal of Adolescent Health, 56*, 483–488. doi:10.1016/j.jadohealth.2014.12.002.

Werth, J. M., Nickerson, A. B., Aloe, A. M., & Swearer, S. M. (2015). Bullying victimization and the social and emotional maladjustment of bystanders: A propensity score analysis. *Journal of School Psychology, 53*, 295–308. doi:10.1016/j.jsp.2015.05.004.

Williams, K. R., & Guerra, N. G. (2007). Prevalence and predictors of internet bullying. *Journal of Adolescent Health, 41*, 14–21.

CHAPTER 2

# Students' Perspectives on Bullying

*Scott W. Ross, Emily M. Lund, Christian Sabey, and Cade Charlton*

The last two decades have seen an overwhelming call to "do something" about bullying. All 50 US states have anti-bullying laws that clearly prohibit bullying and assert its detrimental effect on school environments (http://bullypolice.org, 2015). Hundreds of anti-bullying programs have been developed by researchers and practitioners in response. However, many of the efforts have shown less than ideal results. In fact, some efforts have produced iatrogenic effects, with incidents of bullying increasing after the bullying prevention program was implemented (Farrington & Ttofi, 2009; Merrell, Gueldner, Ross, & Isava, 2008).

There are several potential reasons for the troubling findings of bullying prevention research including (a) teaching students how to recognize, and arguably how to perpetrate aggressive behavior, (b) blaming bullies

S.W. Ross (✉)
Colorado Department of Education, Denver, CO, USA

E.M. Lund
Center for Psychiatric Rehabilitation, Boston University, Boston, MA, USA

C. Sabey • C. Charlton
Brigham Young University, Provo, UT, USA



L.H. Rosen et al. (eds.), *Bullying in School*,
DOI 10.1057/978-1-137-59298-9_2

and excluding them from the social context, and (c) forcing victims to interact with perpetrators who may be further reinforced by the interaction (Merrell et al., 2008). However, in this chapter we will focus on perhaps the biggest reason bullying prevention efforts have failed to result in improved outcomes for students: a lack of focus on involving bystanders, a critical yet too often overlooked component of the bullying dynamic.

Although prevalence rates vary depending on the measurement tool and other variables, around 30% of students report being involved in bullying as either a perpetrator or a victim (Swearer & Espelage, 2004). However, studies indicate that far more students (60–90%) witness bullying on a regular basis (Hoover, Oliver, & Hazier, 1992; National Crime Prevention Council, 2003). These students fall into the category of "bystander", which includes every student other than the bully and victim present during an incident. The aim of this chapter is to discuss the role that these bystanders play in bullying in an effort to inform future prevention and intervention. We will start by considering a functional view of bullying and the antecedents and consequences that fuel it. Once this foundation is established, we will consider the spectrum of roles that bystanders play in bullying incidents, followed by specific strategies that families and schools can employ to change the behavior of everyone involved.

## A Functional Perspective on Bullying

An important concept underlying a functional view of bullying is the idea that all behavior serves a specific purpose. The theory of Applied Behavior Analysis contends that organisms engage in behavior to access reinforcement or avoid punishment (Cooper, Heron, & Heward, 2007). Behaviors that result in reinforcement are more likely to occur in the future under similar circumstances, whereas behaviors that are not reinforced or that result in punishment are less likely to occur in the future under similar circumstances. For example, a student may give a correct answer to a question during math class and receive praise from the teacher. If adult praise functions as a reinforcer for that student, she is more likely to answer questions in the future. Conversely, a student may give an incorrect answer and be teased for not knowing the correct answer. Teasing may serve as a punisher for future responding, making it less likely that the student will answer questions in the future. This principle applies to all behavior and can be conceptualized in a three-step, Antecedent-Behavior-Consequence (ABC) contingency, where the antecedent represents a trigger for a given behavior and the consequence represents the result of the behavior (Cooper et al., 2007; see two examples of the ABC contingency in Tables 2.1 and 2.2).

**Table 2.1** Antecedent, behavior, consequence contingency example: punishment

| *(A)ntecedent* | *(B)ehavior* | *(C)onsequence* |
|---|---|---|
| Student is asked to do a math problem in front of the class | Student tries to do the problem at the board, but struggles | Peers laugh at student and one says aloud, "that one is so easy" |

**Table 2.2** Antecedent, behavior, consequence contingency example: reinforcement

| *(A)ntecedent* | *(B)ehavior* | *(C)onsequence* |
|---|---|---|
| An unpopular peer sits down at a table in the cafeteria next to her more popular peers | One of the popular students teases the unpopular peer, making fun of her appearance | Other popular peers at the table laugh or otherwise join in on the insults |

In the academic example above, teasing (C) serves as a punishment for doing a math problem at the board, as long as it decreases the likelihood that the student will be willing to do a math problem at the board in the future. Conversely, in the example below, sitting at the popular kids' table serves as a trigger for bullying behavior that is immediately reinforced by the laughter of bystanders, increasing the likelihood that bullying behavior will continue and happen again in the future.

The ABC contingency allows for the identification of contextual variables that parents, educators, and professionals can control. Such variables occur outside of the individual and include the events that reliably precede and follow behavior. In bullying, each incident starts with an antecedent or trigger, indicating the availability of reinforcement. In some situations, victims exhibit awkward or unusual behavior that can trigger bullying behavior. In other situations, transitions to unstructured, unsupervised environments are enough to trigger bullying. Once the trigger occurs, perpetrators exhibit some form of physical, verbal, relational, or cyber aggression in order to access peer attention from victims and bystanders. Even when bystanders watch the behavior passively, their mere presence may provide reinforcement through peer interest and passive acknowledgment (O'Connell, Pepler, & Craig, 1999). Similarly, crying and fighting back as the victim or on behalf of the victim may draw additional peer attention that is reinforcing to the perpetrator and thus may unintentionally increase the likelihood of bullying.

Research indicates that incidents of bullying are fundamentally and overwhelmingly reinforced by peer attention. Craig, Pepler, and Atlas (2000) conducted a study in which elementary school students were video- and audio-taped for episodes of bullying and harassment throughout the school. They found that students other than the bully and victim (i.e., bystanders) were present in 79% of incidents that took place on the playground and 85% of those that took place in the classroom. In addition, O'Connell et al. (1999) coded 185 individual instances of bullying behavior with 120 elementary school students and found that 53.5% ($n$ = 99) of segments involved at least two bystander peers. In a study by Ross and Horner (2009), both victim and bystander responses to bullying incidents were measured. Prior to intervention, victim attention (e.g., crying, whining, or fighting back) followed 53% of bullying incidents, and bystander reinforcement (e.g., verbal encouragement and affirmation) followed 57% of incidents (victim and bystander responses were not exclusive). Finally, in O'Connell et al. (1999) study, the number of peers present was positively related to the duration of bullying episodes. The more peers around, the longer the incident lasted. Having more peers present provides more peer attention, resulting in more potent reinforcement.

## Implications of Peer Attention for Perpetrators and Victims

**Perpetrators.** In each incident of bullying, the perpetrator must first determine if aggression (physical, verbal, relational, cyber) is likely to result in peer reinforcement. The perpetrator may see another student in proximity but not directly involved with a group of peers, which may indicate access to both a target for bullying and peers who could potentially provide reinforcement. Additionally, certain characteristics of the victim such as physical weakness, a lack of social skills, or unpopularity may increase the likelihood that peers will join in, and decrease the likelihood that the perpetrator will face physical or social backlash (i.e., punishment; Blake, Lund, Zhou, & Benz, 2012, Craig et al., 2000; Fox & Boulton, 2011). Thus, certain students may become victims because they represent a high probability of reinforcement and a low probability of punishment.

Once the perpetrator engages in bullying behavior, other peers may choose to join in or cheer the perpetrator on. Such peer responses reinforce the bullying behavior and increase the likelihood of future incidents given a similar context (Cooper et al., 2007). Even without bystander active involvement, the perpetrator may be reinforced simply through bystander passive observation (O'Connell et al., 1999). Finally, bullying behavior may also be reinforced by the victims who cry, whine, or fight back. While the reinforcing events may vary, they all provide some form of peer attention and reinforcement of the perpetrator's behavior.

**Victims.** While social reinforcement fuels the behavior of perpetrators, it also has implications for victims. In each incident of bullying, a victim's behavior can be reinforced or punished by the behavior of perpetrators and bystanders. Physical, verbal, relational, and cyber aggression are often harmful and punishing to the victim, resulting in the victim avoiding the perpetrator, the environment, or school altogether (Merrell et al., 2008). However, bullying incidents may also provide a form of peer attention to the victim. Some victims of bullying are unpopular and have few friends. The peer attention provided by incidents of bullying, despite being negative and hurtful, may still reinforce the triggering behavior of victims (Cooper et al., 2007). If the reinforcing effects of the peer attention from perpetrators and bystanders outweigh the punishing effects of the aggression, the victim may learn that being victimized is an effective means of gaining peer attention. In the future that individual may seek out similar interactions, even when those interactions result in some harm. They may also learn to instigate bullying (i.e., bully/victims) if they have poor social skills or are unable to access peer attention more appropriately. Unfortunately, this is commonly the case for students with disabilities, especially those with emotional disturbance, attention deficit hyperactivity disorder, oppositional defiant disorder, autism spectrum disorder, or orthopedic impairments (Blake et al., 2012).

## Implications of Peer Attention for Bystanders

As with perpetrators and victims, the behavior of bystanders is a function of the social consequences (i.e., reinforcement or punishment). Bystanders may play a variety of roles in incidents depending on the environment and their relationship with the perpetrator and the victim (Salmivalli, Lagerspetz, Björkqvist, Österman, & Kaukiainen, 1996). In each incident of bullying, reinforcement from perpetrators, reinforcement from victims and adults, and punishment from perpetrators or victims are in competition with each other. Each bystander's response can be determined by the sum of those consequences. For example, if the acknowledgment, friendship, or fear of the bully outweighs the desire to help, the access to adult recognition, or the positive attention of the victim, the bystander is likely to join in or otherwise support the perpetrator. On the other hand, if the bystander is not highly reinforced by the perpetrator's attention, feels a lot of empathy for the victim, or really wants to impress adults, they are more likely to support the victim. In the end, the actions of the bystander occur along a spectrum, depending on the contingencies in the environment. These actions can range from helping the perpetrator to defending the victim, with various levels of involvement in between. Olweus' early research (Olweus, 1997; Olweus et al., 2007) as well as the research of Salmivalli et al. (1996), illustrates this spectrum of bystander roles (Fig. 2.1).

The students that bully and the students that are victimized are at opposite ends of the spectrum. The "bully" typically instigates the aggressive behavior in its various forms and takes an active part. The "victim" is the target of the bullying but may be simultaneously reinforced and punished by the incident. However, as indicated above, many researchers have argued that the most important roles in the environment are not the victim and perpetrator, but instead the bystanders around the incident that reinforce and discourage it (e.g., Craig et al., 2000; Farrington & Ttofi, 2009; O'Connell et al., 1999; Olweus, 1997; Stueve et al., 2006). In addition, research suggests that even bystanders are negatively affected by bullying, depending on the role they play in it (Stueve et al., 2006).

Next to the "bullies" on the spectrum are bullying followers or henchmen, who take an active part in bullying but do not initiate it (Olweus, 1997; Olweus et al., 2007; Salmivalli et al., 1996). They are often friends of the initiator, and their behavior may be reinforced by the positive peer attention of the initiator and other bystanders or the negative peer attention of the victim. These students will often join in with the initiator once the bullying situation is underway, engaging in teasing, exclusion, or even physical aggression started by the "bully". In a study by Whitney and Smith (1993), 18% of middle and high school students said that they would fulfill this role and join in if their friends were bullying someone.

Next in line after the followers/henchmen are the active supporters of bullying (Olweus, 1997; Olweus et al., 2007; Salmivalli et al., 1996). These students cheer it on but do not take an active part. In an

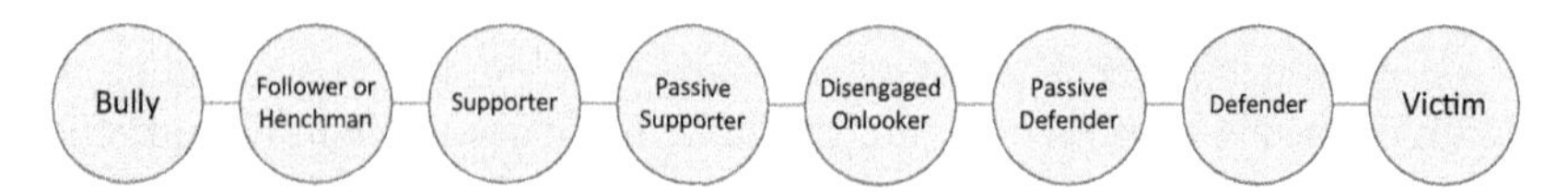


**Fig. 2.1** The spectrum of bystander roles

online environment, they may provide "likes" to the incident but will not go as far as joining in. In a school environment, they may laugh at someone being teased or cheer during a fight. Active supporters of bullying may not engage in the actual bullying because they are fearful of getting in trouble or because they do not want to be grouped with the bully. However, active supporters often end up engaging in the bullying because of peer pressure, or because they see all the peer attention available. Like the henchmen/followers, active support of bullying is often reinforced by the positive attention of the perpetrator, positive attention from other bystanders, and the crying, whining, and fighting back of the victim(s).

Although followers and active supporters are prevalent, the most common bystanders fall into the categories of passive supporters, disengaged onlookers, passive defenders, and active defenders. In a study by Boulton and Underwood (1992), when asked "What do you do when you see a child of your age being bullied?" middle school students responded in the following manner: 49% said they tried to help in some way, 29% said they did nothing but thought that they should try to help, and 22% said they would not help because it was none of their business.

Passive supporters of bullying are unlike active supporters in that they approve of the bullying but do not display open support for it (Olweus, 1997; Olweus et al., 2007; Salmivalli et al., 1996). Students that engage in this behavior do not want to be seen as encouraging bullying so they do not openly cheer or laugh. The fear of getting in trouble may be strong for these students, or they may even be friends with the victim. Even so, they continue to support the behavior through passive observation and involvement. Disengaged onlookers, on the other hand, are those that watch what happens but are not swayed one way or the other. They believe that bullying is none of their business. Unfortunately, they rarely realize that their attention is fueling the behavior despite their disinterest, and that it is increasing the likelihood and intensity of future bullying.

At the helping end of the spectrum are the passive defenders and active defenders (Olweus, 1997; Olweus et al., 2007; Salmivalli et al., 1996). Passive defenders are those in the bullying environment that clearly disapprove of the bullying and think that someone should stand up to it but fail to do so themselves. These students may want to support the victim but may not know how to or may be afraid of associating with the victim for fear of lowering their own status, retribution from the bully, or becoming a victim themselves. They may also fear reporting incidents to adults because they do not want to be a "tattletale" or "snitch". Passive defenders often experience feelings of guilt after bullying incidents because they failed to stand up to the bullying on behalf of the victim.

Finally, active defenders are those students that know how to stand up to bullying, are not strongly reinforced by those supporting it, and are either strongly reinforced by adult approval, strongly reinforced by victim attention, or strongly reinforced by an empathic repertoire and the feeling they get from helping others (Olweus, 1997; Olweus et al., 2007; Salmivalli et al., 1996). If these bystanders intervene the right way, they can effectively remove the reinforcement fueling it. However, if they intervene the wrong way, as is the case with certain victim responses, they can actually provide additional peer attention to the situation, increasing the likelihood of future problem behavior and potentially getting themselves targeted in the process. One common example of this is when a victim and their friend(s) fight back against a student that initiates bullying behavior. They may get angry at the perpetrator, argue with them, start rumors, or even get physically aggressive (e.g., start a fight). In some cases this aggression can serve as punishment to the bully and reduces the likelihood of future behavior. However, if the perpetrator *perceives* the interaction as providing peer attention rather than punishment, the behavior may increase in frequency and intensity in the future. Unfortunately, this is commonly the case in incidents of bullying where the perpetrator has more power or is more popular, bigger, or stronger than the victim and their friends. For this reason, it is critical for educators to not only move young people to the right on the bullying spectrum—away from the bullies and toward the active defenders of victims—but it is also critical to teach those bystanders clear, simple, and non-confrontational strategies that do not result in the perception of peer attention but instead result in the extinction of future problem behavior.

## Bystander-Driven Interventions

Why does the function of bullying behavior matter? The answer is relatively simple: when we understand the contingencies driving problem behavior, we get a much clearer indication of the strategies that can be implemented to improve it. In the examples above, we considered antecedent, behavior, and consequence variables that are prominent in bullying situations. Knowing these variables allows us to contemplate antecedent, behavior, and consequence interventions that can be used to address the problem. Consider again the example provided in Table 2.2. In that scenario, an unpopular peer sits down at a lunch table with popular peers (antecedent). She is teased by the popular peers (behavior), resulting in peer attention in the form of laughter (consequence) from the others. Because we understand these contextual variables, we can develop strategies to address each (see Table 2.3 for a description of intervention types).

**Antecedent interventions.** First, antecedent interventions are those designed to reduce the likelihood of the antecedent occurring, or prompt more appropriate behaviors when the antecedent does occur (Cooper et al., 2007). For example, reorganizing the lunch room so that the popular kids cannot sit together, or implementing a buddy system where all students sit with a partner, would be considered antecedent interventions that reduce the likelihood of the antecedent: the victim sitting down alone at a table filled with popular peers. Antecedent interventions can also include those strategies that prompt alternative, more appropriate responses to the antecedent. Reminding all students at the beginning of lunch that respectful behavior means including everyone is an example of an antecedent intervention that prompts a more appropriate behavior (including everyone) when the antecedent occurs (unpopular peer sitting down at the table).

**Behavior interventions.** Behavior interventions are categorized as interventions that teach more desired, alternative behaviors that still achieve the desired consequence, in this case, peer attention (Cooper et al., 2007). This often involves teaching desired behaviors such as social skills that access peer reinforcement in the environment. For example, schools can implement social skills training that teach students how to make friends and interact with each other appropriately. Using these skills increases access to naturally occurring peer attention. However, if we want

**Table 2.3** Antecedent, behavior, consequence strategies

| *(A)ntecedent interventions* | *(B)ehavior interventions* | *(C)onsequence interventions* |
|---|---|---|
| Interventions that prevent the antecedent from occurring or prompt a more appropriate alternative behavior | Interventions that teach more appropriate and more efficient behavior that access the desired reinforcement | Interventions that reduce access to the desired consequence following problem behavior and increase access following appropriate behavior |

students to actually use the new, more appropriate skills for making friends and accessing peer attention, the new skills must be more effective and more efficient at accessing peer attention than the old, less appropriate behavior. In other words, the desired behavior must be better at accessing peer attention than the bullying behavior. For this reason, simply teaching desired behaviors is rarely enough.

**Consequence interventions.** To result in real behavior change, schools should consider consequence strategies that either increase access to peer attention following appropriate, desired behavior or decrease access to peer attention following inappropriate, bullying behavior (Cooper et al., 2007). To increase access to peer attention following positive behavior, schools can implement strategies that reward students with peer attention for being respectful to others. Students can earn activities for their entire class, activities with a friend, or recognition delivered by their peers. Such strategies can be extremely powerful at increasing the positive behavior of students highly reinforced by peer attention. Conversely, to decrease access to peer attention following bullying behavior, schools can teach all students (including bystanders) specific strategies for responding to disrespectful behavior. These strategies should be simple and non-confrontational and should ensure reduced access to peer attention. For example, in one of the interventions described in the school interventions section below, all students in the school learn a simple, non-confrontational stop response, which is used whenever someone is disrespectful toward you or anyone else (Ross & Horner, 2009, 2013). The response is designed to be easy for students to implement and maintain positive relationships with those they use the stop response with while at the same time significantly reducing access to peer attention following disrespectful behavior.

## Effective School Bullying Interventions

The most common school response to bullying is to do nothing until a major incident occurs, followed by increasingly intense punishment and exclusion of the student(s) caught bullying. Unfortunately, not only has this strategy been ineffective in reducing bullying (APA, 2008), it may contribute to increased aggression, vandalism, truancy, and dropout (Hemphill, Toumbourou, Herrenkohl, McMorris, & Catalano, 2006; March & Horner, 2002; Mayer, 1995; Mayer & Sulzer-Azaroff, 1991; Skiba & Peterson, 1999; Skiba, Peterson, & Williams, 1997). From a functional perspective, adult-driven punishment strategies do little to reduce access to peer attention. In addition, they often decrease student feelings of connectedness to school, a major risk factor for dropout (Blum & Libbey, 2004). Rather, to effectively combat bullying in schools, three strategies appear to be the most promising. First, schools can shift their culture so that students feel safe and empowered to stand up for each other. Second, schools can teach specific strategies for peer recognition and the peer-based reinforcement of positive, stand-up behavior. Third, in addition to creating peer-based recognition, all students (perpetrators, victims, and bystanders) can learn simple strategies for standing up to bullying that effectively remove peer attention rather than providing more of it. The following paragraphs will discuss these strategies and their potential effects.

## Bullying Prevention Culture

The first step a school can take in combating bullying is the creation of a positive school culture where all students feel safe, happy, and empowered to support each other. Research indicates specific social factors that contribute to a "culture of bullying" in some schools, which include shared beliefs and attitudes that support bullying (Bradshaw, Sawyer, & O'Brennan, 2009; Unnever & Cornell, 2008). Aggression and peer victimization become the norm in these schools, and students perceive them as less safe and less supportive. These schools also have increased aggression, retaliation, resistance to reporting bullying incidents, and poor academic performance (Bradshaw et al., 2009).

To shift and improve their culture, schools can implement universal strategies that improve the social environment and broader social climate. Research documents the importance of school-wide prevention efforts that establish and reinforce a common set of behavioral expectations in all contexts and involve all school personnel in prevention activities (Barrett, Bradshaw, & Lewis-Palmer, 2008; Bradshaw et al., 2009; Ross & Horner, 2009). A major example of this work can be seen in School-Wide Positive Behavioral Interventions and Supports (SW-PBIS). While not a pre-packaged program, more than 20 years of research has demonstrated the ability of SW-PBIS to reduce problem behavior and improve school climate (Horner, Sugai, Todd, & Lewis-Palmer, 2005). Recent findings have also indicated significant impacts of SW-PBIS on teacher reports of bullying and rejection (Waasdorp, Bradshaw, & Leaf, 2011).

To create a more positive school climate, SW-PBIS (a) uses empirically tested instructional principles to teach expected, positive behavior to all students (Colvin & Kame'enui, 1993), (b) creates a system of reinforcement for expected behaviors and a continuum of consequences for inappropriate behavior, (c) provides training/feedback to staff regarding their implementation of systems (Crone & Horner, 2010), and (d) employs explicit problem solving around reinforcement and discipline data (Sprague & Horner, 2006). The implementation of these strategies has resulted in demonstrated effectiveness when implemented by state, district, and school educators without the substantial support of researchers (Barrett et al., 2008; Horner et al., 2009), as well as over time (Luiselli, Putnam, & Sunderland, 2002; Taylor-Green & Kartub, 2000).

## Increasing Peer Attention for Stand-Up Behavior

Effective SW-PBIS implementation creates a school environment where all students feel safe and are more likely to act according to expectations. It also provides the data and systems necessary to support sustainability, effective modifications, and interventions for students needing additional supports. However, even with effective SW-PBIS strategies in place, it is not uncommon for a proportion of students to continue exhibiting bullying-like behavior. This is likely due to a lack of emphasis on peer-driven, bystander intervention. In SW-PBIS, adults teach school-wide expectations, reinforce those expectations, and problem solve accordingly. However, SW-PBIS does not include specific strategies for increasing peer attention for stand-up behavior, nor specific strategies for removing the peer attention driving bullying behavior (Ross & Horner, 2009, 2013). To address the first problem, educators should consider adding strategies that increase peer reinforcement for appropriate, positive alternative behaviors that can replace bullying behaviors.

One of the biggest challenges when changing student behavior in response to bullying is the acquisition of student buy-in (Biernesser & Sun, 2009; Nese, Horner, Dickey, Stiller, & Tomlanovich, 2014). When adults tell students how they are supposed to address bullying, students often feel the strategies are too childlike and "uncool". In order for students (especially older ones) to take bullying interventions seriously, they must play a major role in their development, implementation, and evaluation (Biernesser & Sun, 2009; Nese et al., 2014). This process should begin with the creation of a student leadership team that is involved at a very early stage, typically the semester before any strategies are implemented in the school. Previously created teams such as fifth grade classes in elementary schools and student officers or clubs in secondary schools can be used for this purpose; however, the adults that lead the team need to ensure that its members are representative of the school. Sometimes already existent leadership teams in schools are not perceived by other students as representative of them. For the team to be effective in recognizing the positive behavior of others, all students must find their recognition reinforcing. One option is to add to already existing teams through a nomination process where all students nominate those *they feel the most comfortable talking to when they are being treated disrespectfully or having a difficult time.* The students nominated do not need to be the most popular, or the most academically successful. They are simply the students whose recognition other students find reinforcing. In addition, there is no specific limit to the number of students that can be on the leadership team, with some schools having over 100 students involved. The number should only be limited by the number of staff available to supervise them and the venues available to meet with them on at least a monthly basis.

Once the student leadership team is created, they are given four major duties. First, they are put in charge of reviewing dis-identified data about bullying in their school. To do this well, schools should implement surveys that can be aggregated and shared with the student leadership teams. Hundreds of bullying surveys have been created, varying greatly in detail, cost, and time for completion. However, all surveys should provide the student leadership teams with the opportunity to consider the forms of aggression most common, where those behaviors occur, when those behaviors occur, how students (victims and bystanders) typically respond to incidents, and how adults typically respond to incidents.

Once the data has been reviewed, the student leadership team's work can be broken into two major components: intervention and marketing. The intervention component involves the development of specific intervention strategies that provide positive peer attention for stand-up behavior and addresses specific problems in the school as indicated by the data review. One common and promising approach to the provision of positive peer attention is through stand-up behavior nomination boxes placed throughout the school. These boxes provide an opportunity for any student or adult in the school to nominate others for stand-up behavior: "If you experienced someone standing up for you or others, either online or in person, we want you to briefly write down and describe what they did, and put a nomination in the box". Then, once a month, after the supervising adult has ensured only "real" nominations are included, the student leadership team goes out and provides small, school-based reinforcement to those nominated. In addition, a website called Stand for Courage (www.standforcourage.org) was created in 2010 to provide a place where nominations could be uploaded, which could then be recognized further by celebrities on a quarterly basis.

In addition to the development of specific intervention strategies in the school, the student leadership team is also put in charge of creating marketing to increase student, staff, and community buy-in. This often includes the creation of posters, t-shirts, and social media marketing strategies. It can also include announcements to the school, faculty, parents, and community using social media, newsletters, or school newspapers.

Finally, the student leadership team is put in charge of reporting the results of their efforts. This requires another survey be completed after the intervention strategies have been implemented. The team presents the success of their efforts to the students, staff, community, district office, and above. They also continuously problem solve, modify previous efforts, and create new intervention strategies for the upcoming year.

## Strategies that Remove Peer Attention

In addition to creating a more positive school culture and implementing specific strategies for recognizing positive stand-up behavior, it is also important to develop strategies that can effectively remove the peer attention that typically drives bullying behavior. Most popular bullying prevention strategies have an impact on victim and bystander peer attention in one form or another; however, some strategies have proven more effective than others. First, many schools implement zero-tolerance policies, which mandate suspensions and expulsions for children caught bullying. While these strategies may remove the peer attention from the immediate environment and ensure the safety of the victim, they may also result in underreporting of bullying incidents due to the punitive culture they create. In addition, there is limited evidence that such strategies reduce bullying behavior (APA, 2008), and some evidence suggests they contribute to future antisocial behavior (Hemphill et al., 2006; Mayer, 1995) and increase school dropout (Skiba et al., 1997).

A second popular bullying prevention strategy involves brief assemblies or one-day awareness raising events. These programs are easy for schools to implement and are often powerful, emotional experiences for everyone involved. They primarily focus on increasing awareness and empowering students to stand up to bullying. However, while these programs sometimes teach specific strategies for responding to bullying and effectively removing the peer attention reinforcing it, little evidence suggests that they are sufficient for changing the school climate or producing sustainable effects (HRSA, n.d.).

Farrington and Ttofi (2009) indicate that some of the most effective bullying prevention efforts include increased playground supervision, parent and community involvement, the use of consistent disciplinary methods, and classroom behavior management strategies. Although each of these strategies are adult driven, they can potentially reduce bullying behavior by getting adults involved early before peers can provide attention as well as by providing clear expectations about consequences. However, when it comes to bystander-based bullying prevention efforts, the most common, most researched, and most promising strategies may involve teaching students social-emotional and bullying prevention skills through regular classroom instruction and practice (Merrell et al., 2008). If done right, the result of such instruction can be an increase in bystander awareness, an increase in bystander empowerment, an increase in effective responses to bullying incidents, and a reduction in peer attention following incidents.

The most extensively researched program employing bystander instructional strategies is the Olweus Bullying Prevention Program (OBPP; Olweus et al., 2007). The OBPP is clearly one of the important early influences and standards of well-conceived, solidly researched school-wide approaches to preventing bullying behavior in schools. The OBPP is a comprehensive program with multiple components but also includes bullying prevention class meetings with all students conducted throughout the year. These lessons cover several categories of social-emotional skills including: building a positive classroom climate, identifying feelings, identifying bullying hot spots in the school, developing peer relationships, respecting differences, and serving the community. While teaching these lessons can be time and resource intensive for teachers, an increasing number of validation replications and enhancements have been conducted in Norway and in the United States (Nansel et al., 2001; Olweus, 1997, 2005; Solberg & Olweus, 2003), demonstrating the program's effectiveness. However, some research on OBPP has revealed that additional program development and research is still needed. For example, Limber, Nation, Tracy, Melton, and Flerx (2004) reported some initial reductions in self-report measures of peer victimization in boys after implementation of OBPP. However, two years later, differences from the baseline level of peer victimization were insignificant. Additionally, an analysis of results obtained in a study conducted in Rogaland, Norway, indicated an actual increase in bullying behavior three years after the implementation of the Olweus program (Roland, 1993). These types of findings reinforce the need for further enhancements and extensions of bystander-driven bullying prevention instruction and intervention.

A second bullying prevention program designed to improve school culture and teach students how to respond to bullying is Steps to Respect (Frey, Kirschstein, & Snell, 2005). Like the OBPP, Steps to Respect is a comprehensive program that includes classroom-focused lessons to teach all students strategies for supporting each other. The Steps to Respect program has a dual focus on bullying and friendship, training students to make and keep friends, as well as recognize, resist, and report bullying. Like the OBPP, Steps to Respect lessons teach an extensive list of student skills, including social-emotional competence, emotional intelligence, self-management, and social skills. Again, this instruction may be time-consuming for some teachers and schools; however, two studies have demonstrated the program's efficacy. Those trials demonstrated significant impacts on bullying-related attitudes and observations of bullying; however, neither study demonstrated significant improvements on student self-reports of bullying (Brown, Low, Smith, & Haggerty, 2011; Frey et al., 2005).

Finally, in 2008, Ross, Horner, and Stiller developed Bullying Prevention in Positive Behavior Support (BP-PBS), which was designed to fit within the SW-PBIS framework and add simple, bystander-specific, peer attention-related instruction to further reduce bullying behavior. Rather than teach an extensive list of friendship, social-emotional, and bullying prevention skills, the BP-PBS intervention focuses on teaching, practicing, and reinforcing a small set of explicit skills that effectively remove peer attention from bullying environments. First, BP-PBS teaches all students to use a simple, school-wide verbal command and hand signal when they witness or are the target of disrespectful behavior. If this stop signal fails to resolve the problem, students are instructed to walk away or help others walk away from social aggression. Only if walking away fails or if the behavior places people at serious risk of harm are they instructed to tell an adult. This strategy minimizes potential social reinforcement and gives all students a simple, common, and predictable response. In addition, the BP-PBS intervention includes practice and pre-correction for the stop response prior to entering activities likely to include problematic behavior, teaches an appropriate student response when they encounter the stop sequence, and trains all school staff on a universal strategy for responding when students report continued incidents of socially aggressive behavior.

Ross and Horner (2009) found that when BP-PBS strategies were added to the SW-PBIS framework, results indicated a 72% decrease in the frequency of physical and verbal peer aggression perpetrated by at-risk students. Furthermore, they found that following implementation, victims were 19% less likely to cry or fight back, and bystanders were 22% less likely to laugh, cheer, or otherwise join in during incidents (both forms of peer attention). In addition, follow-up studies of BP-PBS have shown significant reductions in self-reported bullying (Ross & Horner, 2013) and bullying-related office discipline referrals and suspensions (Good, McIntosh, & Gietz, 2011). Although these results are promising, none of the studies on BP-PBS were randomized control trials, and more research is needed to validate the effectiveness of the BP-PBS intervention on larger samples of students.

Bystander-focused intervention may be the most promising approach to addressing bullying in schools; however, it is also important to note that some bystander-based efforts can be ineffective or even potentially harmful to students. For example, some peer mediation, conflict resolution, and mentoring strategies have actually resulted in increases in victimization (Farrington & Ttofi, 2009). From a functional perspective, when peers get involved in mediating conflicts, they may inadvertently be providing additional peer attention to the context, increasing the future likelihood of bullying behavior. Additionally, in some cases peer mediators may be viewed by other students as "snitches" and may become victims themselves. Finally, studies on youth violence and delinquency (Dodge, Dishion, & Lansford, 2006) suggest that grouping together students who bully to "teach" them better behavior may actually reinforce their aggressive behavior and result in higher rates of bullying. In these environments, a peer-deviance training occurs, whereby the initiators of bullying learn from each other and are reinforced for their aggressive behavior.

## The Role of Families and the Community in Bullying Prevention

Families are the first line of defense in teaching children how to treat others with respect. Not only can they play a large role in the school interventions described above, they also play an integral role in empowering stand-up behavior, modeling appropriate strategies, and reinforcing implementation of those strategies.

**Engaging with schools to prevent bullying.** Despite the consistent findings that family and community engagement has a powerful effect on student success (Fan & Chen, 2001; Henderson & Mapp, 2002; Jeynes, 2003, 2005), schools often fail to place family engagement as a high priority (Epstein, 2011). Therefore, one of the first steps that parents can take is to engage actively and positively with their schools. Connect for Respect (www.PTA.org/c4R, 2015) is one example of using the Parent Teacher Association (PTA) to create increased opportunities for parent and community engagement in the improvement of school climate and the reduction of bullying. The Connect for Respect (C4R) process involves five steps. First, the PTA builds a C4R team, which can include students, teachers, community members, and parents with an aim to work collaboratively and improve school climate. Next, the C4R team is involved in the assessment of school climate through student, family, and school surveys. They can utilize already existing tools and resources such as the student report surveys employed by the student leadership team. Third, they engage the community in forums where students, families, school staff, and community members can voice concerns about bullying and school climate, as well as brainstorm solutions. Fourth, the C4R team develops an action plan to educate and empower family members and students, create more supportive school environments, and implement specific bullying prevention strategies. Finally, the C4R team can implement marketing and other empowerment strategies that encourage students, family, and the community to be involved in bullying prevention efforts.

**Empower stand-up behavior.** In addition to working with the school, community, and PTA to develop effective, collaborative bullying prevention and school climate strategies, families can also empower their own children to stand up for others and to not be silent, reinforcing (Epstein, 2011). First, it is important to talk with children and teach them that they play a role in bullying, even if they do not act as an instigator, active supporter, or passive supporter. One effective analogy for this is a candle and flame. Disrespectful, bullying behavior is like a flame that is hurtful to those around it. However, in order for a flame to burn, it needs the oxygen for fuel. This is similar to bullying, which needs peer attention to keep burning. Consequently, if you take a glass cup and cover the flame, removing the oxygen fueling it, the flame goes out. This is what happens when bystanders use a stop response, help victims walk away, or otherwise remove peer attention from bullying situations. Like a burning candle, the bullying flame does not go out right away, but over time as students learn their inappropriate behavior will not achieve the peer attention they desire.

In addition to teaching children about peer attention and the role bystanders play in bullying, parents can also work to encourage volunteerism and connections to the school and community. Instilling a sense of connectedness through extracurricular and volunteer activities can result in better relationships with adults and other students (Epstein, 2011; Jeynes, 2005). This will not only make the child a better person but also more comfortable engaging with adults and other students.

**Teach appropriate strategies.** Once students are motivated to engage with the school and stand up for themselves and others, it is important to teach them the right way to do so. Many parents make the mistake of teaching their children to fight back and "stand their ground". While it is important for children to learn to stand up for themselves and others, doing so using physical, verbal, social, or cyber aggression is likely to result in (a) getting hurt and (b) increasing the frequency and intensity of future problem behavior (Boulton & Underwood, 1992; Fox & Boulton, 2011; Hoover et al., 1992). Instead, parents should teach their children simple, clear, and non-confrontational strategies for standing up for themselves and others and removing the peer attention from the environment. It would be ideal if the school was already teaching a response strategy that parents can reinforce and practice at home. However, if this is not the case, parents can still discuss specific strategies their children can use when they witness bullying to take a clear stance against it. For example, if the child knows the instigator, they may be able to diffuse the situation by diverting attention to something else or non-confrontationally encouraging the bullying to stop. If they know the victim, they can take efforts to include them, support them, and offer a way out of situations, such as telling them a teacher is looking for them.

**Reinforce appropriate strategies.** Finally, not only is it important for families to empower and teach, it is also important for them to recognize and reinforce the positive behavior of their children. If parents catch their children doing good deeds and treating others with respect, praising their efforts will increase the likelihood of future positive behavior (Cooper et al., 2007; Epstein, 2011). Parents should ask their children about their days, the interactions they had with adults and other students, and reinforce the behaviors they want to see more of in the future.

## Summary

From a functional perspective, peer attention reinforces bullying behavior, which is triggered by antecedents like awkward victim behavior, the availability of reinforcing peers, or a lack of adult supervision such as during transitions from class to class or class to recess. Peer attention typically comes in the form of positive peer attention from bystanders that support the bullying, negative peer attention from the victims and bystanders that fight back, and neutral peer attention from bystanders that observe the behavior and do nothing about it. For this reason, the specific role that bystanders play can be considered along a spectrum, from henchmen and followers that join in on the bullying, to the active defenders that stand up to it. However, even when bystanders stand up to bullying, if they do so inappropriately, they may inadvertently increase the likelihood and severity of bullying in the future. Therefore, it is critical that students not only be empowered to stand up to bullying but also that they learn to do so in the most effective and efficient manner possible, eliminating the peer attention fueling the behavior while avoiding escalation, revenge, and retaliation.

The past two decades have seen an onslaught of school bullying prevention efforts (Merrell et al., 2008). While some of these efforts have had effects, many results have been mixed, and in some cases, programs have resulted in increased bullying. The most promising strategies are comprehensive ones that (a) create a more positive school culture where students feel safe and feel empowered to stand up for one another, (b) implement peer-driven strategies that provide peer attention for positive stand-up behavior, and (c) teach all students specific skills for removing the peer attention that reinforces bullying.

In addition to school interventions that target bystanders, families and communities also play a major role in shifting the behavior of bystanders. PTAs can create C4R teams that help in assessment, discussion forums, bullying prevention action plans, and marketing to increase buy-in. Parents and families can also work to empower their children to stand up to bullying, teach their children how to respond to incidents appropriately, and praise their children for stand-up efforts.

Bullying remains a major problem in schools and will continue to be a major problem until everyone recognizes the role they play in reinforcing it (O'Connell et al., 1999). Similarly, crying and fighting back as the victim or on behalf of the victim may draw additional peer attention that is reinforcing to the perpetrator and, thus, could unintentionally increase the likelihood of bullying. Research indicates that incidents of bullying are fundamentally and overwhelmingly reinforced by peer attention. (Craig et al., 2000). Bystanders must not only be empowered to stand up to bullying, they must be taught effective and non-confrontational ways of doing so. Schools play a major role in this effort, but family and community involvement is also critical. In the end, only through school, family, and community collaboration can we really impact the perpetrators, victims, and bystanders of bullying, resulting in a more safe and positive environment for everyone.

## References

American Psychological Association (APA) Zero Tolerance Task Force. (2008). Are zero tolerance policies effective in the schools?: An evidentiary review and recommendations. *American Psychologist, 63*, 852–862. doi:10.1037/0003-066X.63.9.852.

Barrett, S., Bradshaw, C. P., & Lewis-Palmer, T. (2008). Maryland state-wide PBIS initiative: Systems, evaluation, and next steps. *Journal of Positive Behavior Interventions, 10*, 105–114. doi:10.1177/1098300707312541.

Biernesser, K., & Sun, L. (2009). Empowering students: Using data to transform a bullying prevention and intervention program. *Professional School Counseling, 12*, 413–420. doi:10.5330/PSC.n.2010-12.413.

Blake, J., Lund, E., Zhou, Q., & Benz, M. (2012). National prevalence rates of bully victimization among students with disabilities in the United States. *School Psychology Quarterly, 27*, 210–222. doi:10.1037/spq0000008.

Blum, R. W., & Libbey, H. P. (2004). School connectedness—Strengthening health and education outcomes for teenagers. *Journal of School Health, 74*, 231–232. doi:10.1111/j.1746-1561.2004.tb08278.x.

Boulton, M., & Underwood, K. (1992). Bully/victim problems among middle school children. *British Journal of Educational Psychology, 62*, 73–87. doi:10.1111/j.2044-8279.1992.tb01000.x.

Bradshaw, C. P., Sawyer, A. L., & O'Brennan, L. M. (2009). A social disorganization perspective on bullying-related attitudes and behaviors: The influence of school context. *American Journal of Community Psychology, 43*, 204–220. doi:10.1007/s10464-009-9240-1.

Brown, E. C., Low, S., Smith, B. H., & Haggerty, K. P. (2011). Outcomes from a school-randomized control trial of Steps to Respect. *School Psychology Review, 40*, 423–443.

Colvin, G., & Kame'enui, E. J. (1993). Reconceptualizing behavior management and school-wide discipline in general education. *Education and Treatment of Children, 16*, 361–381.

Cooper, J. O, Heron T. E., & Heward, W. L. (2007). *Applied behavior analysis* (2nd ed.). Upper Saddle River, NJ: Pearson.

Craig, W. M., Pepler, D. J., & Atlas, R. (2000). Observations of bullying on the playground and in the classroom. *International Journal of School Psychology, 21*, 22–36. doi:10.1177/0143034300211002.

Crone, D. A., & Horner, R. H. (2010). *Building positive behavior support systems in schools: Functional behavioral assessment.* New York: Guilford Press.

Dodge, K. A., Dishion, T. J., & Lansford, J. E. (Eds.). (2006). *Deviant peer influences in programs for youth.* New York: Guilford.

Epstein, J. L. (2011). *School, family, and community partnerships: Preparing educators and improving schools* (2nd ed.). Boulder, CO: Westview Press.

Fan, X., & Chen, M. (2001). Parental involvement and students' academic achievement: A meta-analysis. *Educational Psychology Review, 13*, 1–22. doi:10.1023/A:1009048817385.

Farrington, D. P., & Ttofi, M. M. (2009). *School-based programs to reduce bullying and victimization.* Oslo, Norway: Campbell Systematic Reviews.

Fox, C. L., & Boulton, M. J. (2011). The social skills problems of victims of bullying: Self, peer and teacher perceptions. *British Journal of Educational Psychology, 75*, 313–328. doi:10.1348/000709905X25517.

Frey, K. S., Kirschstein, M. K., & Snell, J. L. (2005). Reducing playground bullying and supporting beliefs: An experimental trial of the "Steps to Respect" program. *Developmental Psychology, 41*, 479–490. doi:10.1037/0012-1649.41.3.479.

Good, C., McIntosh, K., & Gietz, C. (2011). Integrating bullying prevention into school-wide positive behaviour support. *Teaching Exceptional Children, 44*, 48–56.

Health Resources and Services Administration (HRSA). (n.d.). *Misdirections in bullying prevention and intervention.* Retrieved from http://www.stopbullyingnow. hrsa.gov/HHS_PSA/pdfs/SBN_Tip_5.pdf

Hemphill, S. A., Toumbourou, J. W., Herrenkohl, T. I., McMorris, B. J., & Catalano, R. F. (2006). The effect of school suspensions and arrests on subsequent antisocial behavior in Australia and the United States. *Journal of Adolescent Health, 39*, 736–744. doi:10.1016/j.jadohealth.2006.05.010.

Henderson, A., & Mapp, K. L. (2002). *A new wave of evidence: The impact of school, family, and community connections on student achievement.* Austin, TX: Southwest Educational Development Laboratory.

Hoover, J. H., Oliver, R. L., & Hazier, R. J. (1992). Bullying: Perceptions of adolescent victims in the Midwestern USA. *School Psychology International, 13,* 5–16. doi:10.1177/0143034392131001.

Horner, R. H., Sugai, G., Smolkowski, K., Eber, L., Nakasato, J., & Todd, A. W. (2009). A randomized, wait-list controlled effectiveness trial assessing school-wide positive behavior support in elementary schools. *Journal of Positive Behavior Interventions, 11,* 133–144. doi:10.1177/1098300709332067.

Horner, R. H., Sugai, G., Todd, A. W., & Lewis-Palmer, T. (2005). School-wide positive behavior support: An alternative approach to discipline in schools. In L. Bambara & L. Kern (Eds.), *Individualized supports for students with problem behavior: Designing positive behavior plans.* New York: Guilford Press.

Jeynes, W. H. (2003). A meta-analysis: The effects of parental involvement on minority children's academic achievement. *Education and Urban Society, 35,* 202–218. doi:10.1177/0013124502239392.

Jeynes, W. H. (2005). A meta-analysis of the relation of parental involvement to urban elementary school student academic achievement. *Urban Education, 40,* 237–269. doi:10.1177/0042085905274540.

Limber, S. P., Nation, M., Tracy, A. J., Melton, G. B., & Flerx, V. (2004). Implementation of the Olweus Bullying Prevention Program in the Southeastern United States. In P. K. Smith, D. Pepler, & K. Rigby (Eds.), *Bullying in schools. How successful can interventions be?* (pp. 55–80). Cambridge, UK: Cambridge University Press.

Luiselli, J. K., Putnam, R. F., & Sunderland, M. (2002). Longitudinal evaluation of behavior support intervention in a public middle school. *Journal of Positive Behavior Interventions, 6,* 182–188.

March, R. E., & Horner, R. H. (2002). Feasibility and contributions of functional behavioral assessment in schools. *Journal of Emotional and Behavioral Disorders, 10,* 158–170. doi:10.1177/10634266020100030401.

Mayer, G. R. (1995). Preventing antisocial behavior in the schools. *Journal of Applied Behavior Analysis, 28,* 467–478. doi:10.1901/jaba.1995.28-467.

Mayer, G. R., & Sulzer-Azaroff, B. (1991). Interventions for vandalism. In G. Stoner, M. K. Shinn, & H. M. Walker (Eds.), *Interventions for achievement and behavior problems.* Washington, DC: National Association of School Psychologists Monograph.

Merrell, K., Gueldner, B., Ross, S. W., & Isava, D. (2008). How effective are school bullying intervention programs? A meta-analysis of intervention research. *School Psychology Quarterly, 23,* 26–42. doi:10.1037/1045-3830.23.1.26.

Nansel, T. R., Overpeck, M., Pilla, R. S., Ruan, W. J., Simons-Morton, B., & Scheidt, P. (2001). Bullying behaviors among US youth: Prevalence and associations with psychosocial adjustment. *JAMA, 285*, 2094–2100. doi:10.1001/jama.285.16.2094.

National Crime Prevention Council. (2003). *Bullying, not terrorist attack, biggest threat seen by U.S. Teens* (press release). Washington, DC: National Crime Prevention Council.

Nese, R. N., Horner, R. H., Dickey, C. R., Stiller, B., & Tomlanovich, A. (2014). Decreasing bullying behaviors in middle school: Expect respect. *School Psychology Quarterly, 29*, 272–286. doi:10.1037/spq0000070.

O'Connell, P., Pepler, D., & Craig, W. (1999). Peer involvement in bullying: Insights and challenges for intervention. *Journal of Adolescence, 22*, 437–452. doi:10.1006/jado.1999.0238.

Olweus, D. (1997). Bullying/victim problems in school: Facts and intervention. *European Journal of Psychology of Education, 12*, 495–510. doi:10.1007/BF03172807.

Olweus, D. (2005). A useful evaluation design, and effects of the Olweus Bullying Prevention Program. *Psychology, Crime and Law, 11*, 389–402. doi:10.1080/10683160500255471.

Olweus, D., Limber, S. P., Flerx, V. C., Mullin, N., Riese, J., & Snyder, M. (2007). *Olweus Bullying Prevention Program: Schoolwide guide*. Center City, MN: Hazelden.

Roland, E. (1993). Bullying: A developing tradition of research and management. In D. P. Tattum (Ed.), *Understanding and managing bullying* (pp. 15–30). Oxford, UK: Heinemann Educational.

Ross, S. W., & Horner, R. H. (2009). Bully prevention in positive behavior support. *Journal of Applied Behavior Analysis, 42*, 747–759. doi:10.1901/jaba.2009.42-747.

Ross, S. W., & Horner, R. H. (2013). Bully prevention in positive behavior support: Preliminary evaluation of third-, fourth-, and fifth-grade attitudes toward bullying. *Journal of Emotional and Behavioral Disorders, 22*, 225–236. doi:10.1177/1063426613491429.

Salmivalli, C., Lagerspetz, K., Björkqvist, K., Österman, K., & Kaukiainen, A. (1996). Bullying as a group process: Participant roles and their relations to social status within the group. *Aggressive Behavior, 22*, 1–15. doi:10.1002/(SICI)1098-2337(1996)22:1%3C1::AID-AB1%3E3.0.CO;2-T.

Skiba, R. J., & Peterson, R. L. (1999). The dark side of zero tolerance: Can punishment lead to safe schools? *Phi Delta Kappan, 80*, 372–382.

Skiba, R. J., Peterson, R. L., & Williams, T. (1997). Office referrals and suspension: Disciplinary intervention in middle schools. *Education and Treatment of Children, 20*, 295–315.

Solberg, M. E., & Olweus, D. (2003). Prevalence estimation of school bullying with the Olweus bully/victim questionnaire. *Aggressive Behavior*, *29*, 239–268. doi:10.1002/ab.10047.

Sprague, J. R., & Horner, R. H. (2006). Schoolwide positive behavior supports. In S. R. Jimerson & M. J. Furlong (Eds.), *The handbook of school violence and school safety: From research to practice.* Mahwah, NJ: Lawrence Erlbaum Associates.

Stueve, A., Dash, K., O'Donnell, L., Tehranifar, P., Wilson-Simmons, R., Slaby, R. G., & Link, B. G. (2006). Rethinking the bystander role in school violence prevention. *Health Promotion Practice*, *7*, 117–124. doi:10.1177/1524839905278454.

Swearer, S. M., & Espelage, D. L. (2004). Bullying in American schools: A social-ecological perspective on prevention and intervention. *British Journal of Developmental Psychology*, *23*, 316.

Taylor-Green, S. J., & Kartub, D. T. (2000). Durable implementation of school-wide behavior support: The high five program. *Journal of Positive Behavior Interventions*, *2*, 233–235. doi:10.1177/109830070000200408.

Unnever, J. D., & Cornell, D. G. (2008). The culture of bullying in middle school. *Journal of School Violence*, *2*, 5–27. doi:10.1300/J202v02n02_02.

Waasdorp, T., Bradshaw, C. P., & Leaf, P. J. (2011). The impact of school-wide positive behavioral interventions and supports (SWPBIS) on bullying and peer rejection: A randomized controlled effectiveness trial. *Archives of Pediatrics and Adolescent Medicine*, *166*, 149–156. doi:10.1001/archpediatrics.2011.755.

Whitney, I., & Smith, P. K. (1993). A survey of the nature and extent of bully/victim problems in junior/middle and secondary schools. *Educational Research*, *35*, 3–25. doi:10.1080/0013188930350101.

CHAPTER 3

# Teachers' Perspectives on Bullying

*Kathy DeOrnellas and Angelia Spurgin*

As noted in previous chapters, bullying is a significant problem in schools around the world. The purpose of this chapter is to explore bullying as it pertains to the role of the teacher. We will discuss bullying from the perspective of teachers, the training teachers typically receive regarding bullying, and the role of teachers in identifying and contributing to bullying. Finally, we will discuss teachers' roles in intervening in and preventing bullying.

## Teachers' Perceptions of Bullying

Teachers vary significantly in how they perceive bullying, and their perceptions influence how they respond to bullying (Smith et al., 2010). Their attitudes can range from complacent and unconcerned to proactive awareness targeted at bullying prevention (Craig, Bell, & Leschied, 2011). Nonchalant attitudes regarding bullying behavior occur for a variety of reasons and frequently are based on preconceived beliefs. For example, teachers may believe bullying behaviors are typical in child development and the bully will mature, eventually developing more prosocial behaviors. Some teachers may also presume that bullying is a rite of passage for youth

K. DeOrnellas (✉) • A. Spurgin
Texas Woman's University, Denton, TX, USA



L.H. Rosen et al. (eds.), *Bullying in School*,
DOI 10.1057/978-1-137-59298-9_3

and intervention is unnecessary, and as such, being bullied provides an opportunity to "learn how to overcome common obstacles" (Migliaccio, 2015, p. 92). Also, teachers may believe that not intervening in bullying situations forces victims to stand up for themselves, thereby forcing them to develop a stronger and more independent character (Duy, 2013).

Furthermore, teachers often are uncertain about the nature of bullying behaviors. Some teachers find it difficult to determine if students are engaging in good-natured teasing or bullying (Harwood & Copfer, 2011). Some teachers free themselves from the need to intervene by blaming victims for getting themselves into a bullying situation and for letting it continue (Hazel, 2010). Studies have also shown that teachers of young children are hesitant to label preschoolers as bullies or victims, choosing instead to describe negative interactions between peers as inappropriate behavior (Goryl, Neilsen-Hewett, & Sweller, 2013).

Although teachers often focus on the individual student, they are also aware of the social context in which students live. They point to the family, including parenting style and quality of relationship with parents, as a cause for students becoming bullies (Rosen, Scott, & DeOrnellas, 2017). Other factors, such as socioeconomic status and exposure to violence through television, movies, and the Internet, were noted by a group of high school teachers in Turkey, who described bullying as an opportunity for students to demand "rights through violence" (Sahin, 2010, p. 127). Similar beliefs were expressed by a fifth-grade teacher in the USA who stated, "Children are made that way by whatever they are exposed to in the home" (Migliaccio, 2015, p. 95). This perspective not only limits teachers' responses to bullying but also puts the responsibility for students who bully outside the school (Migliaccio). This can be problematic as when teachers attribute bullying to these external factors, more students in the class are victimized (Oldenburg et al., 2015). Given such perceptions, teacher training related to bullying is critical.

## Teachers' Training Related to Bullying

Dealing with student misbehavior is one of the most stressful aspects of teaching. Teachers need more training in classroom management in general and in recognizing and intervening in bullying specifically (Maunder & Tattersall, 2010). Student misbehavior is a primary cause of burnout for teachers and a common reason for novice teachers to leave teaching (Allen, 2010). Previous research has shown that teachers and preservice teachers have incomplete and sometimes inaccurate knowledge of bullying (Ahtola, Haataja, Karna, Poskiparta, & Salmivalli, 2012). Teachers in the field often acknowledge their need for more training on bullying, while preservice teachers may be overly confident in their ability to handle bullying and not see the need for additional training (Ahtola et al.).

Although they typically have the best intentions, teachers may lack the knowledge or skills to handle different bullying behaviors (Berkowitz, 2014). A misunderstanding of the causes and effects of bullying behaviors can lead teachers to trust that students will work out their differences without adult intervention (Waasdorp, Pas, O'Brennan, & Bradshaw, 2011). Teachers with this mindset fail to consider the long-term consequences of bullying and being bullied (Veenstra, Lindenberg, Huitsing, Sainio, & Salmivalli, 2014). Researchers have demonstrated that lack of awareness and ineffective intervention with bullying can lead to negative long-term outcomes, such as escalated violence, poor academic performance, and truancy for the bully and the victim (Goldweber, Waasdorp, & Bradshaw, 2013). When bullies are successful, they quickly learn that bullying is an easy way to get what they want and may develop other forms of antisocial behavior (Kyriakides & Creemers, 2012). Victims may experience depression and feel useless, which adversely affects their ability to take advantage of the academic environment (Kyriakides & Creemers). While it is important to foster independence and autonomy in developing children, it is equally important to be aware of the long-term effects of bullying behaviors that may present within the classroom and across the campus.

Research indicates that teachers would benefit from additional training in bullying, but some have complained that they do not have time to participate (Charmaraman, Jones, Stein, & Espelage, 2013). They have also expressed little hope of change when intervening stating, "Name-calling is never going to stop. Kids are cruel and gangs are real" (Charmaraman et al., p. 440). Despite resistance from some teachers, most indicated a need for mandatory, long-term training on bullying and increased administrative support for bullying incidents (Charmaraman et al.). Many of the teachers in Charmaraman et al.'s study were unaware of policies aimed at providing positive educational experiences for students. A report released at the White House Conference on Bullying Prevention noted that while 98% of teachers believe intervening in bullying is part of their job, almost half had not been trained on their district's bullying policy (Gulemetova, Drury, & Bradshaw, 2011). To complicate matters, many teachers reported difficulty determining whether students' behaviors are normative or bullying, making it difficult to follow the mandate of the school's policy (Charmaraman et al.). Therefore, training must not only identify strategies for intervention and prevention but also must increase teachers' ability to identify bullying behaviors.

Lack of training in intervening with bullying makes it especially difficult for teachers to handle bullying related to issues of sexual diversity. Although Kolbert et al. (2015) reported that teacher training on sexual diversity is associated with an improved school climate for sexual minority students, few teachers have had such training. In 2014, *Education Journal* published a survey of approximately 2000 school staff that revealed only 8% of primary teachers and 17% of secondary teachers had been trained to handle homophobic bullying. These numbers are remarkable given that two-thirds of secondary teachers reported that homophobic bullying was affecting students' academic performance at school (*Education Journal*).

If we accept that many teachers in the field need and want additional training in bullying recognition and intervention and that preservice teachers may be overly confident in their belief that they do not need additional training, where is the training to come from? A first step would be to add additional training in child development and specialized training in bullying to the curriculum of teacher training programs (Sahin, 2010). Next, it is important to provide frequent and comprehensive in-service training for current teachers. Teachers must be trained on their district's bullying policy if they are to be expected to enforce it (Charmaraman et al., 2013). Also, teachers will benefit from in-service training on sexual diversity and homophobic bullying (Kolbert et al., 2015). Finally, it is important that teachers understand the best methods for disciplining bullies.

## The Role of Teachers in Contributing to Bullying

Children and parents view teachers as the educator, decision maker, and protector of students within the classroom. When children report to their parents about difficulties with other students at school, parents customarily refer their children to the teacher as a source of help and assistance. Society has traditionally viewed teachers as the first line of defense in identifying and intervening with bullying among students; however, teachers may unintentionally play a passive and/or active role in contributing to bullying in the school setting (Veenstra et al., 2014). Currently, teachers have a wide-ranging set of responsibilities that involve more than teaching students. While teachers are focused on these additional duties, they may inadvertently overlook serious behavioral issues, such as peer bullying, that are not directly affecting the learning environment (Veenstra et al.). This can be especially true when teachers are under pressure for their students to perform well during high-stakes testing. The emphasis on high-stakes test scores has led to "a narrowed curriculum, increased stress on teachers and students, and reduced teachers' attention to other aspects of students' development" (Hazel, 2010, p. 351). The resulting classroom is likely to be less inclusive and to feel less comfortable for students. In this stressful environment, teachers may be unaware that bullying is occurring within the context of their classroom, thus involuntarily contributing to the bullying situation.

It is likely that many teachers are not intentionally avoiding negative behaviors that are affecting their students; rather, they are simply unaware of what is occurring between their students in the classroom. Bullying behavior also occurs in a variety of settings beyond the four walls of the classroom. For example, the playground, cafeteria, restrooms, and hallways are areas where children may experience negative interactions with peers, and frequently teachers are not present to monitor student behavior (Espelage, Polanin, & Low, 2014). When teachers are not present to observe the bullying behavior, victims are less likely to report the incident to a teacher and bystanders are less likely to intervene (Hektner & Swenson, 2012).

Despite their extensive workloads, teachers play a fundamental role in the overall well-being of their students. While educating students is the primary focus of school, it is important to remember that social and emotional health has a long-lasting impact on a child's future. Teachers play a leading role in facilitating positive and negative atmospheres in their classrooms. Furthermore, a teacher's attitude towards bullies and victims creates the foundation for future attitudes towards bullying for the class as a whole. If the teacher assumes a proactive and anti-bullying position, the class is likely to follow suit (Carrera, DePalma, & Lameiras, 2011).

Unfortunately, there are also incidents in which teachers take on the role of bullies, thus offering poor role models for students on how to interact with others (Charmaraman et al., 2013). Monsvold, Bendixen, Hagen, and Helvik (2011) defined bullying by teachers as "when a teacher uses his or her power to punish, manipulate or disparage a student beyond what would be considered reasonable disciplinary procedures" (p. 323). Bullying by teachers can also be unintentional, taking the form of sarcastic comments, name-calling, refusing to accept late or unidentified work, and making humiliating comments to students they expect to have trouble from in the future (Sylvester, 2011). In an Israeli study, children who reported experiencing bullying behaviors from teachers, including “ridicule, isolation, verbal discrimination, physical assault, and sexual harassment,” were more likely than their peers to develop significant problems in school and to have psychological problems as adults (Monsvold et al., 2011, p. 324).

## The Role of Teachers in Bullying Identification

Teachers are educated in aspects of childhood development; however, there is limited focus on the different traits students may present within a classroom setting. Having a thorough understanding of the different roles bullies and victims play during school is vital for accurate identification. A teacher’s role in bullying identification should be proactive and direct. As accurate identification of bullies and their victims is fundamental to bullying prevention and intervention (Wong, Cheng, & Chen, 2013), it is concerning that many teachers struggle with recognizing bullying behavior when it occurs and have difficulty determining the purported bully and victim. This difficulty contributes to the lower number of bullying incidents typically reported (Ahn, Rodkin, & Gest, 2013). Accurate identification is complicated by disparities in bullying frequency and severity as related to factors such as the race, gender, age, and culture of the students involved (Chen, 2015). In general, correctly identifying a bully requires a teacher to have a working knowledge of the vast array of bullying behaviors that students may exhibit, as well as an understanding of the personalities of the students in his or her classroom and how bullying behaviors may present within those particular students.

Recognition of bullying behaviors is further complicated by the various types of students that engage in bullying; there is not one specific marker that clearly identifies a bully (Duy, 2013). While many definitions have been given for bullying, there is a general consensus that bullying involves negative, harmful behaviors that are prevalent and persistent over a period of time and that typically target a vulnerable person or group of people (Carrera et al., 2011; Oldenburg et al., 2015). With this broad definition of bullying, it is important to note that specific behaviors are not identified within the context of the definition. In the media, bullying is often sensationalized and portrayed as a situation involving public humiliation and/or physical assault of the victim. Perhaps as a result, teachers are better able to identify a bullying situation when the behaviors are flagrant rather than secretive; however, this often is not the norm for bullying behaviors. Teachers are less likely to consider indirect behaviors (e.g., excluding students, making up stories about students, etc.) as bullying (Mishna, Scarcello, Pepler, & Weiner, 2005). They also may mistake social forms of bullying as playful behavior between friends and not interpret it as bullying (Bauman & Del Rio, 2006). Having incorporated a schema that bullying behavior is physically aggressive, many teachers overlook covert, but equally painful, behaviors such as relational bullying (Carrera et al.).

Since bullying in the school does not always consist of physically aggressive behaviors, it is important that teachers develop an understanding of the different ways that students are able to inflict pain on others. For example, Chen (2015) reported that typical bullying behaviors in a Greek primary school consisted of name-calling with racial and sexual undertones, verbal threats, teasing, and peer rejection, while physical assault and theft were the least common acts of bullying reported. In an elementary school in the northwest portion of the USA, significant bullying behaviors included teasing, name-calling, and instigating rumors among peers; peer exclusion and mild physical aggression were considered less significant (Chen). While this does not discount the physical aggression perpetrated by bullies in schools, it is important to note that bullying identification involves more than what is immediately observable. Sometimes, the worst pain imposed on victims of bullies occurs under the radar of teachers and leaves no physically observable wounds or damage.

This type of bullying, generally referred to as covert bullying, is becoming more of a focus in efforts to identify and prevent bullying in the schools (Byers, Caltabiano, & Caltabiano, 2011). Covert forms of bullying occur in settings and situations that are out of view of the teacher, such as in the halls, on the playground, in the cafeteria, or on the Internet. This method of bullying does not involve physical confrontations or insult; however, it can inflict serious damage to a victim's social and emotional health (Barnes et al., 2012; Demaray, Malecki, Secord, & Lyell, 2013). Bullying that is concealed from others may include verbal abuse, cyber bullying, offensive gestures, blackmailing, name-calling, the spreading of rumors, and exclusion of certain students from a group (Byers et al.). Schools and classrooms have been slow to address this form of bullying, choosing to focus instead on the more easily observed behaviors.

In addition to identifying bullies, it is important for educators to be aware of the victims and the multitude of ways they may present within the context of the classroom (Yang & Salmivalli, 2013). In general, there are two primary types of victims that emerge from a bullying scenario: the passive or submissive victim and the aggressive victim. The passive victim may become withdrawn within the classroom, exhibit a significant increase in anxiety, and/or avoid coming to school. The aggressive victim may act out in the classroom, display atypical forms of aggression towards peers and staff, and/or become a bully (Carrera et al., 2011). Many children struggle with telling a teacher they are being bullied (Bauman & Del Rio, 2006), and they also struggle with accurately identifying their emotions surrounding the incident. Changes in a child's behavior should be considered a sign that something is amiss in a child's life, and teachers should respond with care and concern.

Complicating teachers' efforts to identify victims of bullying is that children at different developmental stages may exhibit signs of bullying and victimization in different ways. Research has shown that bullying (both aggressive and relational) begins as early as preschool and experiencing bullying during early childhood can impair children's ability to cultivate friendships and lead to students being unhappy at school (Ostrov, Godleski, Kamper-DeMarco, Blakely-McClure, & Celenza, 2015). Older students who are bullied can display a number of other symptoms. These include lack of connectedness to school, poorer grades, lower attendance, withdrawal from peers, rejection by peers, depression, anxiety, and low levels of resilience (Victoria State Government, 2013).

It is also important to note that, just as male and female students have different types of bullying behaviors, male and female victims may respond differently to bullying (Yang & Salmivalli, 2013). In general, males are more likely to suffer physically aggressive forms of bullying, while females tend to suffer more from relational forms of bullying, such as being excluded from peer groups or having rumors spread about them; however, this is not always the case (Dukes, Stein, & Zane, 2010). Therefore, it is important for teachers to be aware of these differences and to respond accordingly.

## The Role of Teachers in Intervening in the Moment of Bullying Episodes

Teachers' understanding of bullying varies based on level of training, experience, and beliefs regarding bullies and victims. Deficits in their understanding are likely to result in a well-documented tendency to underestimate rates of bullying, particularly with regard to bullying that occurs on school grounds but outside the classroom (Carrera et al., 2011; Chen, 2015; Duy, 2013; Hazel, 2010). In a large study by Demaray and colleagues, the majority of school staff reported bullying rates of less than 10% while students reported rates between 20% and 30% (2013). A number of factors inhibit teachers' response to bullying, and studies have shown that teachers believe they intervene much more frequently than noted by students (Novick & Isaacs, 2010; Pepler, Craig, Ziegler, & Charach, 1994). Pepler et al. found that 84% of teachers reported intervening often or always in bullying situations while only 35% of their students believed this to be true. This finding is supported by a videotaped observation of teacher and student behavior during bullying incidents by Novick and Isaacs who found that teachers intervened in only 18% of episodes that occurred within their classrooms and, even when the teachers were clearly aware of the bullying, failed to intervene 27% of the time.

Just as teachers' schemas about bullying affect their ability to identify bullying behaviors, these belief systems help to determine whether or not they will intervene. When teachers are debating whether or not to intervene in bullying incidents, they draw upon their beliefs about bullying, their previous experiences, and their beliefs about students. Teachers tend to attribute bullying behavior to factors within the teacher's control (i.e., internal factors) or to factors outside their control (i.e., external factors). They are more likely to intervene when they attribute behaviors to internal factors because they are more likely to believe the behaviors can be remediated and are thus more committed to stopping those (Oldenburg et al., 2015). Teachers are likely to put less energy into intervening with bullying behaviors when they believe they are due to external factors, such as characteristics of the student, the student's family, or the community in which the student lives, because they doubt their intervention will make a difference or because they do not believe intervening is part of their job (Oldenburg et al.).

There are a number of internal factors that influence teacher's propensity for intervening in bullying situations. These include characteristics of the teacher, previous experiences, training, and level of confidence regarding intervening in bullying. Teachers' personal histories of bullying influence their decision to intervene. Oldenburg et al. found that teachers that have bullied others may have more permissive attitudes towards bullying, recognizing it as a way to gain power or popularity;

teachers that have been victimized by bullies are more likely to empathize with victims, recognize bullying as it is occurring, and be more likely to intervene (2015).

Teachers' approaches to bullying intervention are influenced by their levels of experience. New teachers typically spend their first year trying to learn the many facets of their job and have little experience intervening in bullying situations, which has led some to conclude that more bullying may occur in the classrooms of new teachers (Oldenburg et al., 2015). However, it has also been argued that, while experienced teachers have intervened in numerous bullying incidents through the years and have developed ways of managing the events, more bullying may take place in the classrooms of experienced teachers because they have, over time, become comfortable with student misbehavior and are less likely to intervene (Oldenburg et al.). Therefore, the teacher's level of experience should be considered in developing training programs for intervening in bullying.

With experience, teachers typically develop confidence in their ability to maintain behavioral control within the classroom. Teachers that feel confident in their ability to intervene effectively are more likely to do so (Ahtola et al., 2012). However, when teachers lack confidence, they are less likely to intervene and their classroom can become unsafe for students. Their lack of confidence may be due to actual skill deficits stemming from inadequate training. Previous attempts at intervention may have failed, and teachers may refrain from intervening due to a fear of making things worse. In some schools, retaliation by students may be a legitimate concern (Pyhältö, Pietarinen, & Soini, 2015). In other cases, teachers may dismiss a child's claim that he or she is being bullied because the reported bullying does not match the teacher's pre-formed schema (Duy, 2013). As previously noted, bullying is typically assumed to mean overt aggression (Bauman & Del Rio, 2006), and teachers have been observed to intervene more frequently with this type of bullying. However, teachers may appear oblivious to mistreatment involving students when it occurs in females, involves behavior outside the classroom or on the Internet, or when the bullying behavior is covert in nature, such as rumor spreading or purposeful exclusion of peers (Waasdorp et al., 2011).

Finally, it is important to mention that teachers may avoid intervening with bullies because they fear becoming a target. de Wet (2010) reported that over 90% of teachers in a London inner-city school were victimized by students. This victimization took the form of deliberate and repeated acts that were aimed at harming the teachers "physically, emotionally, socially, and/or professionally" (de Wet, p. 196). The teacher participants reported feeling powerless and embarrassed, had low self-esteem, and were more likely to withdraw from others. They also reported suffering from physical and psychological ailments such as sleep disturbances, headaches, stress, burnout, and difficulty controlling their anger (de Wet). As would be expected, the victimization limited teachers' ability to teach effectively, increased the number of disciplinary problems in their classrooms, and made it difficult for teachers to look forward to going to work (de Wet). Therefore, multiple aspects of the teacher's previous experiences may determine how and if bullying intervention occurs.

External factors play a significant role in bullying intervention as teachers are less likely to intervene in bullying situations when they believe that bullying and victimization are due to characteristics of the students (Ahtola et al., 2012). Some teachers believe that students are victimized because they are not assertive enough in dealing with bullies (Blain-Arcaro, Smith, Cunningham, Vaillancourt, & Rimas, 2012) and that students would not be picked on or bullied if they would stand up for themselves. However, Espelage (2015) found that encouraging victims to be more assertive led to more aggression and victimization across the school year.

Harwood and Copfer (2011) note that teachers often share the belief that all children bully or are bullied as part of the growing up process (i.e., bullying is normative and intervention is not necessary). Teachers who believe bullying is normative are more likely to let the students work it out on their own, especially when bullying involves girls, and are less likely to reprimand the aggressor (Espelage, 2015).

Another belief held by some teachers is that students would not be victimized if they would just avoid bullies (Harwood & Copfer, 2011). Espelage (2015) found that teachers are more likely to contact parents and separate students when boys are involved; however, with younger students, separating bullies and victims was associated with "lower levels of aggression, declines in classroom-level peer victimization, and declines in aggression for highly aggressive girls" (p. 78). When teachers fully ascribe to these beliefs, they are less likely to intervene and are more likely to blame the victim (Rosen et al., 2017).

Other factors at play include whether the teacher believes the victim is to blame for the bullying, if the victim has what the teacher considers attributes of victimization, if the teacher feels empathy towards the victim, and if the teacher feels the situation is serious (Mishna et al., 2005). Some teachers, including preservice teachers in a study by Smith and colleagues (2010), respond to bullying based on how upset the victim seems to be. Other factors linked to how teachers deal with classroom situations include the gender of the teacher (Harwood & Copfer, 2011), characteristics of the school (e.g., size, climate), and characteristics of the students involved (e.g., age, gender, social status; Holt, Kantor, & Finkelhor, 2009).

Teachers also may be uncomfortable intervening with certain types of students. Bradshaw and colleagues surveyed members of the National Education Association and found that teachers feel more comfortable intervening in bullying involving students with disabilities or weight-based bullying than they do in intervening in bullying regarding sexual orientation (2013). Kolbert et al. (2015) attributed this discomfort to "fear of discrimination, fear of job loss, the possibility of receiving unfavorable reactions from parents, students, and other staff members, their own prejudices, or failure to recognize bullying based on sexual orientation as a serious problem" (p. 249).

In addition to teacher- and student-related factors that influence teacher's intervening in bullying, there are contextual factors, such as school-based anti-bullying policies and adherence to the Student Code of Conduct. Teachers typically consider school policy regarding bullying, particularly when physical aggression is involved (Harwood & Copfer, 2011). All schools have policies that define physical aggression and its consequences. For nonphysical bullying, however, teachers may focus on anti-bullying policies that encourage students to resolve conflicts through prosocial avenues, such as being appropriately assertive and making compromises (Harwood & Copfer).

Whether or not teachers elect to intervene, their behaviors have consequences. If they choose to ignore the incident, bullies are likely to see this as acceptance of the behavior and are more likely to continue while victims come to understand that teachers cannot be trusted to intervene and are less likely to report bullying incidents (Burger, Strohmeier, Sprober, Bauman, & Rigby, 2015). When teachers take an authoritarian (i.e., controlling) stance against bullying by setting firm limits, using verbal reprimands, or incorporating other forms of discipline, bullies tend to curtail their behaviors for a short time. However, this can lead to more covert forms of bullying that are harder to identify (Burger et al.). Some teachers choose a nonpunitive approach in which the bullies' motives are addressed. The goals of this approach are to increase the bullies' understanding of and empathy for the victim and to help bullies develop nonaggressive behavior strategies (Burger et al.). These results must be considered when developing programs for curtailing bullying.

## The Role of Teachers in Prevention and Intervention Programs

Teachers are a key factor in bullying prevention (Kyriakides & Creemers, 2012) and "the factor with the greatest impact on school satisfaction" (Simoes & Gaspar Matos, 2011, p. 38). They do this by creating a learning environment in which all students feel safe. Teachers at all levels strive to maintain a positive atmosphere within their classroom, and the environment of the classroom has profound effects on overall student performance (Goldweber et al., 2013). Students, as a whole, demonstrate greater academic and social gains when teachers provide support and encouragement, thus facilitating an accepting educational environment (Wang et al., 2014). A teacher's attitude lays the foundation for the overall setting in his or her classroom and may have positive or negative implications for the students (Ahn et al., 2013).

As previously noted, many teachers struggle with bullying intervention, and this may be especially true with regard to how to discipline bullies (Kokko & Pörhölä, 2009). Schools that have established harsh criteria for handling bullying situations (i.e., calling the police, suspension, expulsion, corporal punishment) typically do not see a decrease in bullying behaviors because bullies become more secretive and victims are less likely to tell due to fear of retaliation. This approach is ineffective in resolving conflicts and causes further deterioration of the relationship between the bully and victim (Wong et al., 2013). While environments that are strict and overly structured in regard to bullying tend to promote bullying by facilitating negative attitudes and hostility (Harwood & Copfer, 2011), a supportive classroom climate in which the teacher responds to and intervenes effectively with bullying has positive outcomes (Berkowitz, 2014).

Teachers not only create positive environments within their classrooms but can be instrumental in making other parts of the school (e.g., playgrounds, hallways, cafeterias, and restrooms) safe and positive climates (Cortes & Kochenderfer-Ladd, 2014). They also work to promote healthy relationships between students. When students feel comfortable reporting bullying to their teacher, it is a reflection of the positive environment their teacher has created. Students notice how teachers respond to bullying and use this information to decide how likely teachers are to help them if they are in that situation. Seeking help is fostered by the knowledge that their teacher takes bullying seriously (Cortes & Kochenderfer-Ladd). When teachers clearly take a stand against bullying, students learn that bullying is unacceptable and are empowered to speak out against bullying (Maunder & Tattersall, 2010).

Teachers use a number of strategies in preventing bullying. At the classroom level, they set up learning experiences that discourage bullying; supervise students more closely, especially when they are at play; and intervene quickly when bullying occurs (Goryl et al., 2013). Interventions tend to be either proactive or reactive. Since down times (i.e., when students are between assignments or taking a break) can be problematic, teachers can be proactive in organizing activities (e.g., working in cooperative groups to solve puzzles, listening to music, or playing quiet games) that calm students, give them little opportunity for bullying behaviors, and increase their enjoyment of school (Kyriakides & Creemers, 2012). When bullying occurs, teachers who intervene typically do so by verbally reprimanding students, separating students, talking with students about their behaviors, notifying parents, or diffusing the situation (Harwood & Copfer, 2011).

Collaboration with other teachers or with students who are not involved in the bullying can also be very effective. Teachers should be encouraged to work together to observe students, identify bullying behaviors, and exchange ideas about how to best handle situations (Olweus, 1997). Effective strategies can then be shared with staff and administrators.

Since bullying frequently occurs outside of the classroom when no adults are present, one way that teachers can expand their prevention role is by motivating bystander peers to intervene and/or to report incidents (Blain-Arcaro et al., 2012). Peers are usually present when bullying occurs, and they reinforce bullying either by helping the bully or by watching the incident without intervening for the victim (Burger et al., 2015). When they understand how groups operate, teachers can have a powerful impact on students in their classes. They are in a position to influence peer relationships by teaching students social rules and by guiding them to develop their own healthy social norms. Teachers also influence students by being a role model and by developing the teacher/student relationship (Hymel, McClure, Miller, Shumka, & Trach, 2015). When working with students to encourage their assistance, teachers should keep in mind that students may misperceive the seriousness of bullying and should listen to their accounts of the incident carefully. It is important that teachers be very clear in discussing what constitutes bullying and how these behaviors differ from normal relationship difficulties (Maunder, Harrop, & Tattersall, 2010).

In addition to the prevention and intervention measures taken by teachers, both alone and in collaboration with students and other teachers, there are a number of school-wide intervention programs available for adoption (Barnes et al., 2012). Research indicates that long-term programs that involve the entire population of the school are more effective than short-term programs with smaller targeted participants (Sahin, 2010). Teachers have an integral role in the success of these programs.

One of the great advantages of implementing a school-wide program is the knowledge teachers gain (Bowllan, 2011). In a review of the Olweus Bullying Prevention Program, a school-wide intervention program that has been found to change school climates, teachers who participated in the program were better able to recognize and intervene in bullying. In addition, students reported that teachers talked to them more about bullying, and they observed teachers intervening in bullying situations more frequently. It is likely that changes in teacher behavior are related to the training they received on implementing the program (Bowllan).

Teachers also receive training when implementing the KiVa Antibullying Program, a school-wide anti-bullying program that has been found to be effective in replacing bullying in elementary grades (Ahtola et al., 2012). Although the program begins with two days of face-to-face training, the majority of teachers' learning appears to take place while administering the program using a teachers' manual. Through their implementation of the program, teachers develop more confidence in their ability to intervene effectively, more knowledge about identifying bullying, and self-efficacy (Ahtola et al.). Teachers also develop a better understanding of group process while teaching students about the role of the peer group in bullying (Ahtola et al.). Participating in a school-wide program provides teachers with the opportunity to receive sorely needed training on recognizing bullying, to develop confidence in their ability to intervene, and to become a role model for students in dealing with conflict appropriately.

Although it appears that teachers have much to gain from participating in school-wide bullying programs, adherence to the program can be a significant problem. Blain-Arcaro et al. (2012) reported that teachers tend to make use of the elements of the program that fit with their approach to teaching while rejecting those parts that they did not feel would be helpful. This inconsistent adherence to the program is likely responsible for the mixed results seen in program reviews. It is important that school-wide programs take into account teachers' understanding of bullying so as to encourage adherence and fidelity to the program.

## Conclusion

In addition to providing a supportive learning environment, teachers are charged with protecting the students under their care. This requires recognizing, intervening with, and preventing bullying. Unfortunately, many teachers report a lack of knowledge of bullying and a lack of time and resources for intervening (Oldenburg et al., 2015). Other teachers ignore bullying or blame victims for not being assertive enough to avoid being mistreated (Blain-Arcaro et al., 2012; Harwood & Copfer, 2011).

Teachers' perceptions and preconceived attitudes regarding bullying must constantly be challenged in order for them to successfully intervene during bullying situations (Kokko & Pörhölä, 2009). Teachers need to be more open in voicing their concerns to administrators regarding their lack of knowledge and training (Charmaraman et al., 2013). To help teachers be more effective with bullying situations, Maunder and Tattersall (2010) recommend that teachers' roles and responsibilities regarding bullying be clearly defined by school administration. Teachers play a pivotal role in the facilitation of or prevention of bullying through their relationships with students, communication with parents, and collegial relationships with co-workers.

## References


Ahn, H.-J., Rodkin, P. C., & Gest, S. (2013). Teacher-student agreement on "bullies and kids they pick on" in elementary classrooms: Gender and grade differences. *Theory into Practice, 52*, 257–263. doi:10.1080/00405841.2013.829728.

Ahtola, A., Haataja, A., Karna, A., Poskiparta, E., & Salmivalli, C. (2012). For children only? Effects of the KiVa antibullying program on teachers. *Teaching and Teacher Education, 28*, 851–859. doi:10.1016/jtate.2012.03.006.

Allen, K. P. (2010). Classroom management, bullying, and teacher practices. *The Professional Educator, 34*(1), 1–15.

Barnes, A., Cross, D., Lester, L., Hearn, L., Epstein, M., & Monks, H. (2012). The invisibility of covert bullying among students: Challenges for school intervention. *Australian Journal of Guidance and Counseling*, *22*, 206–226. doi:10.1017/jgc.2012.27.

Bauman, S., & Del Rio, A. (2006). Preservice teachers' responses to bullying scenarios: Comparing physical, verbal, and relational bullying. *Journal of Educational Psychology*, *98*, 219–231. doi:10.1037/0022-0663.98.1.219.

Berkowitz, R. (2014). Student and teacher responses to violence in school: The divergent views of bullies, victims, and bully-victims. *School Psychology International*, *35*, 485–503. doi:10.1177/0143034313511012.

Blain-Arcaro, C., Smith, J. D., Cunningham, C. E., Vaillancourt, T., & Rimas, H. (2012). Contextual attributes of indirect bullying situations that influence teachers' decisions to intervene. *Journal of School Violence*, *11*, 226–245. doi: 10.1080/15388220.2012.682003.

Bowllan, N. M. (2011). Implementation and evaluation of a comprehensive, school-wide bullying prevention program in an urban/suburban middle school. *Journal of School Health*, *81*(4), 167–173. doi:10.1111/j.1746-1561.2010.00576.x.

Bradshaw, C. P., Waasdorp, T. E., & O'Brennan, L. M. (2013). Teachers' and education support professionals' perspectives on bullying and prevention: Findings from a National Education Association study. *School Psychology Review*, *42*, 280–297.

Burger, C., Strohmeier, D., Sprober, N., Bauman, S., & Rigby, K. (2015). How teachers respond to school bullying: An examination of self-reported intervention strategy use, moderator effects, and concurrent use of multiple strategies. *Teaching and Teacher Education*, *51*, 191–202. doi:10.1016/j.tate.2015.07.004.

Byers, D. L., Caltabiano, N. J., & Caltabiano, M. L. (2011). Teachers' attitudes towards overt and covert bullying, and perceived efficacy to intervene. *Australian Journal of Teacher Education*, *36*, 105–119. doi:10.14221/ajte.2011v36n11.1.

Carrera, M. V., DePalma, R., & Lameiras, M. (2011). Toward a more comprehensive understanding of bullying in school settings. *Educational Psychology Review*, *23*, 479–499. doi:10.1007/s10648-011-9171-x.

Charmaraman, L., Jones, A. E., Stein, N., & Espelage, D. L. (2013). Is it bullying or sexual harassment? Knowledge, attitudes, and professional development experiences of middle school staff. *Journal of School Health*, *83*, 438–444.

Chen, L.-M. (2015). Self-reported frequency and perceived severity of being bullied among elementary school students. *Journal of School Health*, *85*, 587–594.

Cortes, K. I., & Kochenderfer-Ladd, B. (2014). To tell or not to tell: What influences children's decisions to report bullying to their teachers? *School Psychology Quarterly*, *29*, 336–348.

Craig, K., Bell, D., & Leschied, A. (2011). Pre-service teachers' knowledge and attitudes regarding school-based bullying. *Canadian Journal of Education*, *34*(2), 21–33.

de Wet, C. (2010). Victims of educator-targeted bullying: A qualitative study. *South African Journal of Education*, *30*, 189–201.

Demaray, M. K., Malecki, C. K., Secord, S. M., & Lyell, K. M. (2013). Agreement among students', teachers', and parents' perceptions of victimization by bullying. *Children and Youth Services Review*, *35*, 2091–2100. doi:10.1016/j.childyouth.2013.10.018.

Dukes, R. L., Stein, J. A., & Zane, J. I. (2010). Gender differences in the relative impact of physical and relation bullying on adolescent injury and weapon carrying. *Journal of School Psychology*, *48*, 511–532. doi:10.1016/j.jsp.2010.08.001.

Duy, B. (2013). Teachers' attitudes toward different types of bullying and victimization in Turkey. *Psychology in the Schools*, *50*, 987–1002. doi:10.1002/pits.21729.

Education Journal. (2014, July 7). Just one in eight teachers trained to tackle homophobic bullying. *Education Journal*, (206), 11.

Espelage, D. L. (2015). Taking peer victimization research to the next level: Complex interactions among genes, teacher attitudes/behaviors, peer ecologies, & classroom characteristics. *Journal of Abnormal Child Psychology*, *43*, 77–80. doi:10.1007/s10802-014-9948-8.

Espelage, D. L., Polanin, J. R., & Low, S. K. (2014). Teacher and staff perceptions of school environment as predictors of student aggression, victimization, and willingness to intervene in bullying situations. *School Psychology Quarterly*, *29*, 287–305. doi:10.1037/spq0000072.

Goldweber, A., Waasdorp, T. E., & Bradshaw, C. P. (2013). Examining the link between forms of bullying behaviors and perceptions of safety and belonging among secondary school students. *Journal of School Psychology*, *51*, 469–485. doi:10.1016/j.jsp.2013.04.004.

Goryl, O., Neilsen-Hewett, C., & Sweller, N. (2013). Teacher education, teaching experience and bullying policies: Links with early childhood teachers' perceptions and attitudes to bullying. *Australasian Journal of Early Childhood*, *38*(2), 32–40.

Gulemetova, M., Drury, D., & Bradshaw, C. P. (2011). National Education Association Bullying Study. *Colleagues*, *6*(2), Article 11. Retrieved from http://scholarworks.gvsu.edu/ colleagues/vol6/iss2/11

Harwood, D., & Copfer, S. (2011). Teasing in schools: What teachers have to say. *The International Journal of Interdisciplinary Social Sciences*, *6*, 75–91.

Hazel, C. (2010). Interactions between bullying and high-stakes testing at the elementary school level. *Journal of School Violence*, *9*, 339–356.

Hektner, J. M., & Swenson, C. A. (2012). Links from teacher beliefs to peer victimization and bystander intervention: Tests of mediating processes. *Journal of Early Adolescence*, *32*, 516–536. doi:10.1177/0272431611402502.

Holt, M., Kantor, G., & Finkelhor, D. (2009). Parent/child concordance about bullying involvement and family characteristics related to bullying and peer victimization. *Journal of School Violence*, *8*, 42–63.

Hymel, S., McClure, R., Miller, M., Shumka, E., & Trach, J. (2015). Addressing school bullying: Insights from theories of group processes. *Journal of Applied Developmental Psychology*, *37*, 16–24.

Kokko, T. H. J., & Pörhölä, M. (2009). Tackling bullying: Victimized by peers as a pupil, an effective intervener as a teacher? *Teaching and Teacher Education*, *25*, 1000–1008. doi:10.1016/j.tate.2009.04.005.

Kolbert, J. B., Crothers, L. M., Bundick, M. J., Wells, D. S., Buzgon, J., Berbary, C., ... Senko, K. (2015). Teachers' perceptions of bullying of lesbian, gay, bisexual, transgender, and questioning (LGBTQ) students in southwestern Pennsylvania sample. *Behavioral Sciences*, *5*, 247–263.

Kyriakides, L., & Creemers, B. P. M. (2012). Characteristics of effective schools in facing and reducing bullying. *School Psychology International*, *34*, 348–368.

Maunder, R. E., Harrop, A., & Tattersall, A. J. (2010). Pupil and staff perceptions of bullying in secondary schools: Comparing behavioral definitions and their perceived seriousness. *Educational Research*, *52*, 263–282.

Maunder, R. E., & Tattersall, A. J. (2010). Staff experiences of managing bullying in secondary schools: The importance of internal and external relationships in facilitating intervention. *Educational & Child Psychology*, *27*(1), 116–128.

Migliaccio, T. (2015). Teacher engagement with bullying: Managing an identity with a school. *Sociological Spectrum: Mid-South Sociological Association*, *35*(1), 84–108. doi: 10:1080/02732173.2014.978430.

Mishna, F., Scarcello, I., Pepler, D., & Weiner, J. (2005). Teachers' understanding of bullying. *Canadian Journal of Education*, *28*, 718–738.

Monsvold, T., Bendixen, M., Hagen, R., & Helvik, A.-S. (2011). Exposure to teacher bullying in schools: A study of patients with personality disorders. *Nordic Journal of Psychiatry*, *65*, 323–329.

Novick, R. M., & Isaacs, J. (2010). Telling is compelling: The impact of student reports of bullying on teacher intervention. *Education Psychology*, *30*, 283–296.

Oldenburg, B., van Duijn, M., Sentse, M., Huitsing, G., van der Ploeg, R., Salmivalli, C., & Veenstra, R. (2015). Teacher characteristics and peer victimization in elementary schools: A classroom-level perspective. *Journal of Abnormal Child Psychology*, *43*, 33–44. doi:10.1007/s10802-013-9847-4.

Olweus, D. (1997). Bully/victim problems in school: Facts and intervention. *European Journal of Psychology of Education*, *12*, 495–510.

Ostrov, J. M., Godleski, S. A., Kamper-DeMarco, K. E., Blakely-McClure, S. J., & Celenza, L. (2015). Replication and extension of the early childhood friendship project: Effects on physical and relational bullying. *School Psychology Review*, *44*, 445–463.

Pepler, D. J., Craig, W. M., Ziegler, S., & Charach, A. (1994). An evaluation of an anti-bullying intervention in Toronto school. *Canadian Journal of Community Mental Health, 12, 95–110.*

Pyhältö, K., Pietarinen, J., & Soini, T. (2015). When teaching gets tough—Professional community inhibitors of teacher-targeted bullying and turnover intentions. *Improving Schools, 18,* 263–276.

Rosen, L., Scott, S., & DeOrnellas, K. (2017). Teachers' perceptions of bullying: A focus group approach. *Journal of School Violence, 16,* 119–139.

Sahin, M. (2010). Teachers' perceptions of bullying in high schools: A Turkish study. *Social Behavior and Personality, 38*(1), 127–142.

Simoes, C., & Gaspar Matos, M. (2011). Offending, victimization, and double involvement: Differences and similarities between the three profiles. *Journal of Cognitive and Behavioral Psychotherapies, 11*(1), 29–41.

Smith, H., Varjas, K., Meyers, J., Marshall, M. L., Ruffner, C., & Graybill, E. C. (2010). Teachers' perceptions of teasing in schools. *Journal of School Violence, 9,* 2–22. doi:10.1080/15388220903185522.

Sylvester, R. (2011). Teacher as bully: Knowingly or unintentionally harming students. *The Delta Kappa Gamma Bulletin, 77*(2), 42–45.

Veenstra, R., Lindenberg, S., Huitsing, G., Sainio, M., & Salmivalli, C. (2014). The role of teachers in bullying: The relation between antibullying attitudes, efficacy, and efforts to reduce bullying. *Journal of Educational Psychology, 106,* 1135–1143. doi:10.1037/a0036110.

Victoria State Government. (2013). *The impact of bullying.* Retrieved from http://www.education.vic.gov.au/about/programs/bullystoppers/Pages/impact.aspx

Waasdorp, T. W., Pas, E. T., O'Brennan, L. M., & Bradshaw, C. P. (2011). A multilevel perspective on the climate of bullying: Discrepancies among students, school staff, and parents. *Journal of School Violence, 10,* 115–132. doi:10.1080/15388220.2010.539164.

Wang, W., Vaillancourt, T., Brittain, H. L., McDougall, P., Krygsman, A., Smith, D., ... Hymel, S. (2014). School climate, peer victimization, and academic achievement: Results from a multi-informant study. *School Psychology Quarterly, 29,* 360–377. doi: 10.1037/spq0000084

Wong, C.-T., Cheng, Y.-Y., & Chen, L.-M. (2013). Multiple perspective on the targets and causes of school bullying. *Educational Psychology in Practice, 29,* 278–292. doi:10.1080/02667363.2013.837030.

Yang, A., & Salmivalli, C. (2013). Different forms of bullying and victimization: Bully-victims versus bullies and victims. *European Journal of Developmental Psychology, 10,* 723–738. doi:10.1080/17405629.2013.793596.

CHAPTER 4

# Principals and School Resource Officers' Perspectives on Bullying

*Laura Trujillo-Jenks and Kenneth Jenks*

Being a leader of a school is both an exciting and a frightening concept. Watching students grasp learning objectives and transfer that knowledge successfully to the real world is rewarding. It is also gratifying to work with teachers who are determined to help their students to achieve academic, emotional, and social success. When parents and the community support and promote the success of students and teachers, it is very exciting.

Then, there are the terrifying incidents that seem to multiply with each passing school year. School shootings, fights between students, student suicides, and bullying have become part of the school landscape for administrators. These realities should not be obsessed over, but they are realities that can appear on any campus at any time. To be an effective school leader, one should have a plan of action for handling these realities.

One way of handling the most difficult aspects of a school administrator's job is through the hiring of a school resource officer, or SRO. The SRO can help a school leader's job become more manageable by bringing a sense of order and security to the school campus. When a school leader

L. Trujillo-Jenks (✉)
Texas Woman's University, Denton, TX, USA

K. Jenks
City of Anna, Anna, TX, USA



L.H. Rosen et al. (eds.), *Bullying in School*,
DOI 10.1057/978-1-137-59298-9_4

and SRO understand each other's roles and how those roles can help promote a successful school culture and atmosphere, enforcing rules and policies can become easier. Additionally, when a school leader and SRO work together as a unit, fewer adverse events take place on campus. The next few pages will describe how a good working relationship between a school administrator and SRO can support the success of students, teachers, and the school community.

## The School Principal

The school principal is the leader of a campus and/or the administrator of a school. The principal is in charge of making a campus successful. The school principal is charged with finding ways to help students and teachers to feel safe and supported, feel welcome on campus, and to experience success. The school principal offers support to students and teachers. He or she is there to welcome parents and community members when they come on campus. The expectations and responsibilities of this job require an individual with fortitude and leadership skills. This limits the number of educators willing to take on the challenges of the job.

Because of the changes in our society and the dangerous events that occur on school campuses today, training on how to keep a campus safe is becoming a requirement for the position. The school principal must be knowledgeable about bullying and how it looks in their school community. Unfortunately, principals can find it difficult to access the training that would enable them to detect and eliminate bullying from a campus. There are no specific guidebooks or required trainings that principals must complete before becoming a leader of a campus. The only professional development a principal may obtain concerning bullying is what is mandated through a school district or self-imposed.

Many states have enacted laws that address professional development requirements regarding bullying on school campuses. For example, New Jersey has enacted an Anti-Bullying Bill of Rights Act (P.L. 2010, *c.* 122) that defines the need for educators "to meet requirements [that include] training on harassment, intimidation and bullying" (New Jersey Department of Education, para 1). As another example, Texas addresses bullying through the Texas Education Code (TEC) and offers guidance on how bullying could look on a school campus (see Chap. 37 Sect. 37 of the TEC). The TEC also gives parents the choice of transferring their child to another campus if their child has been a victim of bullying.

Some school districts throughout the nation are also becoming more proactive in ensuring that bullying is being addressed in a timely manner. For instance, in Killeen, Texas, the Killeen Independent School District (KISD) has an electronic *Bully Reporter.* Anyone can go online to report allegations of bullying. Individual schools within KISD have established guidelines on what students and parents can do to address and prevent bullying.

Although there may be local and state guidelines on bullying, it is imperative that the principal address the specific types of bullying seen on campus. This imperative stems from the knowledge that "[b]ullied students are more likely to take a weapon to school, get involved in physical fights, and suffer from anxiety and depression, health problems, and mental health problems" (O'Brien, 2013, para 1). Some students may fail academically and/or may skip school because "[m]any bullied children find that their schools are hostile environments" (Cornell & Limber, 2015, p. 333). In order to address bullying, it is important that principals understand what bullying is and that they be able to recognize it when they see it or hear about it.

**What is bullying?** Principals may have difficulty enforcing rules concerning bullying because of the variety of definitions found for bullying among educators and among bullying programs. Because of this inconsistency, it is best that individual school campuses define bullying according to what is actually occurring on a campus. In fact, it may be best to allow the students to define bullying and to allow the students to educate the educators as to what bullying looks like for a particular campus. Because there are so many forms of bullying, both covert and overt, it is difficult to implement a bullying program that targets all of the different types of bullying seen on a particular campus during a school year. Teachers may have difficulty discerning if interactions between students fall into the bullying category and, as a result, may be hesitant to intervene. This hesitancy makes it difficult for students to report bullying to teachers and other educators (Espelage, Polanin, & Low, 2014; Holt, Raczynski, Frey, Hymel, & Limber, 2013; Kennedy, Russom, & Kevorkian, 2012; Whitson, 2015).

Understandably, educators view bullying in all its forms from different perspectives and may dismiss an incident because, from their perspective, it does not appear serious enough to warrant an intervention. Some educators believe that students are overly sensitive and unable to take a joke or that they are experiencing a rite of passage rather than bullying. This makes defining bullying at the campus level important, since a common definition and program throughout a school will have all stakeholders understanding a common set of expectations.

When students are allowed to define bullying according to their experiences on campus, they are able to provide concrete examples of the types of bullying they have endured so that the principal and other educators can be informed. Encouraging students to talk about their experiences with bullying and talking about strategies they believe should be implemented sends the message that students are valued, helps them to feel better about their school, and could prevent a bullying situation in the future (Uribe-McGilvray, 2004). Principals may want to consider adopting a bullying program that is different from the one adopted by the school district so that it can be tailored to the individual needs of the students on the campus.

Another area of caution is the graduation of bullying acts to penal or criminal code violations. "… Bullying can overlap with many other proscribed behaviors such as criminal assault, extortion, hate crimes, and sexual harassment" (Cornell & Limber, 2015, p. 334). Pellegrini (2002) asserted that bullying, whether physical, verbal, or sexual, increases as youngsters make the transition to middle school. Moreover, as was found in the literature review, large class sizes, school size, along with the lack of school community, contribute to a bullying climate (Tayli, 2013). Hence, the organization health is important when addressing bullying.

Although bullying in general is something that all principals and educators want to be able to stop and to eliminate from the school campus, sexual bullying now needs to be addressed among school-aged students. Bullying that involves sexual harassment or sexual assault is more prevalent in middle schools and high schools. During this time, students are more apt to notice each other's changing bodies, and some students are more comfortable divulging their sexual orientation. Ashbaugh and Cornell (2008) found that "81% of 8th through 11th grade students had experienced sexual harassment at least once in school, and 35% of those students reported first experiencing sexual harassment in 6th grade or younger" (p. 23).

So, then the question becomes what is the difference between sexual harassment, sexual assault, and sexual bullying? Each state has its own definitions, but many schools use them interchangeably. Regardless of the definition used, it has been found that bullying can and does lead to other types of penal code violations, such as sexual harassment and sexual assault

(Bucher & Manning, 2005; Collins, 2006; Rahimi & Liston, 2011). Therefore, sexual bullying may be defined as something that evolves into a criminal act. Although bullying is not found in many state penal codes, what has been seen is that bullies start with teasing or being physically aggressive, which can quickly evolve into a penal code violation, such as a sexual assault.

Sexual bullying can appear in all three formats (i.e., physical, verbal, and relational). Through the three forms of bullying, sexual overtones can be seen (Uribe-McGilvray, 2004), which makes defining sexual bullying even more difficult. According to Cunningham et al. (2010), bullying by girls on girls and boys on boys showed that dominance and popularity may be the main reason for the sexual bullying, but jealousy and homophobia can also be catalysts for bullying. They also found that self-described attractive students would bully if they felt that they were better looking than other students. Duncan and Lang (1998) found that sexual jealousy occurred more often in secondary schools. This is when boys and girls name call, gossip, and try to destroy the sexual reputation of others based on either no or minimal facts. Additionally, they found that girls sexually assaulted other girls and that girls, especially those jealous of other girls, would use physical aggression as a way to bully them into submission (Duncan & Lang, 1998).

Sexual bullying seems to be gaining ground in schools, so learning more about what it is and how it is portrayed on a campus is the duty of the school principal. One resource of information that may shed light on the forms of bullying seen on campus is the SRO.

## The School Resource Officer (SRO)

The SRO program began in the early 1950s but did not become popular until the 1990s (Weiler & Cray, 2011). Hence, the SRO is not a new phenomenon and is an excellent human resource that promotes safety on a school campus. "SROs are now trained to be first responders in an emergency situation, as opposed to just locking a building down and waiting for outside help" (DeNisco, 2014, p. 49). They are law enforcement officers with experience; knowledge of local, state, and federal laws; and knowledge in emergency management procedures (McNair, 2013). With the SRO empowered to act as law enforcement and roles clearly defined, the SRO and administrators can help create a very positive school climate of safety (Weiler & Cray, 2011).

SROs are an excellent addition to any campus because they represent safety and security. They are peace officers, which means that they hold the same privileges that a city or county police officer holds. They receive their training at the police academy and are well-versed in the use of firearms and less-lethal personal protection devices. They have the authority to give citations (tickets) or make physical arrests for violations that occur within their presence or via arrest warrant. An SRO performs three major roles: law enforcement officer, law-related counselor, and law-related educator (Curriculum Review, 2014). SROs serve not only as a security presence but also as role models that serve and protect (Canady & Reiney, 2015). Their focus is to be a helpful resource that builds positive relationships with students and educators.

SROs are an important part of any anti-bullying program since they are partners with educators and parents in keeping a school safe. Robles-Piña and Denham (2012) assert that SROs are needed in schools as key personnel to help reduce bullying. To date there is little research on SROs and how they are trained to implement bullying intervention programs. However, the SRO is a large part of the school safety implementation puzzle and can help in preventing undesired behaviors such as bullying. The SRO is seen as an authority figure, but the officer should also be seen as another trustworthy adult that can help students in time of need. SROs and community law enforcement officers should be involved in the efforts to stop bullying on school campuses (Stopbullying.gov, 2015).

There are many benefits to having an SRO on a school campus, including the handling of 9-1-1 calls, the handling of difficult situations and helping to control possible problems, and having a certified peace officer readily available to answer questions about law enforcement (Black, 2009). SROs are primed to help in ensuring that bullying does not become a cancer on a campus. "Once the SRO and the building administrators understand each other's responsibilities related to school safety, their collaboration and decision making will ensure a safe learning environment for students and staff" (Cray & Weiler, 2011, p. 169).

When SROs are on campus, they should be seen as persons who are available to help school community members. They should not be used as "the punishers" or disciplinarians for common student code of conduct violations. They should be enforcers of the law that address any criminal activity on campus. McNair (2013) stated that SROs are not traditional law enforcement officers who are reactive to situations, but because of their positive role on a school campus and because they are a school community member who is involved in various daily routines, they are in a better position to be proactive.

The proactive SRO is one who intervenes before a situation becomes criminal and helps educate others regarding the penal code and how their actions can be seen as illegal activity. Because the SRO's presence on a campus can help to prevent students from breaking rules and the law, they are proactive in stopping bullying. SROs become part of the school community and get to know the stakeholders, including the students. As the SRO takes time to get to know the different groups of students on a campus, he/she is better able to recognize when a situation may become serious.

It is important that school administrators understand the role of the SRO as it specifically relates to student discipline. Unfortunately, some school administrators must deal with behaviors on their campus that parallel what is taking place in the community (Dunn, 2002). These behaviors exceed the expertise of school administrators, which makes the SRO a vital part of the school community's efforts to promote safety and order while enforcing the law.

Some administrators may see the SRO's presence on campus as permission to abdicate their role as enforcer of rules and policy, placing the burden of campus discipline on the shoulders of the SRO. However, this must be avoided. The SRO is not there to serve as a replacement for the administrator and is not the means by which the administrator gets to be the good guy when student discipline is handed out. Additionally, some administrators may believe that having a SRO on campus ensures that the penal code will be enforced and students can be removed from campus by the SRO, leaving the school principal and administrators free from the need to confront students and parents. This rise of criminal prosecution for illegal behavior in schools, as Carey (2014) refers to it, puts much more responsibility on the SRO and less on the educator.

The educator should never expect an SRO to deal with all student behaviors whether they are violations of the penal code or of the Student Code of Conduct (SCOC). It is better to not involve them until there is "the higher level of actable information and/or probable cause is present ..." (Trujillo-Jenks & Jenks, 2016, p. 133). In short, SROs should never be put in a situation where they are forced to take on the administrator's role as disciplinarian. Principals are the leaders of the school and enforce the SCOC, while the SRO enforces the penal code and supports the educators on campus in enforcing the SCOC. Sometimes there will be concurrent investigations conducted by law enforcement and the school, but neither party is relieved of their duty by the presence of the other. Discipline on the campus is always the lead administrator's responsibility, and they should always work in tandem with the SRO.

When it comes to bullying and the implementation of bullying programs, "Experts say the best plans are designed by local educational leaders working in partnership with law enforcement, community service providers, students, and families to identify potential problems before they become crises" (Brydolf, 2013, p. 8). The SROs and local police departments can be involved in bullying training, which would start in elementary school and carry through high school. Since bullying programs are apt to focus on decreasing and eliminating bullying behavior, implementing a bullying program beginning at the elementary level is a good idea. This will help shape student behavior about bullying and help decrease bullying as the students move from one grade level to the next during the middle and high school years.

At the high school level, students are not always likely to listen or to follow rules, so it may be more difficult for SROs and principals/administrators to implement a bullying program. This is another reason why beginning the bullying program at the elementary level would be best. Additionally, Cloud (2010) suggested that SROs could help bystanders at all levels understand that their role can be crucial in stopping bullying.

SROs are colleagues of school educators and members of the campus family. They should be treated with respect and valued as important members of the school community. Their expertise and knowledge of the law should make them valued members of the crisis team, or violence prevention team. They should be considered key stakeholders and should have a voice in setting policy that concerns school safety and order, specifically when it comes to bullying (Theriot & Anfara, 2011). They are one of the best partners an administrator can have when dealing with bullying and school safety.

## School Safety

To be engaged and successful, students must feel safe in their learning environment. School safety must include the enforcement of the SCOC and the involvement of the SRO in enforcing the laws that govern public safety and interaction. Students who perceive their school as unable to help victims may see an increase in bullying and in violent behaviors among individual students (Debnam, Johnson, & Bradshaw, 2014). In order to help students to see their school as a safe haven, Trujillo-Jenks and Trujillo (2013) suggested that the administration teach teachers to be observant of everything that is occurring on the campus. This means to notice what looks "normal" for the campus and what does not (i.e., a student that wears a school ID is normal). They also encourage administrators to encourage students to use the buddy system. When a buddy system is in place, bullying behavior can be "checked" and possibly stopped by a peer. This is important to note, since the power to stop bullying can be with the student and not an adult who may be seen as the savior of the student. And finally, the use of video cameras on campus will help keep a campus safe because video can be reviewed, as needed, to find evidence of bullying behavior (Trujillo-Jenks & Trujillo, 2013).

The purpose of the SCOC is to ensure that a safe and orderly campus is in force. It also provides a map of what is expected in society, especially since many of the infractions listed in the SCOC are also violations of state or local statutes. The SCOC is a set of rules that must be followed by every single student who attends a school within a school district. This means students as young as three and possibly as old as 22 are subjected to the same rules. Because of this, the enforcement of rules, the consequences of the rules, and the application of the rules may be different from campus to campus.

To increase the safety of the school and to help students feel safe, consistent enforcement of the SCOC is required. This "law of the land" can usually be found as a statute at the state level and includes an outline of the different infractions along with consequences for those infractions. Infractions, or violations of the SCOC, can be minor, such as dress code or ID violations, or they can be serious and result in expulsions and arrests (Trujillo-Jenks & Trujillo, 2013). Students must be informed of the SCOC and the various infractions, the consequences for violating infractions, and what it means to follow the rules and contribute to a healthy school.

Most school districts' SCOCs address bullying. Unfortunately, the bullying rule is often so broadly written that it can be difficult to enforce or to prove a violation, or it does not fully convey how bullying looks on a particular campus. For these reasons, many states have recognized the bullying problem and have either recommended that school districts implement a bullying program on each campus and/or have included a statute for bullying in their education code. Therefore, most schools should address bullying through their individual school rules or through a school handbook. In the "bullying rule," bullying should be defined, and consequences of bullying should be clearly outlined.

The SCOC also can be a guide for how to tackle newer and more abstract types of bullying. If we go back just 20 years, the problems that we are seeing now in public schools are exacerbated by technology. Access to technology makes it easier to demean and hurt another person. Now, the bully may not be one person but several persons. When bystanders are added to the equation, bullying becomes a bigger problem that, to the bullied, seems unsurmountable.

The advent of social media seems to have created individuals who, under the cover of anonymity, refuse to take responsibility for their actions, which allows them to feel free to post the most heinous words, pictures, and videos enticing bullying behavior from others. With the Internet and social media, bullying is much easier because it can be done covertly (Barnes et al., 2012). Additionally, it is easier to bully when encouragement from others on social media creates a situation for the bullied that is unbearable. And, with social media, slander and libel is no longer contained at the school level, but it is open to anyone in the cyber world, which makes bullying a bigger problem for educators (Trujillo-Jenks & Jenks, 2016).

The rules outlined in the SCOC should be taught and explained throughout the year to each student by each teacher and administrator and SRO on the campus. This would work perfectly with a bullying program, since the program should include lesson plans and activities that help teachers and administrators teach students about bullying. The enforcement of the SCOC will hopefully lessen the stark realties of bullying that have manifested on different school campuses across the nation.

## The Realities of Today's Schools

The realities with which the school principal, SROs, and other educators are faced are compounded by the many aspects of bullying. In addition to the various forms of bullying, educators are also dealing with books, news stories, journal articles, and social media generated by parents and society in general stating that schools are not doing enough to stop bullying at the campus level.

The dilemma for some educators is how and what should be done about teaching students about bullying. Do educators teach them that bullying is a way of life and then give them ways to handle bullying? Or, should they be told that they must run to an educator each time that they are bullied in order to be safe? How do educators help students feel strong enough to ward off bullying? How do educators help other students, such as bystanders, to feel comfortable and strong enough to stop bullying instead of encouraging it when they see it?

When educators believe that they are doing their best in protecting students from bullying, how do they convince parents and students? Many educators are finding themselves at the center of legal troubles because of the new sweep of lawsuits that have been filed due to the belief that educators have done little to nothing to prevent and/or stop bullying. What is tragic is that many lawsuits are played out in the media, which does not always tell the whole truth or at least the truth of the educators. This is one reason why educators are sometimes overly cautious in the way they approach bullying.

There are several media stories, old and new, that follow the same pattern: a child is being bullied, the parents report it to the administrator, and nothing is done to alleviate or stop the bullying. Parents feel that their children are being forsaken, that the rules are not being applied fairly, and that their children are not enjoying the due process and equal protection that other children are enjoying. Because of this perception, parents are now fighting back by suing educators who they believe should be doing more to protect their children from bullying. Additionally, more lawsuits are being seen across the nation that focus on parents suing educators for the suicidal deaths of their children.

Robinette (2015) noted that the number of lawsuits that involve bullying is on the rise. While there are no research studies on bullying lawsuits, the National School Boards Association stated that with the increase in cases going to court, the research will be plentiful in the near future. Regrettably, some schools would rather settle out of court to save time and money, instead of finding the truth about a bullying incident. Robinette found that in a case that involved Carlisle schools paying out $10,000 to an alleged bullied student, the district understood that paying the relatively small amount was easier and less time consuming than going to court, even though the student did not make the educators aware of the bullying until after he left the school (Robinette, 2015). This type of lawsuit can set a dangerous precedent, especially since it seems that this court case was winnable for the district. DiBlasio (2011) also noted an uptick of lawsuits focused on bullying and attributed it to an increased awareness and more expert lawyers. She also established that many parents are unhappy when they hear a family is suing a school district over bullying because it means that tax dollars are being spent to pay the district's court costs and fees.

How did we get to this point? How did bullying get to the point where lawsuits are being filed taking the battle to court instead of settling the battle at its origination—in the schools? The legal troubles some educators are finding themselves in have themes. Parents believe that educators are doing nothing, could have done more, and/or refuse to follow established policy and the law. Parents also feel that going to the city police department and to lawyers is more helpful because they believe that the school administrators and educators are weak in enforcing policy and intervening when bullying is reported.

There have been many court cases that highlight the bullying factor, and unfortunately, this is not a new phenomenon. Although there are court cases, such as Gebser v. Lago Vista (1998) that deal with a type of bullying that was allegedly sexual harassment from a teacher toward a student and DeGooyer v. Harkness (1944), which dealt with the initiation of an athlete that caused his death, this section will focus on student bullying. The following examples give light to the realities occurring in today's schools.

One case that has become seminal when it comes to bullying is Ledfors v. Emery County School District (1993), which affirmed that the school district was protected from a lawsuit even when a student was physically assaulted by two other students at a high school. After being in a physical education (P.E.) class and left alone in a gym with other students who were playing a game, two assailants entered the gym and beat Ledfors to the point that he was hospitalized. The other students did try to stop the assault and they tried to find an educator to help without luck. The Ledfors family sued the two assailant students, the school district, the principal, and the P.E. teacher for negligence, which resulted in the severe assault and hospitalization of their son. The parents sued using three main points, but the third point is something that schools should take note of. In the third point, the parents challenged that the school principal's and coach's lack of action and supervision contributed to the battery of their son and voiced that "but for the government's breach of its duty to supervise and protect minor students in public schools," their son may have not been hospitalized after a severe beating (Ledfors v. Emery County School Dist., 1993). The lesson: Educators should never leave students unsupervised.

Another seminal case is Davis v. Monroe County Board of Education (1999) where a fifth-grade female was subjected to a consistent pattern of sexual harassment, both verbal and physical, by another fifth-grade male classmate. For five months, she and her mother reported the incidents to school personnel, but nothing was done to help stop the sexual harassment. As the fifth-grade female's grades began to drop and after her father found a suicide note, the mother filed a lawsuit against the school for showing deliberate indifference toward her daughter, meaning the school did nothing to prevent the sexual harassment her daughter was subjected to. Further, the courts found that Title IX can be used by plaintiffs to collect monetary damages if the harassment is so "severe, pervasive, and objectively offensive that it effectively bars the victim's access to an educational opportunity or benefit" (Davis v. Monroe County Board of Education, 1999, Opinion). The lesson from this case is that schools must take action. When a report of bullying or any other type of harassment is given, investigate, speak to all involved, find witnesses, and/or do something that will help the bullied student feel less helpless.

The majority of the cases that are brought to court allege that the school officials, including the teachers, did nothing to intervene or stop the bullying which led to dire consequences such as continued bullying, depression, and/or suicide. One case that focuses on getting administrators to do more involves a 14-year-old boy who was constantly bullied by a group of boys who were in athletics with him (Chawla, 2015). They used racial slurs, manhandled him using his backpack, and attempted to throw him over a balcony. All of this was allegedly reported to the assistant principal by the 14-year-old, and the assurance of something being done was always given. However, because of the inactions of the administration and other educators, the Givens family filed suit (Chawla, 2015) after their child committed suicide. This case illustrates that educators must receive professional development that helps them understand the signs of depression and how to address those signs more than adequately.

Retaliation against a family who wants something done about bullying is a factor that has gotten some educators in a predicament. A family outside of Chicago, whose son attended Robert Frost Elementary, sued an alleged bully, his parents, the school principal, and the school district for $50,000 in damages (FoxNews.com, 2014). According to the allegations, the bully had choked, punched, tripped, pushed, spat, and threatened to kill their third-grade son, who was afraid of attending school and who had frequent nightmares. The parents allege that the school principal failed to discipline the third-grade bully and did not try to stop the behavior. Additionally, the mother, who works in the cafeteria of the school, was immediately fired after her family filed the complaint (FoxNews.com, 2014). The educators were seen as retaliating against the family, which made them look guiltier in the eyes of the community.

Public schools are not the only places where bullying lawsuits or retaliation is being seen. In Louisiana, at Hammond Holy Ghost Catholic School, the administrators allegedly did nothing to stop the bullying from two boys who consistently harassed a 12-year-old girl, who eventually was hospitalized for depression and suicidal tendencies (Stewart, 2014). Additionally, the school requested the Holmes family withdraw their children from the private Catholic school, which sent the message that the Holmes children were not welcomed due to the lawsuit and the negative comments that Mrs. Holmes was leaving on social media about the school administration (Stewart, 2014). Retaliation, or the appearance of retaliation, should never be a move that educators take since it will only make things worse for them.

In another incident that occurred in Tennessee at Hendersonville High School, a 14-year-old student who was a basketball star with grades to match was being bullied by several teammates (WSMV, 2014). Allegedly, the teammates harassed the 14-year-old based on race. Although the mother of the 14-year-old reported the alleged bullying to the basketball coach, she did not report it to any administrator. The basketball coach did have a team meeting with the girls to discuss the allegations of bullying, but she did not report the incident to her administration. Additionally during the fall season, the coach cut the 14-year-old star from the team and told her she could try again in the spring. This star student had received letters from colleges since she was in eighth grade, yet she was cut from the team. The retaliation, or the appearance of retaliation, and the bullying of the 14-year-old student resulted in her receiving counseling for depression.

While parents understand that a suicide can never be reversed, they are concerned that other students will follow suit. In a lawsuit by parents who lost their high school son to "bullicide," the parents sought no compensation, but sought, instead, the implementation of an anti-bullying program to prevent any further bullicides. As one parent stated, "What it boils down to is the football players, cheerleaders and kids with money have a different set of rules than everybody else," and everyone else is subjected to harsh bullying (Donaldson James, 2009, para 12). Additionally, through this case, it was found that "... every day an estimated 160,000 kids nationwide stay home from school because they are afraid of being bullied. In addition, researchers at the Yale School of Medicine, in a review of studies from 13 countries, have found signs of an apparent connection between bullying, being bullied, and suicide" (Donaldson James, 2009, paras. 15–16).

At the state level, some are taking bullying very seriously. New Jersey is taking a different stance through a Superior Court judge who has ruled that school districts may file suit against bullies. In a case brought by a student identified as V.B. against a school district, the school district's attorney requested that the identified bullies and their parents should share in the culpability of the bullying if proven true (Mueller, 2014). The sharing of culpability would allow for fewer damages to be paid by the school district. V.B. had endured the bullying since he was in fourth grade and while in high school his health deteriorated and the school allowed him to graduate early. Thus, the sharing of culpability would seem fair and acceptable, according to the school district, especially if there was a ruling in favor of V.B. A lawyer in Texas is following a similar thought process and advises his clients to sue the parents of the bully. He cites the Texas Family Code, Section 41.001, which states that "parents are liable for 'the willful and malicious conduct' of a child who is at least 10 years of age but younger than 18" (Land, 2011, para 6).

Group bullies or bullies who bully while in groups are also a problem for educators. Making sure that group bullies are swiftly punished for bullying is a stance that some school districts have taken. In a case that dealt with a group of students who were a part of a secret society, the courts found that school administrators rightly disciplined the students in question (The Council of School Attorneys, 2003). This case, which focused on hazing and secret societies, involved a "powder puff" high school annual event, where students would be hazed off campus and not during a school day. This event was well known, but, because it was not a school-sponsored event, seniors thought they could haze underclassmen to the point of status humiliation and physical assaults. Additionally, the hazing was videotaped, which made the matter easy to discipline. Although this took place off campus, the school rightly and justly intervened in disciplining 32 students, which included expulsions (The Council of School Attorneys, 2003). This case also confirmed the usefulness of wording that appears in the SCOC of many school districts that prohibits secret societies, gangs, fraternities, sororities, and other groups of students that gather for the purpose of hazing or bullying.

Some school districts are settling lawsuits, even when they feel they have done nothing wrong. In Ohio, the Green Local School District settled a $500,000 lawsuit, which was filed in 2011, due to a female student who was allegedly regularly harassed for over three years because she did not believe in Jesus Christ (Nethers, 2015). The bullying included verbal assaults, physical assaults, a stabbing in the leg with a pencil, cyberbullying, and her name listed on a "kill list." Along with the district administrators paying the settlement, they also agreed for the United States Department of Education to review the policies on bullying that the district had in place and to provide professional development on how to address bullying in the future. As the female student's lawyer, Ken Meyer, succinctly stated,

> ... if you send a message from the school administration that it [bullying] will not be tolerated then it generally is controllable; if you send a message that we are not going to do anything about it ... then the opposite message is sent and you have ongoing systemic problems. (as cited in Nethers, 2015, para 22)

Not all bullying lawsuits have a positive outcome, however. In the case that involved a Henderson Middle School student who committed suicide in December 2013, a US District Judge remanded the case back to the state court, since the parents were unable to show how Clark County School District violated their child's Constitutional rights (Morton, 2015). The judge ruled that because the school district had no duty to protect a student from bullying, and because it had no duty to provide assistance in the prevention of suicide, the parents could not prove wrongdoing. Additionally, the judge stated that the parents only alleged inaction and not action when dealing with the bullying incidents that their child endured (Morton, 2015). This unfortunate ruling should caution parents to be sure that the evidence they gather when building a bullying case shows a clear violation of a law.

Finally, not all lawsuits involve the filing of a lawsuit by the bullied person, but more are making it in court with the accused bully filing a lawsuit. In Tenafly, New Jersey, a male student made a truthful comment about a female student having lice and was labeled a bully. According to the school's bullying specialist, the male student engaged in bullying behavior because he made a truthful statement that insulted the female student and made her feel bad about herself (Yellin, 2015). Ironically, the boy was openly humiliated in front of his class after his teacher was required to lecture the class about being kind to one another (Yellin, 2015). Because some educators are overwhelmed with what to do when it comes to bullying, some can go overboard in thinking they are protecting a victim and making an example of an alleged bully.

As educators, specifically principals and SROs, look at how bullying has evolved, they must be reminded that the safety of all students cannot be guaranteed and not everyone will be safe and free from bullying (Trujillo-Jenks & Trujillo, 2013). Administrators and SROs cannot be in every part of the school at all times, which is why the health of the organization and the implementation of a bullying program is so important (Frank, 2013). When principals and SROs work together in implementing a bullying program and a Student Code of Conduct that all stakeholders understand and enforce consistently, all forms of bullying can be lessened on school campuses. Instead of waiting for the students to take extreme actions, principals and SROs are in a formidable position to help students feel like schools are safe places and free of bullying.

It is also good to go to the Internet and find what students are viewing. There are many informative tools, applications, and suggestions on how EC-12th graders can help stop bullying in schools. As Grace Helbig reminds us in her Public Service Announcement (PSA) about bullying and bystanders, "I want to help foster a sense of positive community based on responsibility and accountability" (Strehlke, 2015, para 6). She also has promoted the anti-bullying emoji, along with the *I Am a Witness* app, which helps witnesses of bullying to do something to intervene and stop bullying.

## Principals, SROs, and Bullying Prevention

To address the realities of schools today, principals and SROs must work toward bullying prevention. Because they are seen as leaders of a campus and charged with keeping law and order, both the principal and SRO are key in preventing bullying. Hence, the principal and SRO are bullying program facilitators for a campus, and they are the persons who can and will help the stakeholders of a campus to identify and prevent bullying.

Since it has been established that the definition of bullying can be evasive, professional development on the implementation of a bullying program is necessary for principals and SROs as well as all other stakeholders on the school campus. Involving other stakeholders is necessary so that everyone within the school organization understands how bullying is defined and what is being done to remove it from campus. It is also pertinent for principals and SROs to know how bullying has and is being dealt with in other schools and what bullying "trends" may be appearing on campuses.

In a review of the literature, Espelage et al. (2014) found that bullying is less evident in schools where school administrators work closely with teachers and other educators, including SROs, on campus. The problem of bullying is exacerbated when the adults on the campus either refuse to recognize that there is an issue of bullying or believe that bullying cannot happen on their campus. Additionally, it is always good to understand how the students on a campus may react to bullying. Craig, Pepler, and Blais found that girls self-reported to intervene when bullying was evident by telling an adult, whereas boys were more often to stop bullying with aggressive behaviors of their own (as cited in Kennedy et al., 2012, p. 3). This is good information to understand when deciding on a bystander intervention program.

So, where do educators and SROs begin? Kennedy et al. (2012) stated that educators need professional development in bullying prevention. In their study, they found that there was a different understanding between teachers and administrators on what bullying prevention should entail, which made enforcing a bullying program less effective. Teachers seem to want professional development to increase their knowledge about bullying and understanding of how to support students in bullying prevention. This is good to know, since through professional development, teachers would understand that bullying can be curbed significantly, if teachers intervene as soon as they see bullying on their campus (Strohmeier & Noam, 2012).

Not all SROs are required to go through anti-bullying training. However, in addition to his/her specialized training in crime prevention, they have access to training in bullying prevention. As with principals and educators, there is no requirement that all SROs are trained in preventing bullying, but as a principal and SRO work together, their focus for a particular campus should be on implementing professional development focused on a campus-wide bullying program.

Once the definition, program, and professional development have been chosen, the bully should be seen as the aggressor and not as a victim (Massari, 2011). Although the bully should be educated and shown the proper ways to interact with others, it is important that their bullying actions are stopped. Teachers need to show empathy toward a victim by taking the perspective of the victim (Lam, Law, Chan, Wong, & Xiao, 2015), which will humanize the bullied and dehumanize the bully. Unfortunately, if educators refuse to or do not want to intervene when bullying is apparent, they may find themselves in a lawsuit involving negligence. "Negligence is generally viewed as a failure to exercise a reasonable standard of care that results in harm to another person or a breach of duty to protect another person from unreasonable address of harm" (Essex, 2011, p. 195).

Hence, administrators, SROs, and teachers must acknowledge that bullying is occurring on the campus and must stop it each time they see it. Yerlikaya (2014) stated that because schools have a purpose of socializing students, there should be a goal toward ensuring that socializing does not involve any kind of aggression or bullying. Additionally, because educators and SROs behave in loco parentis while students are away from their parents, they are obligated to "anticipate or foresee that certain acts involving student conduct may be harmful to other students" by providing a reasonably safe environment for all students on campus (Essex, 2011, p. 194). Furthermore, the good faith effort must always be in place, which means that educators should do something to help students feel and be safe from harmful acts of others.

One caution about implementation of any bullying program is the consistency of implementation among the faculty and other stakeholders on a campus. Holt et al. (2013) found that differences in how a bullying program was implemented could be seen between classrooms on the same campus. Teachers addressed bullying differently because there was no buy-in and not all teachers believed that bullying was an issue that needed to be addressed on campus. Therefore, when implementing a bullying program, lesson plans, team meetings, faculty meetings, parent meetings, and community meetings should be set so that all stakeholders are involved in the implementation of the program. This will help ensure that every stakeholder becomes accountable in ensuring the success of a bullying program.

Including parents, community, and business members on the team will allow for a voice from outside the school community to give insight on what bullying looks like outside of the school walls. Parents and other family members can help teach anti-bullying strategies at home that will empower their child and may help in decreasing peer harassment (Studer & Mynatt, 2015). Especially when meeting with business persons who employ students, understanding the perceptions of workplace bullying will allow for the bullying program to be extended to the students' other frequented settings outside of school.

These stakeholders, then, can help in deterring and stopping bullying, if they are taught the same skills in bullying prevention that the educators understand. Having a collaborative partnership that focuses on a common threat, such as bullying, will not only ensure support for all of the partners but also support for the students. Moreover, Smith and Smith (2014) found that when a school definition on bullying is established by a committee that includes students, parents, and other stakeholders, the buy-in is more profound. Also, they found that when school officials communicate the definition and share it through printed posters and during times when parents are on campus (i.e., Open House), the bullying program becomes a part of the culture of the school and automatically enforced by all.

In short, the role of the principal and the SRO in intervening and preventing bullying on a campus is to:

- Lead the discussion and professional development for all stakeholders, including educators, students, parents, and community members.
- Include different stakeholders by giving them a voice as to how they perceive bullying on a campus and how they suggest addressing bullying.
- Identify the bullying behaviors that have been seen on a campus and determine how to define it.
- Identify and employ a ready-made bullying program or create a bullying program that is unique and that specifically addresses the bullying concerns for a campus.
- Ensure that the bullying program is consistently and constantly employed by all stakeholders and that regular professional development checkups or reminders are given throughout a school year.
- Ensure that all stakeholders understand their role in intervening and preventing bullying on a campus by consistently communicating the main ideas about the bullying program.
- Create benchmarks for evaluations throughout the school year in order to gauge how the bullying program is working and change tactics as needed with all stakeholder buy-in for the new school year.

Bullying is a problem for many principals and SROs, as well as for many students, parents, community members, and other educators. There are many who are "fed up" with bullying in the schools and beyond. It is up to principals, with the help of SROs, to help educate others about bullying and stop it at the EC-12 level, which may lead to fewer bullying incidents in the workplace and other social situations. Bullying may not be eradicated fully from schools, but with the dedication of the principal and SRO, it can be addressed and lessened.

## References

Ashbaugh, L. P., & Cornell, D. G. (2008). Sexual harassment and bullying behaviors in sixth-graders. *Journal of School Violence*, *7*(2), 21–38. doi:10.1300/J202v07n02_03.

Barnes, A., Cross, D., Lester, L., Hearn, L., Epstein, M., & Cowan, E. (2012). The invisibility of covert bullying among students: Challenges for school intervention. *Australian Journal of Guidance and Counseling*, *22*(2), 206–226. doi:10.1017/jgc.2012.27.

Black, S. (2009). Security and the SRO. *American School Board Journal, 196*(6), 30–31. Retrieved from http://www.asbj.com/

Brydolf, C. (2013). Preparing for the unthinkable: School safety after Sandy Hook. *Education Digest*, *79*(3), 4–8. Retrieved from http://www.eddigest.com/

Bucher, K. T., & Manning, M. L. (2005). Creating safe schools. *Clearing House*, *79*(1), 55–60.

Canady, M., & Reiney, E. (2015). Take action today: Creating safe school environments and building bridges. *Stopbullying Blog*. Retrieved from http://www.stopbullying.gov/blog/2015/02/03/take-action-today-creating-safe-school-environments-and-building-bridges

Carey, J. (2014). A student's right to remain silent. *Journal of Law & Education*, *43*, 575–580. Retrieved from https://www.ebscohost.com/

Chawla, K. (2015). The investigators: Bullying lawsuit filed against school district after teen attempted suicide. *CBS-WAFB 9*. Retrieved from http://www.wafb.com/story/29589960/the-investigators-bullying-lawsuit-filed-against-school-district-after-teen-attempted-suicide

Cloud, J. (2010). When bullying turns deadly: Can it be stopped? *TIME*. Retrieved from http://content.time.com/time/magazine/article/0,9171,2024210,00.html

Collins, C. L. (2006). Threat assessment in the post-Columbine public school system: The use of crisis management plans in the public school sector as a means to address and mitigate school gun violence. *International Journal of Educational Advancement*, *7*(1), 46–61. doi:10.1057/palgrave.ijea.2150043.

Cornell, D., & Limber, S. (2015). Law and policy on the concept of bullying at school. *American Psychologist*, *70*(4), 333–343. doi:10.1037/a0038558.

The Council of School Attorneys. (2003). *Principal Leadership*, 72–76. Retrieved from https://www.principals.org/portals/0/content/48693.pdf

Cray, M., & Weiler, S. C. (2011). Policy to practice: A look at national and state implementation of school resource officer programs. *Clearing House*, *84*(4), 164–170. doi:10.1080/00098655.2011.564987.

Cunningham, N. J., Taylor, M., Whitten, M. E., Hardesty, P. H., Eder, K., & DeLaney, N. (2010). The relationship between self-perception of physical attractiveness and sexual bullying in early adolescence. *Aggressive Behavior*, *36*, 271–281. doi:10.1002/ab.20349.

Curriculum Review. (2014). Examining school safety and gun violence in America. *Curriculum Review: Special Report*, *54*(4), 8–9. Retrieved from http://www.curriculumreview.com/

Davis v. Monroe County Board of Education (97-843) 526 U.S. 629. (1999). 120 F.3d 1390.

Debnam, K. J., Johnson, S. L., & Bradshaw, C. P. (2014). Examining the association between bullying and adolescent concerns about teen dating violence. *Journal of School Health*, *84*, 421–428. doi:10.1111/josh.12170.

DeGooyer v. Harkness, 70 S.D. 26 (S.D. 1944).

DeNisco, A. (2014). Police presence powers up. *District Administration*, *50*(11), 49–52. Retrieved from https://www.districtadministration.com/

DiBlasio, N. (2011). More bullying cases have parents turning to courts. *USA Today*. Retrieved from http://usatoday30.usatoday.com/news/education/story/2011-09-11/bullying-lawsuits-parents-self-defense-courts/50363256/1

Donaldson James, S. (2009). *Teen commits suicide due to bullying: Parent's sue school for son's death*. Retrieved October 11, 2015, from http://abcnews.go.com/Health/MindMoodNews/story?id=7228335

Duncan, N., & Lang, P. (1998). Sexual bullying in secondary schools. *Pastoral Care in Education*, *16*(2), 27–31.

Dunn, M. J. (2002). The role of SRO. *American School & University*, *75*(2), 50. Retrieved from http://asumag.com/

Espelage, D. L., Polanin, J. R., & Low, S. K. (2014). Teacher and staff perceptions of school environment as predictors of student aggression, victimization, and willingness to intervene in bullying situations. *School Psychology Quarterly*, *29*(3), 287–305. doi:10.1037/spq0000072.

Essex, N. (2011). Bullying and school liability—Implications for school personnel. *Clearing House*, *84*(5), 192–196. doi:10.1080/00098655.2011.564678.

FoxNews.com. (2014). Parents sue their son's alleged third-grade bully. *FoxNews.com*. Retrieved from http://www.foxnews.com/us/2014/06/20/parents-sue-their-son-alleged-third-grade-bully/

Frank, D. B. (2013). A principal reflects on shame and school bullying. *Psychoanalytic Inquiry, 33*(2), 174–180. doi:10.1080/07351690.2013.764710.

Gebser v. Lago Vista Independent School Dist. 524 U.S. 274 (1998).

Holt, M. K., Raczynski, K., Frey, K. S., Hymel, S., & Limber, S. P. (2013). School and community-based approaches for preventing bullying. *Journal of School Violence, 12*(3), 238–252. doi:10.1080/15388220.2013.792271.

Kennedy, T. D., Russom, A. G., & Kevorkian, M. M. (2012). Teacher and administrator perceptions of bullying in schools. *International Journal of Education Policy & Leadership, 7*(5), 1–12. Retrieved from http://journals.sfu.ca/ijepl/index.php/ijepl

Kennedy-Paine, C., & Crepeau-Hobson, F. (2015). FBI study of active shooter incident: Implications for school psychologists. *Communiqué, 43*(7), 22–23.

Lam, S.-F., Law, W., Chan, C.-K., Wong, B. P. H., & Zhang, X. (2015). A latent class growth analysis of school bullying and its social context: The self-determination theory perspective. *School Psychology Quarterly, 30*(1), 75–90. doi:10.1037/spq0000067.

Land, M. (2011). Lawyer to parents: Sue the bully. *NBCDFW.com*. Retrieved from http://www.nbcdfw.com/news/local/Lawyer-to-Parents-Sue-the--Bully-119889184.html

Ledfors v. Emery County School District, Supreme Court of Utah, 849 P.2d 1162 (1993). Retrieved from http://law.justia.com/cases/utah/supreme-court/1993/900503.html

Lösel, F., & Bender, D. (2014). Aggressive, delinquent, and violent outcomes of school bullying: Do family and individual factors have a protective function? *Journal of School Violence, 13*(1), 59–79. doi:10.1080/15388220.2013.840644.

Massari, L. (2011). Teaching emotional intelligence. *Leadership, 40*(5), 8–12.

McNair, D. (2013). Including school resource officers in school-based crisis intervention. *Communique, 41*(6), 14–14.

Morton, N. (2015). Judge dismisses federal lawsuit over bullying death. *Las Vegas Review-Journal*. Retrieved from http://www.reviewjournal.com/news/education/judge-dismisses-federal-lawsuit-over-bullying-death

Mueller, M. (2014). Bullies beware: Groundbreaking ruling allows schools to sue students who harass peers. *NJ.com True Jersey*. Retrieved from http://www.nj.com/news/index.ssf/2014/03/bullies_beware_groundbreaking_ruling_allows_schools_to_sue_students_who_harass_peers.html

Nethers, D. (2015). Local school district settle lawsuit that claimed classmates bullied girl for years. *Fox 8 Cleveland*. Retrieved from http://fox8.com/2015/06/16/local-school-district-settles-lawsuit-that-claimed-classmates-bullied-girl-for-years/

Nordahl, J., Poole, A., Stanton, L., Walden, L., & Beran, T. (2008). A review of school-based bullying interventions. *Democracy & Education, 18*(1), 16–20.
O'Brien, A. (2013). Bullying preventions: 5 tips for teachers, principals, and parents. *Edutopia*. Retrieved from http://www.edutopia.org/blog/bullying-prevention-tips-teachers-parentsanne-obrien
Pellegrini, A. D. (2002). Bullying, victimization, and sexual harassment during the transition to middle school. *Educational Psychologist, 37*(3), 151–163. doi:10.1207/S15326985EP3703_2.
Rahimi, R., & Liston, D. (2011). Race, class, and emerging sexuality: Teacher perceptions and sexual harassment in schools. *Gender & Education, 23*(7), 799–810. doi:10.1080/09540253.2010.536143.
Ramirez, O. (2013). Survivors of school bullying: A collective case study. *Children & Schools, 35*(2), 93–99. doi:10.1093/cs/cdt001.
Rigby, K. (2011). What can schools do about cases of bullying? *Pastoral Care in Education, 29*(4), 273–285. doi:10.1080/02643944.2011.626068.
Rigby, K. (2012). Bullying in schools: Addressing desires, not only behaviors. *Educational Psychology Review, 24*(2), 339–348. doi:10.1007/s10648-012-9196-9.
Riordan, C. A. (2014). Creating safe learning environments: Making school safe. *Techniques: Connecting Education & Careers, 89*(7), 26–31. Retrieved from http://www.acteonline.org/
Robinette, E. (2015). Bullying lawsuits increasing. *Dayton Daily News*. Retrieved from http://www.daytondailynews.com/news/news/local/bullying-lawsuits-increasing/njppD/
Robles-Piña, R. A., & Denham, M. A. (2012). School resource officers for bullying interventions: A mixed-methods analysis. *Journal of School Violence, 11*(1), 38–55. doi:10.1080/15388220.2011.630311.
Schuiteman, J. G. (2005). The security of Virginia's public schools. *The Virginia News Letter, 81*(2), 1–8.
Sinkkonen, H.-M., Puhakka, H., & Meriläinen, M. (2014). Bullying at a university: Students' experiences of bullying. *Studies in Higher Education, 39*(1), 153–165. doi:10.1080/03075079.2011.649726.
Smith, R., & Smith, K. (2014). Creating the cougar watch: Learning to be proactive against bullying in schools. *Middle School Journal*, 46(1), 13–19. Retrieved from http://www.amle.org/
Stampler, L. (2014). Anti-bullying campaign for high school rape victims goes viral with #YesAllDaughters. *Time.com*. Retrieved from http://time.com/3604666/yesalldaughters-normal-high-school/#3604666/yesalldaughters-normal-high-school/
Stewart, R. (2014). Hammond girl's bullying leads to lawsuit against school: Suit says Catholic school officials failed to protect teen. *The Advocate*. Retrieved from http://theadvocate.com/news/8729801-123/hammond-girls-bullying-leads-to

Stopbullying.gov. (2015). Involvement of law enforcement officers in bullying prevention. Retrieved from http://www.stopbullying.gov/resources-files/involvement-of-law-enforcement-tipsheet.pdf

Strehlke, S. (2015). This brand new emoji is specifically designed to help you fight bullying: Even Grace Helbig is a fan. *Teen Vogue*. Retrieved from http://www.teenvogue.com/story/anti-bullying-campaign-emoji-grace-helbig

Strohmeier, D., & Noam, G. (2012). Bullying in schools: What is the problem, and how can educators solve it? *New Directions for Youth Development, 133*, 7–13. doi:10.1002/yd.20003.

Studer, J. R., & Mynatt, B. S. (2015). Bullying prevention in middle schools: A collaborative approach. *Middle School Journal, 46*(3), 25–32. doi:10.1080/00940771.2015.11461912.

Tayli, A. (2013). School size as a predictor of bullying. *International Journal of Academic Research, 5*(5), 124–130. doi:10.7813/2075-4124.2013/5.

Theriot, M. T., & Anfara, V. A. (2011). School resource officers in middle grades school communities. *Middle School Journal, 42*(4), 56–64. doi:10.1080/00940771.2011.11461775.

Thompson, A., & Alvarez, M. (2013). Considerations for integrating school resource officers into school mental health models. *Children & Schools, 35*(3), 131–136. doi:10.1093/cs/cdt009.

Trujillo-Jenks, L., & Jenks, K. (2016). *Case studies on safety, bullying, and social media in schools: Current issues in educational leadership*. New York: Routledge Publishers.

Trujillo-Jenks, L., & Trujillo, M. (2013). *The survival guide for new campus administrators: How to become a professional, effective, and successful administrator*. Austin, TX: Park Place Publications.

Twemlow, S. W., & Sacco, F. C. (2013). Bullying is everywhere: Ten universal truths about bullying as a social process in schools & communities. *Psychoanalytic Inquiry, 33*(2), 73–89. doi:10.1080/07351690.2013.759484.

United States Department of Education (USDOE). (2014). A resource for improving school climate and discipline. *The Education Digest*. Retrieved from http://www2.ed.gov/policy/gen/guid/school-discipline/guiding-principles.pdf

Uribe-McGilvray, T. (2004). The bully—A need for intervention. *Human Development, 25*(2), 15–19.

Vaillancourt, K., & Gibson, N. (2014). Model school district policy for suicide prevention. *Communique, 43*(2), 23–27.

Weiler, S. C., & Cray, M. (2011). Police at school: A brief history and current status of school resource officers. *Clearing House, 84*(4), 160–163. doi:10.1080/00098655.2011.564986.

Whitson, S. (2015). Bringing an end to bullying. *Reclaiming Children & Youth, 24*(1), 50–54.

Whitted, B., Takiff, N., & Hansen, J. (2015). Bullying and school liability case summaries. Retrieved from http://www.wthlawfirm.com/resources/publications/bullying-school-liability-case-summaries/

Willard, N. (2014). A new 21st century approach for battling bullying: How we can empower our kids. *Parenting for High Potential*. Retrieved from http://www.nagc.org/resources-publications/nagc-publications/teaching-high-potential

Wong, C., Cheng, Y., & Chen, L. (2013). Multiple perspectives on the targets and causes of school bullying. *Educational Psychology in Practice*, *29*(3), 278–292. doi:10.1080/02667363.2013.837030.

WSMV.com. (2014). Parents sue over treatment of daughter at Sumner County school. Retrieved from http://www.wsmv.com/story/25583033/parents-sue-over-treatment-of-daughter-at-sumner-co-school

Yellin, D. (2015). Tenafly family's lawyer says settlement with school district over bullying lawsuit is near. *NorthJersey.com*. Retrieved from http://www.northjersey.com/news/tenafly-family-s-lawyer-says-settlement-with-school-district-over-bullying-lawsuit-is-near-1.1390640

Yerlikaya, I. (2014). Evaluation of bullying events among secondary education students in terms of school type, gender and class level. *International Journal of Progressive Education*, *10*(3), 139–149.

CHAPTER 5

# School Psychologists and School Counselors' Perspectives on Bullying

*Kathy DeOrnellas and Ronald S. Palomares*

## Introduction

School psychologists have specialized training that combines education and psychology at the individual student level and at the systems level (Kub & Feldman, 2015). Their roles include evaluating students for academic, behavioral, and emotional concerns; consulting with parents, teachers, and other professionals regarding students' needs; and providing individual and group counseling to address these needs. The National Association of School Psychologists (NASP) also charges school psychologists with helping to create learning environments where students can feel safe and perform to the best of their abilities (2012). As noted by Sherer and Nickerson (2010), school psychologists "are in an ideal position to assume leadership roles in violence and bullying prevention and intervention" (p. 217). School psychologists have training that prepares them to assess the prevalence of bullying on campus; promote awareness among students, school personnel, and parents; lead efforts to prevent bullying; and intervene with bullies and victims as warranted (Diamanduros, Downs, & Jenkins, 2008).

K. DeOrnellas (✉) • R.S. Palomares
Texas Woman's University, Denton, TX, USA





L.H. Rosen et al. (eds.), *Bullying in School*,
DOI 10.1057/978-1-137-59298-9_5

School counselors also provide services to students, parents, school staff, and community members. They are "uniquely qualified to address all students' academic, career, and personal/social development needs by designing, implementing, evaluating, and enhancing a comprehensive school counseling program that promotes and enhances student success" (American School Counselor Association [ASCA], n.d., p. 1). As part of their duties, school counselors work to create a safe learning environment and to support the rights of all students (Sandhu, 2000). School counselors provide direct services to students, which include providing counseling core curriculum or guidance lessons that are designed to teach students "knowledge, attitudes, and skills appropriate for their developmental level" (ASCA, p. 2). Direct services also include working with individual students to plan their academic and/or post-academic careers, and services that are geared to meet students' immediate needs, such as crisis intervention (ASCA).

Although from these descriptions it would appear that there is considerable overlap between school psychologists and school counselors, their actual roles vary significantly depending on the types of schools in which they are employed, how many schools they report to, and the types of services they provide. It is not unusual for school psychologists to cover several schools—working with preschoolers one day and high school students the next. School counselors are more likely to be based on one campus. School psychologists have traditionally spent most of their days evaluating students for academic, social, and/or behavioral problems or consulting with teachers; however, individual and group counseling is part of their repertoire. School counselors' roles vary based on the level of their school. Those assigned to elementary schools are likely to spend more of their time giving guidance lessons to classrooms of children or providing individual and group counseling. When school counselors work with adolescents, however, they are more likely to spend their time working with academic schedules and college preparation. Despite these differences, school psychologists and school counselors are well qualified to take the lead in bullying prevention and intervention.

## Defining Bullying

From the perspective of school psychologists and counselors, bullying is typically defined as "pervasive or persistent hurtful acts directed at another student that have caused, or can reasonably be forecast to cause, distress resulting in a significant interference with the ability of the student to receive an education or participate in school activities" (Willard, n.d.). This or similar language is found in most state statutory definitions and provides the basis upon which schools must enforce policies against bullying. Although state statutory definitions vary, "most are based on federal case law (Tinker v. Des Moines Ind. Comm. Sch. Dist 393 U.S. 503 [1969]; Davis v. Monroe, 526 U.S. 629, 633, 650 [1999]; Saxe v. State College 240 F.3d 200 [3d Cir. 2001])" (Willard).

This definition of bullying differs from the one used most frequently in the literature and in research studies. On StopBullying.gov (n.d.), bullying is defined as "unwanted, aggressive behavior among school aged children that involves a real or perceived power imbalance. The behavior is repeated, or has the potential to be repeated, over time." Many research studies use surveys that ask students if they have suffered a variety of hurtful acts without providing students with a definition of bullying or clarifying that the behaviors have to have been repeated over time (see Hamburger, Basile, & Vivolo, 2011, for a review of surveys used to measure bullying). The statutory definition used by school districts is a more objective way of defining bullying, and school psychologists and counselors are encouraged to look at bullying from this perspective. By using an agreed upon definition, school staff can be more accurate when intervening in incidents of bullying, incidents can be accurately recorded to track the presence of bullying behavior on campus, and the effectiveness of bullying programs can be evaluated.

## Typical Training Related to Bullying

A large majority of school psychologists and counselors (87%) reported having been trained in assessing and intervening in bullying when surveyed by Lund, Blake, Ewing, and Banks (2012). Less than half of those reported that their training occurred pre-service with the majority reporting that they received training through school-based in-service trainings or professional conferences. Although practitioners reported receiving training in bullying prevention and in counseling bullies and victims (Lund et al.), evidence-based interventions and empirically supported programs were seldom endorsed (Kratochwill, 2007), and practitioners tended to rely on more general interventions such as social skills training (Whitted & Dupper, 2005). When creating interventions, practitioners were more likely to use materials from staff trainings or from books in the popular press than to rely on scholarly references (Lund et al.). Similar numbers were reported by Bauman, Rigby, and Hoppa (2008) who found that 69% of school counselors had received some type of training in bullying but only 2% had done so as part of their pre-service training. Almost half of those surveyed had received their training at professional workshops, while less than half were trained through school-based in-service trainings.

Lack of in-depth training in the aspects of bullying can lead practitioners to endorse interventions that are likely to be ineffective. Bauman et al. (2008) found that many school counselors believe it is important to work with bullies to improve their self-esteem, which is contrary to evidence that bullies tend to have average self-esteem. Mediation is also chosen as a way to intervene in bullying, but the power differential between bullies and victims can make it a poor choice (Bauman et al., 2008). In an effort to improve training for school psychologists and other school personnel, one professional organization has developed an online training program that strives to provide in-depth training on the complexities of bullying and helps practitioners to develop strategies for bullying prevention (New York Association of School Psychologists [NYASP], n.d.). The program consists of four modules with a final project; each module covers one aspect of bullying and provides three hours of continuing professional development credit (NYASP, para. 1).

## Identifying Bullying

With adequate training and experience, school psychologists and counselors should be able to identify bullying as it occurs. Their training in mental health allows them to discern those students who are in conflictual peer interactions and are thus at risk for bullying. In their survey of 560 school psychologists and counselors, Lund et al. (2012) found that the majority of school mental health practitioners believe they are aware of bullying situations within their schools. Participants reported that bullying adversely affects 10–15% of their students and they are involved in developing strategies for handling bullying situations. However, this number is lower than statistics reported by a number of studies. For example, 86.2% of lesbian, gay, bisexual, and transgendered (LGBT) students reported being bullied in a school climate survey conducted by the Gay, Lesbian, and Straight Education Network (Teaching Tolerance, n.d.). In a study by the National Center for Education Statistics, 42.9% of sixth graders were bullied in 2009 (Teaching Tolerance). These numbers make it clear that school mental health practitioners are not aware of all the students being victimized at school. This is due in part to victims that are hesitant to report bullying and to the inability of school psychologists and counselors to be present at the moment that bullying occurs.

Nevertheless, school psychologists and counselors can be instrumental in identifying students who are being victimized by bullies. Many schools rely on anonymous self-reports from victims, which can be problematic if "bullying" is not clearly defined for students. In one study, Cornell and Mehta found that only 56% of students who self-identified as victims were actually confirmed as victims by trained school counselors (2011). Baly and Cornell (2011) attribute this, in part, to some students' inability to understand the difference between bullying and ordinary conflict between peers. When students were shown an educational video that distinguished between the two, they reported significantly less victimization than a control group that did not watch the video (Baly & Cornell). It is important that students be educated regarding what constitutes bullying.

Using peer nominations was used successfully in another study. Phillips and Cornell (2012) found that school counselors, when given adequate training and experience in identifying bullying, were a valuable resource in "identifying and aiding victims of bullying" (p. 129). The middle school in this study used school-wide surveys and a peer nomination form to help identify those students who might be victims of bullying. Use of peer nominations meant that several sources of information were available and that the victim could be identified. Rather than having students identify bullies and risk the social stigma of being an informer, they were asked to identify other students who they believed to have been bullied (Phillips & Cornell).

Peer nominations of victims are not sufficient, however, since it is possible that students could be nominated as a prank by their classmates (Phillips & Cornell, 2012). With this in mind, the school counselors interviewed those students that received multiple nominations. For students with two or more nominations, 43% were confirmed as victims while 90% of students with nine or more nominations were found to be victims (Phillips & Cornell). While this process was time-consuming, the authors found peer nominations to be an effective screening tool. In addition to identifying incidents of bullying, they can be useful in helping school mental health practitioners learn about students that are experiencing conflicts with peers that could develop into bullying.

## Intervening in Bullying Episodes

School psychologists and counselors have a different set of skills that can be used when intervening with bullies and victims. There are a number of methods that have the possibility of both preventing and intervening with bullying. These include teaching students to regulate their emotions, particularly their anger; develop more tolerant attitudes toward others; build trust and develop empathy; and develop better communication and relationship skills (Modin & Ostberg, 2009). The most common approach used by school psychologists and counselors is to talk to the bully and the victim to ensure they have a clear understanding of the situation. Then, if needed, individual counseling for both parties can be introduced (Lund et al., 2012).

Intervening in bullying can take place at several levels. Having a school-wide policy against bullying has been found to make school personnel more aware of bullying as it occurs and to increase the likelihood that educators who observe the incident will get other adults (e.g., school psychologist, school counselor, administrator) involved (Bauman et al., 2008). Making changes in the school environment can also serve as bullying interventions. Kyriakides and Creemers (2012) assert that increasing adult monitoring of students during passing periods and recess can help educators to identify bullying as it occurs and to make a swifter intervention.

School psychologists and school counselors can be effective in developing positive school climates, which have been found to be a deterrent to bullying. They can work with teachers and administrators to improve learning environments and visit classrooms to develop a better understanding of the dynamics that can lead to bullying (Kyriakides & Creemers, 2012). They can also provide strategies for teachers and parents who are dealing with bullying. This can be especially helpful for new teachers who may not understand how students feel about bullying. Developing this understanding helps teachers to respond effectively (Kahn, Jones, & Wieland, 2012). School psychologists and counselors also have the expertise to provide education to school staff, students, parents, and community leaders about bullying through interactive trainings, newsletters, and other resource materials (Diamanduros et al., 2008).

When students are involved in bullying, there is often disagreement among school personnel as to what should be done. Depending on their dispositional coping styles, teachers may feel strongly that bullies should be punished, a view not so readily accepted by school psychologists and counselors. School psychologists and counselors are less likely to feel comfortable with punishing students and are less likely to advocate for a punitive approach to bullying than teachers (Rigby & Bauman, 2010). This is likely due to their role as student advocates rather than disciplinarians. In contrast, teachers see discipline as an important part of their role in order to maintain order and manage their classrooms. When Harris and Willoughby (2003) surveyed teachers on track to become administrators, they found a preponderance of them (56%) advocated for automatically punishing bullies; however, some of the teachers acknowledged that counseling might be helpful prior to the punishment. Rigby and Bauman (2010) found that 82% of teachers were prepared to punish the bully compared with 67% of counselors. When consulting with teachers, it is important that school psychologists and school counselors be cognizant of teachers' unique perspectives on bullying and how they cope with stressors (Kahn et al., 2012).

The type of training school psychologists and school counselors receive leads them to view students and bullying in a more empathic manner and to respond to bullying in different ways. Counselors have been found to have more empathy for victims of bullying, particularly when the bullying is physical or relational, than do teachers (Jacobsen & Bauman, 2007). They take relational bullying more seriously than do teachers and are more likely to intervene in incidents of relational bullying. They are also more likely to suggest interventions for bullies in relational bullying (Jacobsen & Bauman, 2007). Bauman et al. (2008) interpret this to mean that "school counselors may be more perceptive and more sensitive to issues of bullying than teachers" (p. 838). When intervening with bullying, teachers and school counselors agreed that enlisting other adults and working with the bully were important but disagreed as to the importance of working with the victim; counselors were more likely to work with the victim (i.e., through encouraging more assertive behavior from the victim) than were teachers (Rigby & Bauman, 2010).

While school psychologists, because of the nature of their job, may not be on campus at the time an intervention is required, school counselors are often called upon to intervene. Bauman et al. (2008) attribute the differences between teacher and counselor responses to bullying to the training that counselors receive. School counselors receive extensive training in active listening skills and learn to respond to students in a supportive, nonjudgmental way. In addition to focusing on students' academic success, they work to promote students' social and emotional growth. Their training in these areas may make it easier for them to notice the more subtle forms of bullying and make it more difficult for them to ignore bullying incidents.

## Prevention and Intervention

Many school psychologists and school counselors are engaged in the anti-bullying prevention and intervention services found in public schools today. Due to their expert knowledge and experiences in serving the psychological needs of students, these school professionals should be the first resources the schools turn to when bullying is an issue. School psychologists and school counselors should be involved in selecting the most appropriate program for their school and/or actively engaged in the implementation of the selected program. Understanding the variety of published and researched programs, as well as the current research findings on these programs, will help provide a broader understanding of the roles school psychologists and school counselors play in the implementation of anti-bullying programs in the schools.

## Three Tiers of School-Based Programs

Anti-bullying programs typically tend to focus on one of three levels within the school environment (Lund et al., 2012). The broadest types are the school-wide bullying interventions, referred to as Universal or Tier 1 level programs. These broad-based programs have the goal of creating a positive school environment through respectful behaviors and no tolerance for bullying behaviors across a system, for example, school district. Tier 2 secondary programs have interventions designed for the classroom or small group settings. The individual-focused programs, Tier 3, concentrate on individual students, with separate interventions for the victim and for the bully (Lund et al., 2012).

By far, the most commonly used approach in schools are Universal/Tier 1 programs, with research supporting their use because they are comprehensive and address multiple layers of the school system (Whitted & Dupper, 2005). By changing the environment of the school, these systemic programs are able to impact students individually and in groups. Universal/Tier 1 programs are not only applied at the school district level but can also be found implemented at the state (Pennsylvania—Schroeder et al., 2012) and national levels (Finland—Salmivalli, Karna, & Poskiparta,

2010). These types of anti-bullying programs have a focus on increasing students', teachers', and school staff's knowledge around bullying behaviors and prevention, creating a positive school environment and promoting respect for all (Cross, Pintabota, Hall, Hamilton, & Erceg, 2004). However, research has not been able to fully support the broad application of current Universal/Tier 1 programs in schools due to mixed positive results based on gender, age, race/ethnicity, and types of bullying incidents (Bowllan, 2011).

Both Secondary/Tier 2 and Individual/Tier 3 level programs predominantly have a focus on building social skills, conducting peer mentoring, or having the victim or bully engage in individual or small group counseling (Lund et al., 2012). Lund and her colleagues report that there has been little research on Secondary/Tier 2 level programs and even less on Individual/Tier 3 level programs. From the research that has occurred to date, results are also mixed as to the effectiveness of programs at these levels in changing bullying behaviors. However, several studies have reported improvement in self-efficacy and self-concept of victims of bullying after involvement in Secondary/Tier 2 programs. Lund et al. posit that the reason for the primary focus on developing and researching Universal/Tier 1 programs is due to the commonly held premise that bullying occurs as a group phenomenon, which includes the victim, the bully, bystanders, and the environmental support; thus, targeting the Universal/Tier 1 level is the more effective approach to take. Another reason for research into the effectiveness of Universal/Tier 1 programs is the level of commitment, both financial and in staff time and effort, required for the implementation of the program. Administrators want to be certain that they are getting their money's worth and school psychologists can be instrumental in determining the effectiveness of these programs given their training in program evaluation.

## Evaluating School-Based Programs

There has been quite extensive research conducted over the years focused on both developing and evaluating anti-bullying programs. The quantity of studies have allowed for several meta-analyses focused on the efficacy and evaluation of existing programs to help school psychologists and counselors make evidence-based decisions on the efficacy of programs to be incorporated in their schools. One recent summary from Child Trends (Lawner & Terzian, 2013) presents several generalizations that can be made from the research on anti-bullying programs and a chart with several of the most prominent programs evaluated across various dimensions. In short, Lawner and Terzian report that programs that included parents and used a "whole-school approach" were considered to be effective. When reviewing the prominent programs, they used a three-part (Found to Work, Not Found to Work, and Mixed Findings) grading system measured across five dimensions of the program's impact of bullying outcome. The dimensions included overall bullying, social/relational bullying, bullying victimization, being a bystander, and attitudes toward bullying. Of the nine programs evaluated, only Success in Stages (Evers, Prochaska, Van Marter, Johnson, & Prochaska, 2007), an interactive computer program designed to decrease and prevent bullying, was found to be effective on three dimensions. However, based on the specific dimensions one would want their program to target, there were several that were identified as "Found to Work" on one or two dimensions as well.

Interestingly, the program evaluation conducted by Lawner and Terzian (2013) did not include the two most commonly researched and used Universal/Tier 1 programs, both with extensive and comprehensive national and international research studies investigating them. The Olweus Bullying Prevention Program (OBPP: Olweus & Limber, 2002), which uses the Olweus Bully/Victim Questionnaire (BVQ; Olweus, 2002), is noted to be the most widely used, worldwide bullying behavior self-report. Research in the United States strongly supports the use of the OBPP for anti-bullying interventions with reports of reducing school-based bullying by 30%–50%, resulting in the program gaining an endorsement by the American Academy of Pediatrics in 2009 (Schroeder et al., 2012).

In addition to the OBPP, another internationally developed and researched school-based program is the KiVa Antibullying Program (Salmivalli et al., 2010). Commissioned by the Finnish government, the KiVa program has been incorporated into the Finnish public schools' curriculum with an emphasis on preventative student lessons and specific actions to be taken when a bullying incident takes place (Ahtola et al., 2012). The largest success noted in the current research with the KiVa is the reduction of bullying incidents and behaviors in first through sixth grades (Karna et al., 2011). Research has also noted the positive impact this program has on teachers and the school climate in general (Ahtola et al., 2012) and the higher success found when using a non-confrontational approach (Garandeau, Poskiparta & Salmivalli, 2014).

Examples of other anti-bullying programs include the School-Wide Positive Behavioral Interventions and Supports (SW-PBIS; Kennedy & Swain-Bradway, 2012) and multicomponent Rural Early Adolescent Learning Program (Project REAL; Farmer, Hall, Petrin, Hamm & Dadisman, 2010). The SW-PBIS is a Tier 1/Universal proactive organizational framework for implementing practices to support the social and academic success of all students. It has been noted to reduce the rate of problem behaviors, including bullying in elementary schools (Bradshaw, Mitchell & Leaf, 2010), but not when homegrown videos are incorporated in the presentation modules (Kennedy & Swain-Bradway). Project REAL targets middle school students and is designed to raise teachers' awareness of the peer groups with which rural school students are involved to better understand bullying behaviors as they occur (Farmer et al., 2010).

Measuring bullying behaviors and attitudes is most often conducted through a self-report form. As previously mentioned, the Olweus Bully/Victim Questionnaire (BVQ; Olweus, 2002) is viewed both nationally and internationally as one of the most commonly used measures to obtain this information. However, in a concurrent validity study, Lee and Cornell (2010) found there to be only a modest correspondence between the self-reported behaviors indicated on the BVQ when compared to peer nominations for bullying and academic grades, two additional common factors associated with bullying behaviors. This research calls into question the overreliance on self-reported behavioral data and the importance of the roles school psychologists and counselors play in supporting the identification of and interventions with bullies and their victims.

## Role of School Psychologists and Counselors in School-Based Anti-bullying Programs

The governments of countries around the world (e.g., United Kingdom, Finland, Canada, France, Australia, Philippines, etc.) have begun mandating anti-bullying efforts or legislating policies related to bullying (Garandeau et al., 2014). Their primary efforts are to impact bullying at the Tier1/Universal level, which means policies are set for school systems to enact programs and actions to curtail or end bullying within their systems. Richard, Schneider, and Mallet (2011) revisited the whole-school approach to bullying prevention within the generally agreed upon understanding that bullying is systemic; therefore, interventions must be directed at the systems. Their research in a French school system found that mutual respect among school staff members and a greater focus on the quality of teacher-student interactions were needed for more success when an anti-bullying program was put in place.

The types of interactions with school staff, especially teachers, in which school psychologists and school counselors engage may also be seen as critical roles fostering a more collegial atmosphere and improving teacher-student interactions. Trained with consultation and collaboration skills, school psychologists and school counselors are able to identify and interact, often modeling most appropriate behaviors to staff, in order to help foster the most conducive environment for reducing bullying behaviors (Dougherty, 2014). As the mental health experts with advanced training in psychological principles of behavior and observational skills, school psychologists and school counselors are critical to the identification and understanding of the covert, as well as overt, bullying behaviors occurring in schools (Barnes et al., 2012).

Although school psychologists and counselors are involved in their school's anti-bullying prevention and intervention services, few report that they are involved in activities to select programs or engaged in the implementation of the program. The primary decision makers are school administrators when it comes to anti-bullying efforts (Lund et al., 2012), with the majority of school psychologists and school counselors reporting to have only a minor role in the anti-bullying programs within their schools. School psychologists and counselors are the school-based mental health professionals in the school system, and it is imperative that school administrators recognize their expertise and experience. School psychologists and school counselors must also begin to step up and advocate to the administrators, informing them of their training and skills to help identify evidence-based anti-bullying programs, as well as the critical role they can play to support the establishment of adopted programs across the district and within their schools.

## Role of School Psychologists and School Counselors in Working with Bullies and Victims

While school psychologists have pushed to take a more active role in developing school-wide approaches to bullying, most of those who are working within schools have focused on individual approaches to intervention, such as counseling the bully and/or the victim (Swearer, Espelage, & Napolitano, 2009). Seeking to understand the actual roles of school counselors, as well as school psychologists, in their schools as they relate to anti-bullying activities and programs, Lund et al. (2012) surveyed both school professional groups and found that they are seldom included in the selection of bullying prevention programs within their school districts or buildings. Even when their schools had anti-bullying programs in place, the majority (86%) reported their primary role was to talk with the student to learn about the situation, similar to the Sherer and Nickerson (2010) results. The next most common intervention was conducting individual therapy with the bully (47%) or the victim (58%; Lund et al., 2012).

Sherer and Nickerson (2010) sought to identify the most common anti-bullying practices school psychologists witness in their school settings. Their survey results found the most frequent strategies implemented were school staff talking with the bullies after an event, disciplinary consequences for the bully, individual counseling for the victims, and individual counseling for the bullies. Sherer and Nickerson reported that the most frequent interventions used by school psychologists include "individual interventions with bullies and victims, such as talking with them or providing counseling, avoiding contact between the bully and victim, identifying at-risk students, and disciplining students who bully others" (p. 224). In addition to these individual interventions, "95.8% of responding school psychologists indicated that increased supervision in unstructured areas was a strategy used" (Sherer & Nickerson, 2010, p. 225). Some of the least engaged in strategies included peer-led courts, anti-bullying committees, student peer counseling for victims, and student-led anti-bullying activities (Sherer & Nickerson, 2010).

Counselors have suggested a number of interventions for bullies and victims (Bauman et al., 2008). For bullies, individual meetings with the counselor and referrals to mental health professionals have been suggested; for victims, extra attention, support groups, and training to develop assertiveness and self-esteem are warranted. Counselor-led mediation has also been suggested although it may be of limited effectiveness due to the power differential between bullies and victims (Bauman et al., 2008). Broader interventions such as targeted classroom guidance lessons, school-wide education programs to build character, and panel discussions have also been suggested (Bauman et al., 2008). When counseling is considered, school counselors were more likely to use group rather than individual sessions for treating bullies (Jacobsen & Bauman, 2007). Support groups can also be a protective factor for victims. Goodenow, Szalacha, and Westheimer (2006) found that LGBT students were less likely to be threatened by peers when their school had a support group for them. They were also less likely to make multiple suicide attempts.

In addition to individual interventions, school psychologists and school counselors may elect to assist in training students to participate in peer support programs. These programs help students to become more assertive, develop resilience, make good decisions, solve problems, and become leaders (Peer Support Australia, n.d.). Peer support systems have been found to be effective in challenging bullying in schools and creating a caring environment in UK schools (Naylor & Cowie, 1999) but were not found to be engaged in frequently by Sherer and Nickerson. This is likely due to the additional adult support required for peer support programs (Naylor & Cowie). Although school psychologists and school counselors have the expertise to play important roles in school-wide anti-bullying programs, research indicates they are seldom consulted when Universal/Tier 1 programs are selected. As a result, it appears their primary role is to provide individual and group interventions for bullies and victims. While they are trained to provide these services, it is likely they are being underutilized by school districts.

## Conclusion

As previously noted, school psychologists and school counselors vary in their job roles, the number of schools they serve, and their ability to intervene in bullying as it happens; nevertheless, they serve as the mental health professionals for most school campuses and are arguably the best trained to manage bullying within the school. School counselors are likely to have received training related to bullying and to perceive themselves as being competent to counsel bullies and victims (Lund et al., 2012). Historically, school psychologists spent much of their time on campus assessing students and were more often viewed as assessment personnel than mental health practitioners. As the role of school psychologists broadens, it is likely they will spend more time intervening in bullying and helping schools to develop intervention programs. Their expertise in program evaluation should make them leaders at the campus or district level in developing and evaluating anti-bullying programs (Swearer, Espelage, &

Hymel, 2009). School psychologists and school counselors can also be instrumental in educating and training staff (Sherer & Nickerson, 2010) and in improving school climate (Espelage, Polanin, & Low, 2014).

## References

Ahtola, A., Haataja, A., Karna, A., & Salmivalli, C. (2012). For children only? Effects of the KiVa antibullying program on teachers. *Teaching and Teacher Education*, *28*, 851–859.

American School Counselor Association. (n.d.). *The role of the professional school counselor*. Retrieved from http://schoolcounsellor.org/asca/media/asca/home/RoleStatement.pdf

Baly, M., & Cornell, D. (2011). Effects of an educational video on the measurement of bullying by self-report. *Journal of School Violence*, *10*, 221–238. doi:10.1080/15388220.2011.578275.

Barnes, A., Cross, D., Lester, L., Hearn, L., Epstein, M., & Monks, H. (2012). The invisibility of covert bullying among students: Challenges for school interventions. *Australian Journal of Guidance and Counselling*, *22*, 206–226. doi:10.1017/jgc.2012.27.

Bauman, S., Rigby, K., & Hoppa, K. (2008). US teachers' and school counselors' strategies for handling school bullying incidents. *Educational Psychology*, *28*, 837–856. doi:10.1080/01443410802379085.

Bowllan, N. M. (2011). Implementation and evaluation of a comprehensive, school-wide bullying prevention program in an urban/suburban middle school. *Journal of School Health*, *81*, 167–173. doi:10.1111/j.1746-1561.2010.00576.x.

Bradshaw, C., Mitchell, M., & Leaf, P. (2010). Examining the effects of a school-wide positive behavioral interventions and supports on student outcomes: Results from a randomized controlled effectiveness trial in elementary schools. *Journal of Positive Behavior Interventions*, *12*, 131–132. doi:10.1177/1098300709334798.

Cornell, D. G., & Mehta, S. (2011). Counselor confirmation of middle school student self-reports of bullying victimization. *Professional School Counseling*, *14*, 261–270. doi:10.5330/PSC.n.2011-14.261.

Cross, D., Pintabota, Y., Hall, M., Hamilton, G., & Erceg, E. (2004). Validated guidelines for school-based bullying prevention and management. *International Journal of Mental Health Promotion*, *6*(3), 34–42. doi:10.1080/14623730.2004.9721937.

Diamanduros, T., Downs, E., & Jenkins, S. J. (2008). The role of school psychologists in the assessment, prevention, and intervention of cyberbullying. *Psychology in the Schools*, *45*, 693–704. doi:10.1002/pits.20335.

Dougherty, A. M. (2014). *Psychological consultation and collaboration in school and community settings* (6th ed.). Belmont, CA: Cengage.

Espelage, D. L., Polanin, J. R., & Low, S. K. (2014). Teacher and staff perceptions of school environment as predictors of student aggression, victimization, and willingness to intervene in bullying situations. *School Psychology Quarterly, 29*, 287–305. doi:10.1037/spq0000072.

Evers, K. E., Prochaska, J. O., Van Marter, D. F., Johnson, J. L., & Prochaska, J. M. (2007). Transtheoretical-based bullying prevention effectiveness trials in middle schools and high schools. *Educational Research, 49*, 397–414. doi:10.1080/00131880701717271.

Farmer, T. W., Hall, C. M., Petrin, R., Hamm, J. V., & Dadisman, K. (2010). Evaluating the impact of a multicomponent intervention model on teachers' awareness of social networks at the beginning of middle school in rural communities. *School Psychology Quarterly, 23*, 94–106. doi:10.1037/a0020147.

Garandeau, C. F., Poskiparta, E., & Salmivalli, C. (2014). Tackling acute cases of school bullying in the KiVa Anti-Bullying Program: A comparison of two approaches. *Journal of Abnormal Child Psychology, 42*, 981–991. doi:10.1007/s10802-014-9861-1.

Goodenow, C., Szalacha, L., & Westheimer, K. (2006). School support groups, other school factors, and the safety of sexual minority adolescents. *Psychology in the Schools, 43*, 573–589. doi:10.1002/pits.20173.

Hamburger, M. E., Basile, K. C., & Vivolo, A. M. (2011). *Measuring bullying victimization, perpetration, and bystander experiences: A compendium of assessment tools.* Atlanta, GA: Centers for Disease Control and Prevention, National Center for Injury Prevention and Control.

Harris, S., & Willoughby, W. (2003). Teacher perceptions of student bullying behaviors. *ERS Spectrum, 21*(3), 11–18.

Jacobsen, K., & Bauman, S. (2007). School counsellor's responses to school bullying scenarios. *Professional School Counseling, 11*, 1–9. doi:10.5330/PSC.n.2010-11.1.

Kahn, J. H., Jones, J. L., & Wieland, A. L. (2012). Preservice teachers' coping styles and their responses to bullying. *Psychology in the Schools, 49*, 784–793. doi:10.1002/pts.21632.

Karna, A., Voeten, M., Little, T. D., Poskiparta, E., Alanen, E., & Salmivalli, C. (2011). Going to scale: A nonrandomized nationwide trial of the KiVa antibullying programs for grades 1–9. *Journal of Consulting and Clinical Psychology, 79*, 796–805. doi:10.1037/a0025740.

Kennedy, M. J., & Swain-Bradway, J. (2012). *Rationale and recommended practices for using homegrown video to support school-wide positive behavioral interventions and supports* (pp. 20–28). Winter: *Beyond Behavior.*

Kratochwill, T. R. (2007). Preparing psychologists for evidence-based practice: Lessons learned and challenges ahead. *American Psychologist, 62*, 826–843. doi:10.1037/0003-066X.62.8.829.

Kub, J., & Feldman, M. A. (2015). Bullying prevention: A call for collaborative efforts between school nurses and school psychologists. *Psychology in the Schools, 52*, 658–671. doi:10.1002/pits.21853.

Kyriakides, L., & Creemers, B. P. M. (2012). Characteristics of effective schools in facing and reducing bullying. *School Psychology International, 34*, 348–368. doi:10.1177/0143034312467127.

Lawner, E. K., & Terzian, M. A. (2013). What works for bullying programs: Lessons from experimental evaluations of programs and interventions. Child Trends Research Brief. Publication #2013–39. Bethesda, MD: Child Trends.

Lee, T., & Cornell, D. (2010). Concurrent validity of the Olweus Bully/Victim Questionnaire. *Journal of School Violence, 9*, 56–73. doi:10.1080/15388220903185613.

Lund, E. M., Blake, J. J., Ewing, H. K., & Banks, C. S. (2012). School counselors' and school psychologists' bullying prevention and intervention strategies: A look into real-world practices. *Journal of School Violence, 11*, 246–265. doi:10.1080/15388220.2012.682005.

Modin, B., & Ostberg, V. (2009). School climate and psychosomatic health: A multilevel analysis. *School Effectiveness and School Improvement, 20*, 433–455. doi:10.10880/09243450903251507.

National Association of School Psychologists. (2012). *Bullying prevention and intervention in schools [Position statement]*. Retrieved from http://nasponline.org/about_positionpapers/BullyingPrevention.pdf

Naylor, P., & Cowie, H. (1999). The effectiveness of peer support systems in challenging school bullying: The perspectives and experiences of teachers and pupils. *Journal of Adolescence, 22*, 467–479. doi:10.1006/jado.1999.0241.

New York Association of School Psychologists. (n.d.). *NYASP bullying prevention specialist program*. Retrieved from nyasp.wildapricot.org/bullying prevention

Olweus, D. (2002). A profile of bullying at school. *Educational Leadership, 60*, 12–17.

Olweus, D., & Limber, S. P. (2002). *Bullying prevention program (Blueprints for violence prevention)*. Washington, DC: Center for the Study and Prevention of Violence.

Peer Support Australia. (n.d.). *Program overview*. Retrieved from http://peersupport.edu.au/the-program/overview/

Phillips, V. I., & Cornell, D. G. (2012). Identifying victims of bullying: Use of counselor interviews to confirm peer nominations. *Professional School Counseling, 15*, 123–131. doi:10.5330/PSC.n.2012-15.123.

Richard, J. F., Schneider, B. H., & Mallet, P. (2011). Revisiting the whole-school approach to bullying: Really looking at the whole school. *School Psychology International, 33*, 263–284. doi:10.1177/0143034311415906.

Rigby, K., & Bauman, S. (2010). How school personnel tackle cases of bullying. A critical examination. In S. R. Jimerson, S. M. Swearer, & D. L. Espelage

(Eds.), *Handbook of bullying in schools: An international perspective* (pp. 455–467). New York: Routledge.

Sandhu, D. S. (2000). Alienated students: Counseling strategies to curb school violence. *Professional School Counseling, 4*, 81–85.

Salmivalli, C., Karna, A., & Poskiparta, E. (2010). Development, evaluation, and diffusion of a national anti-bullying program, KiVa. In B. Doll, W. Pfohl, & J. Yoon (Eds.), *Handbook of youth prevention science* (pp. 238–252). New York: Routledge.

Sherer, Y. C., & Nickerson, A. B. (2010). Anti-bullying practices in American schools: Perspectives of school psychologists. *Psychology in the Schools, 47*, 217–229. doi:10.1002/pits.20466.

Schroeder, B. A., Messina, A., Schroeder, D., Good, K., Barto, S., Saylor, J., & Masiello, M. (2012). The implementation of a statewide bullying prevention program: Preliminary finding from the field and the importance of coalitions. *Health Promotion Practice, 13*, 489–495. doi:10.1177/1524839910386887.

StopBullying.gov. (n.d.). *What is bullying?* Retrieved from http://www.stopbullying.gov/what-is-bullying/definition/index.html

Swearer, D. L., Espelage, T. V., & Hymel, S. (2009). What can be done about school bullying? Linking research to educational practice. *Educational Researcher, 39*(1), 38–47. doi:10.3102/0013189X09357622.

Swearer, S. M., Espelage, D. L., & Napolitano, S. A. (2009). *Bullying prevention and intervention: Realistic strategies for schools.* New York, NY: Guilford Press. doi:PSIN-2009-01976-000; 2009-01976-000.

Teaching Tolerance. (n.d.). *Bullying by the numbers.* Retrieved from http://www.tolerance.org/sites/default/files/kits/tt_BULLIED_Statistics.pdf

Whitted, K., & Dupper, D. (2005). Best practices for preventing or reducing bullying in schools. *Children & Schools, 27*, 167–175. doi:10.1093/cs/27.3.167.

Willard, N. (n.d.). *Professional practice: Addressing critical issues in bullying.* Retrieved from http://www.nasponline.org/publications/periodicals/communique/issues/volume-43-issue-2/addressing-critical-issues-in-bullying

CHAPTER 6

# School Nurses' Perspectives on Bullying

*Nora Zinan*

## The Role of Nurses in Schools

School nurses are valuable members of the teams of professionals who educate our children (National Association of School Nurses (NASN), 2011). They share the goal of ensuring that children receive the education that is required by law and that will lay a strong foundation for becoming productive members of a community. The effectiveness and quality of this education is largely influenced by the students' physical, social, and emotional health (NASN, 2011).

School nurses provide a variety of services to students to support good health. Historically, the focus of school nurses has been to prevent the spread of communicable disease. The first school nurse, Lina Rogers, was hired in 1902 into the New York City school system to contain outbreaks of diseases such as diphtheria, mumps, smallpox, scarlet fever, and measles (School Nurse News, 1999). This is still a main function for school nurses today. They monitor compliance with required immunizations and administer them as needed. They are part of the broader health care delivery system that aims for a high rate of immunization compliance to provide herd immunity against diseases that killed large portions of communities in the past (US Department of Health and Human Services, 2015).

N. Zinan (✉)
University of Saint Joseph, West Hartford, CT, USA



L.H. Rosen et al. (eds.), *Bullying in School*,
DOI 10.1057/978-1-137-59298-9_6

As the prevalence of communicable diseases has decreased, the focus of school nurses has evolved to monitor and treat any condition that can interfere with learning or increase absenteeism (NASN, 2011). School nurses administer daily medications for students with conditions such as ADHD, asthma, depression, anxiety, diabetes, hypertension, and others. They screen for scoliosis, vision impairments, and hearing deficits. They manage emergencies and provide first aid. They are responsible for overseeing or giving care to students who require medical devices such as feeding tubes, tracheostomy tubes, blood sugar monitors, and urinary catheters (NASN, 2014a). They ensure that annual physical examinations are completed to allow students to participate in sports and they manage student care and reentry into school following a concussion (NASN, 2016). School nurses also act as health educators when they teach about puberty, hygiene, dental care, and healthy behaviors in the classroom and offer programs to faculty, staff, and families. Finally, school nurses are the liaisons between the school, a student's family, and their primary care providers, and an important link in providing consistent, continuous, and comprehensive health care (American Academy of Pediatrics (AAP), 2008).

These responsibilities place nurses at the front lines of public health to detect, monitor, treat, and educate about conditions that affect students, families, communities, and beyond. Bullying is considered a public health problem because of its frequency and the effect it has on well-being (Srabstein & Leventhal, 2010). It creates an unsafe environment that may result in long-lasting health problems (Russell, Ryan, Toomey, Diaz, & Sanchez, 2011; Sourander et al., 2007). Thus, preventing bullying and dealing with it has become another responsibility for school nurses (NASN, 2014b). In this chapter, school nurses are quoted and share their insights about students, bullying, and the school nurse role.

## Health Symptoms and Bullying Involvement

> I had a student in my office one day because she was beat up by two girls who were tired of her bullying them. And students clapped because they were happy that someone stood up to her. This girl was crying and saying that no one wanted to be her friend. So, the bully was the victim.
>
> *Zoey W., School Nurse*

In the school setting, students who are involved with bullying often present to the school nurse's office with health symptoms (Vernberg, Nelson,

Fonagy, & Twemlow, 2011). The students may be bullies, victims, or both bully and victim. The more frequent the involvement with bullying, the greater the risk that a student will present with health symptoms (Due et al., 2005; Williams, Chambers, Logan, & Robinson, 1996). Even bystanders can experience psychological distress from witnessing bullying behavior (Rivers, Poteat, Noret, & Ashurst, 2009).

Although the symptoms experienced by individual students may vary, the types of symptoms that accompany bullying are experienced by children around the world (Due et al., 2005). Victims who report being bullied sometimes or more frequently report not sleeping well, bed-wetting, feeling sad, and experiencing more than occasional headaches and stomach aches (Williams et al., 1996). Other symptoms can include backache, feeling low, bad temper, nervousness, difficulties in getting to sleep, dizziness, loneliness, tired in the morning, feeling left out of things, and feeling helpless (Due et al., 2005). The association between bullying and health symptoms was demonstrated in a study where students who had no health complaints at the beginning of the year, and were bullied during the year, were found to be more likely to develop depression, anxiety, bed-wetting, abdominal pain, and feeling tense (Fekkes, Pijpers, & Verloove-Vanhorick, 2005). In another study, girls, in particular, presented with abdominal pain from being bullied (Fekkes, Pijpers, Fredriks, Vogels, & Verloove-Vanhorick, 2006).

## Mental Health Symptoms and Bullying Involvement

Sadness and suicidal thoughts are common symptoms for students involved with bullying as a victim, bully, or bully-victim (Camodeca & Goossens, 2005; Glew, Fan, Katon, Rivara, & Kernic, 2005; Klomek, Marrocco, Kleinman, Schonfeld, & Gould, 2007; Rigby & Slee, 1991). In one study, students who said they were sad most days had higher odds of being bullies or victims (Glew et al., 2005). Another study reported that the more frequently the student was involved with bullying, the more likely the student was reported to be depressed, have suicidal ideation, or have attempted suicide (Klomek et al., 2007). In another study, victims were found to be the saddest of all the groups, feeling sadder than bullies when something unpleasant happens (Camodeca & Goossens, 2005). High levels of suicidal ideation in victims were supported by peer and self-reports in another study (Rigby & Slee, 1991). Although weaker, the association between bullying and suicidal thoughts was also found to be significant for bullies (Rigby & Slee, 1991).

Anxiety and anxiety disorders have also been associated with bullying involvement. One study showed that girls involved as bullies or victims in either traditional bullying (verbal, physical, relational) or cyberbullying situations had higher anxiety scores than boys (Kowalski & Limber, 2013). However, boys who were both bullies and victims had higher anxiety scores than girls in that category. Students who were both cyberbullies and cybervictims had the highest anxiety and depression scores (Kowalski & Limber, 2013). Another study correlated anxiety and depression with abdominal pain, a common complaint of health office visitors. The study reported that pediatric patients in a primary care setting with recurrent and unexplained abdominal pain related to bullying also had significantly higher levels of anxiety, as well as depression, compared to control subjects (Campo et al., 2004).

Another study found that frequent victimization as a child predicted a diagnosis of anxiety disorder later in life (Sourander et al., 2007). The study followed eight-year-old boys in Finland until their military call-up examination at ages 18–23. It also found that being a bully predicted antisocial personality, substance abuse, and depressive and anxiety disorders, and being both a bully and a victim predicted anxiety and antisocial personality disorder. A later study by Sourander (2009) found that victimization of females at age eight "independently predicted psychiatric hospital treatment and use of antipsychotic, antidepressant, and anxiolytic drugs" when followed up between the ages of 13 and 24 (p. 1005).

These findings were reinforced in another study that followed children who were bullied between the ages of 9 and 16, until their early adulthood years (19–26) (Copeland, Wolke, Angold, & Costello, 2013). It demonstrated that after controlling for child psychiatric or family hardships, victims of bullying demonstrated higher levels of anxiety disorders than bullies, bully-victims, or students who were neither bullies nor victims (Copeland et al., 2013). Students who were bully-victims had higher levels of depressive and panic disorders, in addition to suicidality. Being a bully was shown to increase the risk of future antisocial personality disorder (Copeland et al., 2013).

## Frequent Office Visits and Bullying

Students who are being bullied usually come in at the same time each day with a different complaint. Often they complain of headaches and stomach aches. Another key sign is that they are withdrawn.

*Judith H-S., School Nurse*

School nurses are often faced with students who are persistent and frequent visitors to the health office with symptoms that vary with each visit (Sweeney & Sweeney, 2000; Vernberg et al., 2011). While a single symptom may not indicate bullying involvement, persistent and multiple symptoms require investigation. One study used a case study method to examine the characteristics of students who are frequent visitors to the school nurse's office at two middle schools (Sweeney & Sweeney, 2000). Of the 3014 visits made to the nurse's office in the 3-month period, just 12% of the students made 56.1% of the visits. Health complaints included headache, stomach ache, dizziness, chest pain, sore/painful limbs, hyperventilation, gray pallor, sweatiness, crying, diarrhea, and complaints of not feeling well. Nurses categorized these complaints as students' responses to stress/anxiety, somatic complaints, or learned illness behaviors and associated the symptoms with six areas of difficulties the students had: academics, teachers, home issues, personal constitution, stress/anxiety, and peer relations with a link to possible bullying involvement. The authors recommended that schools assist the frequent visitors by instituting educational workshops on how students can learn to deal with behaviors from other students that cause them to feel vulnerable, bothered, or embarrassed. Peer mediation was recommended as a means of helping students learn the skills needed to work out their own problems (Sweeney & Sweeney, 2000).

Another study demonstrated that bullying involvement as a bully, victim, or both significantly predicted visits to the school nurse's office with health symptoms (Vernberg et al., 2011). The relationship between office visits and bullying involvement was demonstrated significantly enough that frequent office visits are recommended to be used as an indicator of bullying involvement (Vernberg et al., 2011).

## Pre-existing Health Conditions and High-Risk Groups

> The students who are bullied are usually the smaller children and those with the "not so cool" appearance. They are often hesitant to report the matter because they fear retaliation. They also still hold out hope of being friends.
>
> *Zoey W., School Nurse*

Bullying behavior is based on a real or perceived imbalance of physical, emotional, or social power (National Bullying Prevention Center, 2015; Olweus, 1993). Children who are different are most likely to be bullied according to 10-year-olds in a study by Erling and Hwang (2004). Differences in physical appearance were most likely to lead to victimization, but other differences, including eating different foods, speaking differently, and thinking or acting differently, were also considered reasons for bullying (Erling & Hwang, 2004). Victims were also described as easily provoked or submissive.

Having a pre-existing health condition or disability has also been identified as a factor that can increase a child's chance of being bullied (US Department of Health and Human Services, n.d.). In one study, children with special health-care needs were identified as being significantly more likely to be bullied than children without those needs (Van Cleave & Davis, 2006). Special health-care needs were defined as the need for prescription medication; the need for extra medical, mental health, or educational services; limitations in doing age-appropriate activities; the need for physical, occupational, or speech therapy; and emotional, developmental, or behavioral problems that necessitate treatment. In another study, children with autism spectrum disorder were identified as being at risk for being bullied or left out by peers (Twyman et al., 2010), as were children with epilepsy and diabetes (Hamiwka et al., 2009; Storch et al., 2004). Other studies have also reported that students who have physical or learning disabilities are bullied more often than their non-disabled peers (Carter & Spencer, 2006; Rose, Monda-Amaya, & Espelage, 2010).

Students with mental health issues can also be targets of bullying. In one study, students were followed from the beginning to the end of the school year (Fekkes et al., 2006). The study found that students who had psychological symptoms of depression and anxiety at the beginning of the school year had a significantly higher chance of being newly bullied during the school year. A prior study reported that children who are shy, withdrawn, anxious, fearful, insecure, and depressed and have low self-esteem or low social skills are more likely to be bullied through social exclusion or physical harm (Olweus, 1997). In addition to students who are victims of bullying, having an emotional, developmental, or behavioral problem has also been found to be significantly associated with students who bully others (Van Cleave & Davis, 2006).

Weight status also increases the risk of being bullied. This has been demonstrated for students who are either overweight or underweight (Wang, Iannotti, & Luk, 2010). In one study, both boys and girls who were underweight were at an increased risk for being bullied. However, boys were more likely to be physically bullied, while girls were more likely to be bullied through social exclusion or spreading of rumors. For overweight boys and obese girls, the risk for verbal bullying was increased (Wang et al., 2010). Another study reported that the odds of being bullied increased with the amount of excess weight (Janssen, Craig, Boyce, & Pickett, 2004).

Finally students who identify as gay, lesbian, bisexual, transgendered, or questioning (GLBTQ) are also at risk. They are more likely than students who identify as straight to have been involved in a fight that requires medical treatment or to have been violently attacked in the past year (Russell, Franz, & Driscoll, 2001). In a national survey of school climate, 89.1% of GLBTQ students reported verbal harassment and 18.3% reported being physically assaulted (Kosciw, Greytak, Bartkiewicz, Boesen, & Palmer, 2012). Because of the high rates of victimization, GLBTQ students have a higher risk of anxiety, depression, and suicidal thoughts (Russell et al., 2011).

## The School Nurse's Office as a Safe Haven

> It takes a lot of courage for a student to go to the Assistant Principal or the Principal to report bullying. But students trust the school nurse and so some will come here first.
>
> *Judith H-S, School Nurse*

The school nurse holds a unique position in the school system in that the nurse's office carries no academic or disciplinary risk for students (Cooper, Clements, & Holt, 2012; King, 2014). The role is complementary to other personnel and consists of monitoring, nurturing, facilitating, educating, and intervening. This engenders trust and often leads to the school nurse being the first person to whom the student may report bullying (King, 2014). Many students underreport bullying because they feel that the situation will not be taken seriously (Barboza et al., 2009). In the school health office, however, they find a listening ear and someone with assessment skills and a desire to help.

When students confide in the school nurse, research shows that they benefit (Borup & Holstein, 2007). One study looked at five possible outcomes for students who talk with the school nurse about bullying. These outcomes included: (a) reflecting on the content of the dialogue, (b) discussing the dialogue with a parent, (c) following the advice of the school nurse, (d) doing what the student thought was best, and (e) visiting the school nurse again. Students who were bullied were more likely to do at least one of the suggested outcomes. The study also reported that students who were bullied at least weekly were more likely to visit the school nurse again (Borup & Holstein, 2007).

## School Nurses and Their Role in Preventing and Dealing with Bullying

> It's the nurse's responsibility to look beyond the immediate symptoms and the frequent visits and dig deeper about the possibility of bullying. I had one student who kept coming in with stomach aches and headaches. I finally sat down beside her and asked her pointedly about being bullied. She denied it at first, but then the tears started to roll. She admitted that she was being bullied and I was able to get mediation for the student and the bully. The student's stomach aches and headaches have not returned.
>
> *Leslie B., School Nurse*

In its position paper on school nurses and bullying, the NASN states that the role of the school nurse should include prevention of bullying, as well as identification of those who are involved (NASN, 2014a). School nurses should assume a leadership role in establishing school policies to deal with bullying. In general, these responsibilities include becoming knowledgeable about bullying and the students involved, assessing students, becoming part of the school-wide team to address the problem, coordinating care, and becoming involved with policy. The American Academy of Pediatrics (2008) also holds a position that school nurses should participate in planning and implementing school policies regarding school violence and bullying.

School nurses follow the nursing process when dealing with visitors to the health office (American Nurses Association (ANA), 2016). Assessment of the problem is followed by analysis of information obtained from talking to and examining the student. This information then guides the design and selection of nursing interventions. The interventions are subsequently evaluated to determine if they have been of benefit to the patient. Finally, the assessment, analysis, interventions, and evaluation are documented according to legal standards.

**Assessment and analysis .** The school nurse is responsible for evaluating student complaints of illness and injury and conducting a general or focused assessment (Massachusetts Department of Public Health, 2007).

During the assessment phase, nurses collect information on the physical, psychological, social, and other factors that affect health as a way to evaluate the illness in a holistic manner (ANA, 2016; NASN, 2013). Assessment of illnesses involves talking to the student about when the symptoms began, how often they occur, what may be triggers, and what the student feels would improve the symptoms. This is followed by a focused physical exam, which provides objective information. Together, the subjective and objective information guides the actions of the nurse. For example, students who complain of a headache will be asked if other symptoms are present, how long they have had the headache, how painful it is, if it is due to an injury, and if anything makes it feel better or worse. Students will then have their temperature taken and throat examined to determine if the headache is part of an illness. Absent other physical symptoms, the nurse will then dig deeper to determine potential causes such as hormonal changes, vision straining, or hunger. One possible consideration will be if the headache seems to occur frequently at the same time of the day and is accompanied by anxiety or a feeling of sadness. This combination of symptoms and timing may indicate bullying involvement.

Assessment of injuries will include not only the type of injury, the location, and the severity but also the frequency, timing, and the cause (ANA, 2016). School nurses may be able to identify if injuries are happening away from school or during the same time period of the school day (NASN, 2014c; Shannon, Bergren, & Matthews, 2010). For example, if a child consistently comes in from recess with an injury, it is possible that the child is being bullied at that time. However, if the student visits the health office at the beginning of the day with a new complaint, the bullying may be occurring at home.

The holistic approach of the nursing process instructs nurses to assess students for factors beyond physical health that may contribute to illness complaints (ANA, 2016; Shannon et al., 2010). The National Association of School Nurses lists eight questions that school nurses should ask when deciding whether or not a student has been bullied. These questions add to the verbal information collected from the student and the physical assessment data to create a complete picture that will either confirm or rule out bullying involvement (NASN, 2014c, p. 1).

1. Are there any factors that particularly place the student at risk?
2. Are there behavioral changes?
3. Are there increased absences?

4. Are there more psychosomatic complaints or illnesses?
5. Are there unexplained injuries?
6. Has academic performance diminished?
7. Are selected activities avoided?
8. Are clothes torn or belongings "lost"?

**Nursing interventions and the ecological perspective.** After analyzing assessment data, the nurse's role turns to determining effective interventions (ANA, 2016). The ecological perspective is often used as a framework to understand public health problems and create solutions (National Cancer Institute [NCI], 2005; Sallis, Owen, & Fisher, 2008). It describes health problems as occurring due to the influence of factors that are present on multiple levels—individual (intrapersonal), interpersonal, community, and policy level. It recognizes that the factors interact in both directions across the multiple levels of influence, that each level has specific factors that are most influential to the behavior, and that solutions to health behavior problems should address the multiple levels of influence (NCI, 2005).

Individual-level (intrapersonal) factors that affect health behaviors such as bullying include personal health habits, current health status, personality traits, attitudes, beliefs, and knowledge (NCI, 2005). Interpersonal-level factors include the relationships among family members, peers, and society that support a person's social identity and the roles they establish. The community-level factors include rules, regulations, social norms, networks, and standards that deter or encourage a behavior, as well as the resources that are available to deal with a bullying problem. Public policy is also considered a community-level factor of influence and includes local, state, and federal laws that regulate violence and bullying, and those that provide funds for bullying prevention programs (NCI, 2005).

An example of an individual-level factor that may increase the chance of becoming a target of bullying may be that the student is frequently alone. On an interpersonal level, if violence is an accepted way to deal with problems in a family, a student is more likely to use that method for dealing with personal problems in school (Nansel et al., 2001). On a community level, training students to actively intervene during bullying episodes, termed bystander intervention, has been shown to significantly decrease victimization (Polanin, Espelage, & Pigott, 2012). Finally, on a policy level, a well-designed anti-bullying policy that is consistently enforced has been shown to decrease bullying (Fekkes et al., 2005).

The school nurse can use the ecological perspective to guide her interventions to prevent and manage bullying (Zinan, 2010). It can be applied to empower the student on multiple levels or to guide her/his own behavior. On an individual level, school nurses can help victims to understand their feelings in response to bullying, and to recognize that they have the ability to do something about it (Zinan, 2010). They can help students to understand the power issues involved and determine ways to increase their own personal power. They can encourage students to document the events and support them as they report it to the school administrators. They can also help students to address issues that decrease their self-esteem such as weight, acne, and physical strength. Regarding the factors that influence the nurse's personal behavior, the school nurse can examine her/his feelings and biases related to bullying, become knowledgeable about the topic, identify strengths, and make a commitment to become part of the solution (Zinan, 2010).

On an interpersonal level, school nurses can help victims practice relationship skills (Zinan, 2010). They can also help the student to practice ways to respond to bullies. If the pace of the nurse's office does not allow enough time, the student can be encouraged to seek help from school counselors and psychologists in practicing these social skills. School nurses can ensure that students receive the health care they need to improve their emotional state and decrease their risk of being bullied. They can also ensure that an educational plan for students with physical and learning disabilities includes an element of emotional support. School nurses can encourage high-risk students, such as GLBTQ students, to join support groups or receive outside counseling support. Regarding her/his own behavior, the school nurse can foster trusting relationships and create a welcoming and safe environment in the school health office.

On a community level, school nurses can encourage the student to speak out publicly as a way to have input into how bullying is handled in schools (Zinan, 2010). For example, the student may advocate for better supervision on buses, at recess, and in hallways and cafeterias. On a policy level, the student may advocate for a strong policy that is consistently enforced (Zinan, 2010). School nurses should also participate in these efforts and influence the local, state, and federal policies and laws pertaining to bullying. They should document visits to the health office that are associated with bullying and support educational events that encourage bystander and community involvement.

I think one of the reasons that students bully others is because they really don't know each other well. I had a situation between a 7th and 8th grader where I had them both eat lunch with me for a couple of weeks. At the end of the two weeks, they knew each other and the bullying stopped.

*Judith H-S, School Nurse*

**Evaluation and documentation .** After implementing nursing interventions, nurses evaluate them to determine their effectiveness (ANA, 2016). With regard to bullying, nurses will document any healing of injuries or decrease in symptom patterns as a result of nursing actions. Indications that the intervention was not effective would prompt further investigation and a different intervention. For example, if health complaints and frequent office visits persist, the nurse will continue to explore the cause and bring the child to the attention of the school crisis team.

## The Value of School Health Office Records

School health office records are a source of information about bullying on the school campus. They can indicate the types, frequency, and timing of complaints and visits to the health office. The information that nurses collect and report can provide proof of a potential problem and improvement of an existing problem (Zinan, 2014). It can guide program planning and determine if current efforts are having a positive effect. Health office records can also be used to document the association between bullying involvement and increased absenteeism (Steiner & Raspberry, 2015).

Identifying the extent and effect of bullying is valuable information that can be used to secure grants and resources to deal with the issue (Zinan, 2014). One possible use of the data would be to secure assistance in the school health office in order to decrease the school nurse workload. This would free the nurse to participate in broader bullying prevention efforts. It can also be used to justify additional school psychologist and counselor positions and secure resources to conduct educational programs.

## School Nurses: Part of a Team

In high school, you might not find out about bullying until there's a fight because students don't report it. Our job at that time is to assess injuries and calm the student down. Then we direct the care they need by connecting them to the social worker or other services.

*Maxine V., School Nurse*

School nurses are part of a team that can address the issues that accompany bullying involvement (Bohnenkamp, Stephan, & Bobo, 2015; Dresler-Hawke & Whitehead, 2009; Kub & Feldman, 2015). They may be the first contact for students in distress and a continual support for ongoing issues (Cooper et al., 2012; Zinan, 2010, 2014). School nurses develop positive relationships with family members and thus may provide insight and understanding to both the family and school officials.

Teachers, principals, school psychologists, and school staff recognize the value of the school nurse in addressing complaints that have physical and mental health implications (Baisch, Lundeen, & Murphy, 2011; Bohnenkamp et al., 2015; Kub & Feldman, 2015). School nurses are considered vital to keeping students in the classroom, maintaining accurate school health records, and improving immunization rates. The time that school nurses devote to their assigned duties saves time that would be shifted to others. In one study, principals reported that school nurses save them an hour of time per day that may be devoted to health issues; teachers each reported a savings of 17 minutes, and school secretaries reported a savings of 47 minutes (Baisch et al., 2011). The presence of a nurse in the school also has economic benefits. The time saved from shifting the management of health complaints to others was estimated to save schools over $60,000 annually after accounting for the school nurse salary (Baisch et al., 2011).

As a member of the team, school nurses provide a holistic perspective in addressing student health issues, including bullying (NASN, 2013). They are the pediatric health experts on the school campus and understand that maintaining physical and mental well-being is essential to minimizing absenteeism and enhancing learning (NASN, 2014b). Their focus extends beyond the classroom to include the multiple components of health (physical, emotional, social) and the multiple influences on health (individual, family, community, and policy) (Dresler-Hawke & Whitehead, 2009; NASN, 2014b). They have the potential to broaden the capacity for schools to understand and intervene in bullying.

The NASN believes that school nurses should assume a leadership role in preventing bullying (2014b). The responsibilities of school nurses include becoming educated about the different roles (bully, victim, bystander) and how students are affected by bullying. School nurses are encouraged to be key players in identifying bullies and victims but are cautioned to avoid labeling them as such. They should provide leadership in educating other stakeholders about the lasting effects of aggressive behavior among students, assist in developing prevention and intervention strategies for bullying behaviors, and help to form connections between the school, students' families, and the community. When treating students with unexplained health complaints, school nurses should provide a safe place where students can be assessed for bullying and where they will feel comfortable confiding in an adult. When bullying is suspected, school nurses have a responsibility to share this information with other stakeholders so that action can be taken to ensure that all students feel safe at school. Finally, NASN encourages school nurses to advocate for students by being active at the community, state, and national levels to help develop programs that prevent and/or intervene in bullying (2014b).

## Barriers to Bullying Intervention

School nurses are motivated to help with the issue of bullying, and they see it as an element of their job (National Education Association, n.d.; Zinan, 2014). However, barriers may exist to prevent them from becoming involved. In one study, the most commonly cited barrier was that the bullying occurred in locations other than the nurses' supervising area (Hendershot, Dake, Price, & Lartey, 2006). School nurses also cited as a barrier that they felt that someone else was more qualified to deal with bullies, victims, or bullying situations. Other barriers included not having enough time and not being prepared to handle the problem. Only 15% of nurses stated there were no barriers to dealing with bullying (Hendershot et al., 2006). In another study, the number of barriers to dealing with bullying decreased following a nurse-focused training (Zinan, 2014). However, the three most common barriers cited before and after the program included that bullying occurred in places not supervised by the nurse, the feeling that others were more qualified, and not having enough time (Zinan, 2014).

Lacking the time to deal with bullying is a reflection of school nurse workload. This may prohibit them from participating beyond addressing illnesses and injuries in the health office. One study reported that two-thirds of the nurses interviewed identified their workload as "too heavy" (Ball, 2009, p. 20). This may be particularly true of school nurses who are not employed full time, or who are responsible for more than one school. The recommended ratio of school nurses to students is 1:750 (NASN, 2015). Lower ratios are recommended for student populations with complex health needs (NASN, 2015). In addition to their mandates to screen students for vision and hearing deficits and scoliosis, and monitor immunization compliance, nurses must meet documentation standards required by law for these activities. Combined with the medication administration responsibilities, and the need to oversee the care of students with medical needs, managing emergencies, coordinating sports physicals, and conducting concussion assessments, nurses have little time to take on bullying prevention efforts.

## Needs of School Nurses to Address Bullying

The belief that someone other than the nurse is more qualified to deal with bullying issues may reflect a lack of training for school nurses (Hendershot et al., 2006; Zinan, 2014). Professional training about bullying is required by law in many states (US Department of Health and Human Services, n.d.). However, few trainings are offered that are specific to school nurses. School nurses should receive training specific to their role in assessing and intervening with bullies and victims (Hendershot et al., 2006; Zinan, 2014). School nurses should be taught to recognize victims and bullies by their symptoms and learn intervention techniques that can be easily implemented in the health office (Zinan, 2014). They should be allowed time to process their own feelings regarding bullying, as they may have been victimized in the past, and to assess their own biases regarding bullying (Zinan, 2014).

Training improves school nurses' knowledge levels and empowers them to deal with bullying issues (Zinan, 2014). Following a training designed for school nurses, the participants reported a significant increase in their ability to recognize the signs and symptoms of students who are bullies and victims (Zinan, 2014). They also indicated an increase in the number of strategies that they felt were effective in reducing bullying.

Training should also include a review of laws that address bullying and that apply to school environments (Deitch, 2012). Finally, training should provide the opportunity to explore the resources within and outside the school system, such as websites, national organizations, and community agencies, to broaden their role in preventing bullying.

In order to more fully participate in bullying prevention and intervention, school nurses need assistance in the school health office (Zinan, 2014). School nurses should receive administrative support to develop and maintain an accurate documentation system for health office visits. This may necessitate transferring some duties to administrative staff.

As school health records become computerized, school nurses can run reports of the number of visits per complaint, per student and per time period. School nurses should also be allowed to hire substitute nurses to assist them in high-activity periods. These actions could free up time for them to participate in violence prevention task forces and child assistance teams, develop educational materials to be sent home, monitor data trends in health office visits, foster connectedness between schools and families, and influence policy.

In summary, school nurses need the following in order to fully participate in a bullying prevention program that addresses the problem with an ecological perspective:

- Training specific to school nurses
  - signs and symptoms
  - effects of bullying
  - intervention techniques
  - laws related to bullying
  - addressing personal uncertainties and biases
  - working as a team member
  - online and community resources to address the problem
- Computerized health record-keeping system and training
- Administrative support
- Flexible hiring of substitutes
- Time allotted to participate in violence prevention task forces and educational programs

## Summary

School nurses are valuable members of the teams of professionals who educate our children (National Association of School Nurses (NASN), 2011). Involvement with bullying as either a victim, a bully or both increases the likelihood of physical and emotional symptoms that can impair learning, increase absenteeism and bring the student to the school health office. High risk students are those who have poor social skills; are withdrawn, anxious or depressed; have learning difficulties; identify as lesbian/gay/bisexual/transsexual/questioning or who look and act "differently." The school nurse can provide a safe haven for students who are involved with bullying, and assist in resolving the problem on a personal, interpersonal, community or policy level. School nurses should be supported to undertake a leadership role in bullying prevention efforts. They may need nurse-specific training in order to feel prepared and qualified to intervene with those involved (Zinan, 2014). Providing administrative assistance and the option to hire substitutes for high-activity periods may increase the time that a nurse can devote to bullying beyond assessing and documenting student injuries. This has potential to increase their involvement while minimizing any impact on school budgets, and potentially save money. Administrative assistance may be in the form of establishing a computerized health record-keeping system to monitor health office visits in order to correlate them with trends in bullying. The collected data can also be used for grant applications as a way to obtain additional resources to deal with bullying.

## References

American Academy of Pediatrics. (2008). *Role of the school nurse in providing school health services.* Retrieved from http://aappolicy.aappublications.org/cgi/reprint/pediatrics;121/5/1052.pdf

American Nurses Association. (2016). *The nursing process.* Retrieved from http://www.nursingworld.org/EspeciallyforYou/StudentNurses/Thenursingprocess.aspx

Baisch, M. J., Lundeen, S. P., & Murphy, M. K. (2011). Evidence-based research on the value of school nurses in an urban school system. *Journal of School Health, 81*, 74–80.

Ball, J. (2009). *School nursing in 2009.* Retrieved from http://www.nursingtimes.net/Journals/1/Files/2009/9/14/School_Nurses_2009_final_report_pdf.pdf

Barboza, G., Schiamberg, L., Ochmke, J., Korzeniewski, S., Post, L., & Heraux, C. (2009). Individual characteristics and the multiple contexts of adolescent bullying: An ecological perspective. *Journal of Youth and Adolescence, 38*, 101–121. doi:10.1007/s10964-008-9271-1.

Bohnenkamp, J., Stephan, S., & Bobo, N. (2015). Supporting student mental health: The role of the school nurse in coordinated school mental health care. *Psychology in the Schools, 52*, 714–726. doi:10.1002/pits.21851.

Borup, I., & Holstein, B. (2007). School children who are victims of bullying report benefit from health dialogues with the school health nurse. *Health Education Journal, 66*, 58–67.

Camodeca, M., & Goossens, F. (2005). Aggression, social cognitions, anger and sadness in bullies and victims. *Journal of Child Psychology and Psychiatry, 46*, 186–197. doi:10.1111/j.1469-7610.2004.000347.x.

Campo, J., Bridge, J., Ehmann, M., Altman, S., Lucas, A., Birmaher, B., ... Brent, D. (2004). Recurrent abdominal pain, anxiety, and depression in primary care. *Pediatrics, 113*, 817–824.

Carter, B., & Spencer, V. (2006). The fear factor: Bullying and students with disabilities. *International Journal of Special Education, 21*, 11–23.

Cooper, G. D., Clements, P. T., & Holt, K. E. (2012). Examining childhood bullying and adolescent suicide: Implications for school nurses. *Journal of School Nursing, 28*(4), 275–283. doi:10.1177/1059840512438617.

Copeland, W., Wolke, D., Angold, A., & Costello, J. (2013). Adult psychiatric and suicide outcomes of bullying and being bullied by peers in childhood and adolescence. *Journal of the American Medical Association Psychiatry, 70*, 419–426. doi:10.1001/jamapsychiatry.2013.504.

Deitch, M. (2012). *School nurses and bullying*. Retrieved from http://nursing.advanceweb.com/Features/Articles/School-Nurses-Bullying.aspx

Dresler-Hawke, E., & Whitehead, D. (2009). The behavioral ecological model as a framework for school-based anti-bullying health promotion interventions. *The Journal of School Nursing, 25*(3), 195–203. doi:10.1177/1059840509334364.

Due, P., Holstein, B., Lynch, J., Diderichsen, F., Gabhain, S., Scheidt, P., ... The Health Behavior in School-Aged Children Bullying Working Group. (2005). Bullying and symptoms among school-aged children: International comparative cross sectional study in 28 countries. *European Journal of Public Health, 15*, 128–132.

Erling, A., & Hwang, C. P. (2004). Swedish 10-year-old children's perceptions and experiences of bullying. *Journal of School Violence, 3*, 33–43.

Fekkes, M., Pijpers, F., Fredriks, M., Vogels, T., & Verloove-Vanhorick, P. (2006). Do bullied children get ill, or do ill children get bullied? A prospective cohort study on the relationship between bullying and health-related symptoms. *Pediatrics, 117*, 1568–1574.

Fekkes, M., Pijpers, F. I., & Verloove-Vanhorick, S. P. (2005). Bullying: Who does what, when and where? Involvement of children, teachers and parents in bullying behavior. *Health Education Research, 20*, 81–91.

Glew, G., Fan, M., Katon, W., Rivara, F., & Kernic, M. (2005). Bullying, psychosocial adjustment, and academic performance in elementary school. *Archives of Pediatric and Adolescent Medicine, 159*, 1026–1031.

Hamiwka, L., Yu, C., Hamiwka, L., Sherman, E., Anderson, B., & Wirrell, E. (2009). Are children with epilepsy at greater risk for bullying than their peers? *Epilepsy & Behavior, 15*, 500–505.

Hendershot, C., Dake, J., Price, J., & Lartey, G. (2006). Elementary school nurses' perceptions of student bullying. *The Journal of School Nursing, 22*(4), 229–235.

Janssen, I., Craig, W., Boyce, W., & Pickett, W. (2004). Associations between overweight and obesity with bullying behaviors in school-aged children. *Pediatrics*, *113*, 1187–1194.

King, K. (2014). Violence in the school setting: A school nurse perspective. *OJIN: The Online Journal of Issues in Nursing*, *19*(1), 4. doi:10.3912/OJIN.Vol19No01Man04.

Klomek, A., Marrocco, F., Kleinman, M., Schonfeld, I., & Gould, M. (2007). Bullying, depression and suicidality in adolescents. *Journal of the American Academy of Child & Adolescent Psychiatry*, *46*, 40–49.

Kosciw, J., Greytak, E., Bartkiewicz, M., Boesen, M., & Palmer, N. (2012). *The 2011 national school climate survey: The experiences of lesbian, gay, bisexual and transgender youth in our nation's schools.* Retrieved from http://www.glsen.org/press/2011-national-school-climate-survey

Kowalski, R., & Limber, S. (2013). Psychological, physical, and academic correlates of cyberbullying and traditional bullying. *Journal of Adolescent Health*, *53*, S13–S20. doi:10.1016/j.jadohealth.2012.09.018.

Kub, J., & Feldman, M. (2015). Bullying prevention: A call for collaborative efforts between school nurses and school psychologists. *Psychology in the Schools*, *52*, 658–670. doi:10.1002/pits.21853.

Massachusetts Department of Public Health. (2007). *Comprehensive school health manual.* Retrieved from http://files.hria.org/files/SH3001.pdf

Nansel, T. R., Overpeck, M., Pilla, R. S., Ruan, W. J., Simons-Morton, B., & Scheidt, P. (2001). Bullying behaviors among us youth: Prevalence and association with psychosocial adjustment. *Journal of the American Medical Association*, *285*, 2094–2100.

National Association of School Nurses. (2011). *Role of the school nurse.* Retrieved from https://www.nasn.org/PolicyAdvocacy/PositionPapersandReports/NASNPositionStatementsFullView/tabid/462/ArticleId/87/Role-of-the-School-Nurse-Revised-2011

National Association of School Nurses. (2013). *Mental health of students.* Retrieved from http://www.nasn.org/Portals/0/positions/2013psmentalhealth.pdf

National Association of School Nurses. (2014a). *Transition planning for students with chronic medical conditions.* Retrieved from https://www.nasn.org/PolicyAdvocacy/PositionPapersandReports/NASNPositionStatementsFullView/tabid/462/smid/824/ArticleID/644/Default.aspx

National Association of School Nurses. (2014b). *Bullying prevention in schools: Position statement.* Retrieved from http://www.nasn.org/Portals/0/positions/2014psbullying.pdf

National Association of School Nurses. (2014c). *See something, say something ... the school nurse role in bullying prevention.* Retrieved from https://www.nasn.org/portals/0/resources/bullyingflyerpledge.pdf

National Association of School Nurses. (2015). *School nurse workload: Staffing for safe care. Position statement.* Retrieved from http://www.nasn.org/Portals/0/positions/2015psworkload.pdf

National Association of School Nurses. (2016). *Concussions—The role of the school nurse: Position statement.* Retrieved from https://www.nasn.org/PolicyAdvocacy/PositionPapersandReports/NASNPositionStatementsFullView/tabid/462/ArticleId/218/Concussions-The-Roleof-the-School-Nurse-Revised-June-2016

National Bullying Prevention Center. (2015). *Bullying info and facts.* Retrieved from http://www.pacer.org/bullying/resources/info-facts.asp

National Cancer Institute. (2005). *Theory at a glance: A guide for health promotion practice.* Retrieved from: http://www.cancer.gov/cancertopics/cancerlibrary/theory.pdf

National Education Association. (n.d.). *Health and student services ESPs and bullying prevention.* Retrieved from https://www.nea.org/assets/docs/ESP_STOP_Bully_Health-final.pdf

Olweus, D. (1993). *Bullying at school: What we know and what we can do.* Oxford, England: Blackwell Publishers.

Olweus, D. (1997). Bully/victim problems in school: Knowledge base and an effective intervention program. *The Irish Journal of Psychology, 18*(2), 170–190.

Polanin, J., Espelage, D., & Pigott, T. (2012). A meta-analysis of school-based bullying prevention programs' effects on bystander intervention behavior. *School Psychology Review, 41*(*1*), 47–65.

Rigby, K., & Slee, P. (1991). Bullying among Australian school children: Reported behaviour and attitudes toward victims. *Journal of School Psychology, 131*, 614–627.

Rivers, I., Poteat, V., Noret, N., & Ashurst, N. (2009). Observing bullying at school: The mental health implications of witness status. *School Psychology Quarterly, 24*(4), 211–223. doi:10.1037/a0018164.

Rose, C. A., Monda-Amaya, L. E., & Espelage, D. L. (2010). Bullying perpetration and victimization in special education: A review of the literature. *Remedial and Special Education, 32*(2), 114–130. doi:10.1177/0741932510361247.

Russell, S., Franz, B., & Driscoll, A. (2001). Same-sex romantic attraction and experiences of violence in adolescence. *American Journal of Public Health, 91*, 903–906.

Russell, S., Ryan, C., Toomey, R., Diaz, R., & Sanchez, J. (2011). Lesbian, gay, bisexual, and transgender adolescent school victimization: Implications for young adult health and adjustment. *Journal of School Health, 81*(*5*), 223–230.

Sallis, J., Owen, N., & Fisher E. (2008). Ecological models of health behavior. In K. Glanz, B. Rimer, & K. Viswanath (Eds.), *Health behavior and health education* (pp. 465–552). Retrieved from http://riskybusiness.web.unc.edu/files/2015/01/Health-Behavior-and-Health-Education.pdf#page=503

School Nurse News. (1999). *The experiment that endured: The beginnings of school nursing*. Retrieved from http://www.schoolnursenews.org/BackIssues/1999/SNMarch99history.pdf

Shannon, R., Bergren, M., & Matthews, A. (2010). Frequent visitors: Somatization in school-age children and implications for school nurses. *The Journal of School Nursing, 26*(3), 169–182.

Sourander, A., Jensen, P., Ronning, J., Niemala, S., Helenius, H., Sillanmaki, L., ... Almquist, F. (2007). What is the early adulthood outcome of boys who bully or are bullied in childhood? The Finnish "From a Boy to a Man" study. *Pediatrics, 120*, 397–404. doi:10.1542/peds.2006-2704.

Sourander, A., Ronning, J., Brunstein-Klomek, A., Gyllenberg, D., Kumpulainen, K., Niemela, S., ... Almqvist, F. (2009). Childhood bullying behavior and later psychiatric hospital and psychopharmacologic treatment. *Archives of General Psychiatry, 66*, 1005–1012.

Srabstein, J., & Leventhal, B. (2010). Prevention of bullying-related morbidity and mortality: A call for public health policies. *Bulletin of the World Health Organization, 88*, 403–403. doi:10.2471/BLT.10.077123.

Steiner, R. J., & Rasberry, C. N. (2015). 163. Associations between in-person and electronic bullying victimization and missing school because of safety concerns among US high school students. *Journal of Adolescent Health, 43*, 1–4.

Storch, E. A., Lewin, A., Silverstein, J. H., Heidgerken, A. D., Strawser, M. S., Baumeister, A., & Geffken, G. R. (2004). Peer victimization and psychosocial adjustment in children with type 1 diabetes. *Clinical Pediatrics, 43*(5), 467–471.

Sweeney, J., & Sweeney, D. (2000). Frequent visitors to the school nurse at two middle schools. *Journal of School Health, 70*, 387–389.

Twyman, K. A., Saylor, C. F., Saia, D., Macias, M. M., Taylor, L. A., & Spratt, E. (2010). Bullying and ostracism experiences in children with special health care needs. *Journal of Developmental Behavioral Pediatrics, 31*, 1–8.

US Department of Health and Human Services. (n.d.). *Bullying and children and youth with disabilities and special health needs.* Retrieved from http://www.stopbullying.gov/at-risk/groups/special-needs/BullyingTipSheet.pdf

US Department of Health and Human Services. (n.d.). Policies and laws. https://www.stopbullying.gov/laws/

US Department of Health and Human Services. (2015). *Community immunity ("Herd Immunity")*. Retrieved from http://www.vaccines.gov/basics/protection/

Van Cleave, J., & Davis, M. (2006). Bullying and peer victimization among children with special health care needs. *Pediatrics, 118*, 1213–e1219. doi:10.1542/peds.2005-3034.

Vernberg, E., Nelson, T., Fonagy, P., & Twemlow, S. (2011). Victimization, aggression, and visits to the school nurse for somatic complaints, illnesses, and physical injuries. *Pediatrics, 127*, 842–848. doi:10.1542/peds.2009-3415.

Wang, J., Iannotti, R., & Luk, J. (2010). Bullying victimization among underweight and overweight US youth: Differential associations for boys and girls. *Journal of Adolescent Health, 47*, 99–101. doi:10.1016/j.jadohealth.2009.12.007.

Williams, K., Chambers, M., Logan, S., & Robinson, D. (1996). Association of common health symptoms with bullying in primary school children. *British Medical Journal, 313*, 17–19.

Zinan, N. (2010). *Bully victim identification and intervention program for school nurses* (Doctor of Nursing Practice Capstone Project). Retrieved from http://scholarworks.umass.edu/cgi/viewcontent.cgi?article=1000&context=nursing_dnp_capstone

Zinan, N. (2014). Bully victim identification and intervention program for school nurses—A case study. *Clinical Nursing Studies, 2*(1), 45–52.

CHAPTER 7

# Coaches' Perspectives on Bullying

*Christopher Kowalski*

## Introduction

Bullying is seen as a method of degrading, abusing, or humiliating someone to demonstrate superiority, and it can be witnessed in the athletics environment through harmful acts such as physical, emotional, and sexual abuse, as well as team rituals or "traditions" (i.e., hazing). Because of the values associated with major sports in Western culture (i.e., winning at all costs, using power and dominance to control others, and employing a hierarchical structure of authority), bullying and hazing practices are often utilized within the athletics environment (Steinfeldt, Vaughan, LaFollette, & Steinfeldt, 2012; Stirling & Kerr, 2009). To that end, a central figure in the development of athletes, and whether or not they engage in bullying activities to achieve sport-related goals, is the coach. A coach may not recognize the danger of bullying or hazing in athletics, foregoing an analysis of the negative consequences of these behaviors because of the prioritization on winning. The importance of winning may be so great that a coach will push for victories while sacrificing the dignity and integrity of the athletic program.

A coach's primary focus may be winning, but there are also important responsibilities to the athletes associated with the sport. Coaches are

C. Kowalski (✉)
University of Northern Iowa, Cedar Falls, IA, USA



L.H. Rosen et al. (eds.), *Bullying in School*,
DOI 10.1057/978-1-137-59298-9_7

tasked with aiding in the development of athletes' mental, physical, technical, and tactical abilities, as well as healthy socialization skills (Becker, 2009). Coaches who have favorable win-loss records or athletes under their tutelage that elicit positive psychological responses are considered effective in their role (Horn, 2008). For many coaches, the development of a positive culture among their athletes serves as the vehicle towards a successful psychological experience by the athlete along with a favorable win-loss record. Unfortunately, there are coaches who choose the path towards success that invites bullying and hazing among their athletes. While short-term success may occur, the long-term effects to the athletes and the athletic program are detrimental and debilitating.

This chapter will highlight a number of items related to coaches and bullying in the athletic arena. First, a description of bullying will be outlined from an athletics standpoint, inclusive of reasons why bullying may occur in the sport environment. Additionally, key individuals who can impact the prevalence or deterrence of bullying in athletics will be highlighted. Following this definition will be a discussion of the role a coach plays in addressing bullying that may occur within their team or among their athletes, inclusive of the power dynamic associated with the coach-athlete relationship. Lastly, strategies for bullying prevention, intervention, and elimination will be illustrated.

## What Is Bullying in the Athletic Setting?

Bullying in the athletic setting involves physical, verbal, or psychological behaviors between teammates and, in some cases, between a coach and an athlete, which has the potential to abuse and demoralize an individual (Stirling, 2009). Studies have shown bullying in the athletic setting to include acts that are physical (i.e., hitting, damaging an individual's personal property), verbal (i.e., name-calling, inappropriate jokes or gestures, threatening), social (i.e., spreading rumors, exclusion), electronic/digital (i.e., using email, Facebook, or text messages as a vehicle for embarrassment/humiliation), and social actions such as hazing rituals (Shannon, 2013; Steinfeldt et al., 2012; Stirling & Kerr, 2009; Swigonski, Enneking, & Hendrix, 2014). The stress associated with being a victim of bullying can be daunting, and the emotional pain that one endures during and after a bullying incident may be a long-term hurdle an athlete will have to overcome in life (Fuller, Gulbrandson, & Herman-Ukasick, 2013).

As McMullen (2014) points out, the definitions of bullying, hazing, and harassment in athletics often overlap due to the similarities associated with the tendencies and consequences of each action. There are slight differences associated with bullying and hazing, with hazing taking on a more ritualized activity that is associated with induction of new members by older or current members into an existing social group. Hazing occurs due to the motivation to preserve traditions and enhance the team cohesion. Bullying tends to isolate or separate an individual from a group.

Nearly all definitions of bullying in the athletic setting include a discussion of the imbalance in power between teammates or between a coach and an athlete. The imbalance in the power dynamic creates a situation of vulnerability for athletes who become victims of bullying. When it comes to reporting bullying incidences, this power dynamic also influences whether a victim speaks up or silently accepts the abuse (Stirling & Kerr, 2009).

**Why is bullying in athletics continuing?** The belief that participation in sports helps build one's character is a common thought. While the positive elements of sports participation may help young people develop, the dark side of this statement is the perpetuation of bullying and hazing rituals that provide "proof" of character development (Rees, 2010). The longevity of bullying and hazing in athletics, and the support given to the acts by athletes, coaches, and communities, can make it challenging to step forward and move towards social change within the athletics program.

Kevorkian and D'Antona (2010) highlight ten key facts about bullying in athletics; they are:

- Bullying occurs when there is minimal adult supervision,
- Hazing and bullying in athletics occurs in all forms,
- Bullying behaviors are detrimental to the benefits of athletics participation,
- Many coaches are not provided with bullying prevention training or education,
- Males and females are involved in all forms of bullying,
- Bullying occurs among athletes of all ages, abilities, and levels,
- Many athletes do not report bullying for fear of retaliation,
- Parents and caregivers may be the perpetrators of bullying behaviors towards athletes,
- Good sportsmanship must be modeled, taught, and reinforced among athletes, and

- It is important to implement and enforce bullying policies in and out of the athletic setting, as well as in the cyber setting.

These factors illustrate the far-reaching roots, as well as repercussions, that bullying has in the athletic setting. Consideration of the source of bullying behaviors and the extension of bullying behaviors into a person's life are important points to ponder when deliberating how to prevent bullying from occurring. Bullying may not be compartmentalized to just the athletic team; it may be the result of years of "traditional practices" by athletes, coaches, and community members.

One perspective regarding the continuance of bullying in athletics is rooted in Bronfenbrenner's *ecological systems theory* (1979). Supporters of ecological systems theory highlight that individual characteristics of youth are weighed in consideration of social contexts that involve other "key players" in a child's life. Those contexts include home life, school, and community. To understand bullying in athletics, ecological systems theorists point out that consideration should be given to the context or setting where youth development occurs (Barboza et al., 2009; Espelage & Swearer, 2010; Garbarino & deLara, 2002; Shannon, 2013).

Studies exploring bullying in the sport and recreation settings found core themes influencing the nature and extent of bullying incidents (Barboza et al., 2009; Espelage & Swearer, 2010; Garbarino & deLara, 2002; Shannon, 2013). These themes include organizational culture, program elements, spillover from other settings, and peer group dynamics. Organizational culture includes the values, beliefs, and attitudes staff members and administrators hold in conjunction with the prevalence of bullying. Values associated with a positive organizational culture include creating a safe and enjoyable environment for youth, as well as open communication with parents and caregivers about codes of conduct within the organization. Communication procedures also include developing steps to document bullying incidents, inclusive of any harm or injury that occurred. Organization administrators also provided staff trainings on addressing bullying if it occurred, and encouraged staff to attend conferences outside of the organization.

A handful of program elements were perceived to increase the opportunities for bullying, including competitive programs and activities, lack of leader supervision, and unstructured time (Barboza et al., 2009; Espelage & Swearer, 2010; Garbarino & deLara, 2002; Shannon, 2013). There are sports that involve physical contact, and as administrators pointed out, when coaching a sport with physical contact, coaches may also encourage athletes to engage in aggressive behaviors. It is the athletes who take the aggressive nature of the sport too far who facilitate bullying, via threats and altercations. Making sure that the ratio of athletes to coaches is adequate is important for supervisory purposes. The coaches also need to embody the values of the organization and be mature in their decision-making. Administrators may value coaches and staff members who come with backgrounds in psychology and youth development as these individuals have an understanding of strategies to address bullying behavior. When there is unstructured time, bullying opportunities increase. Some coaches wanted to eliminate unstructured events, such as team sleepovers, due to the potential for problems. Other coaches stated it would be more beneficial to discuss with youth how to interact with each other during unstructured time (Shannon, 2013).

Bullying behavior that may have originated in other settings was identified as a major factor for bullying in the recreation and sport setting (Shannon, 2013). Eliminating this type of behavior would need to include the same message regarding bullying in all settings and from all leaders. If this consistency emerged, the potential for bullying behavior may decrease.

Lastly, the individual personalities of youth and how youth communicate with each other in a group setting may influence whether bullying occurs (Garbarino & deLara, 2002; Shannon, 2013). When group dynamics fluctuate based on the youth in the group, the challenge is for coaches to maintain a solid stance on policies and goals of the organization. Developing strategies for creating positive group dynamics as the group members change is an important stabilizing factor in combating bullying. Some coaches engage in these types of activities when the group initially comes together, and they continue these types of activities with the group throughout the time together. Noticing negative peer group dynamics is also an important step for coaches to take; the development of cliques or socially excluding certain individuals is a detrimental step in group development and can be a precursor to bullying.

As Kreager (2007) pointed out, high school athletics can serve as a vehicle for the development of peer social networks and hierarchies among students based on social status. Coaches—and to some extent, athletes—create expectations for participation in athletics. In an effort to navigate the path of participation in athletics and developing friends, athletes may conform to expectations—in some cases, that are counterproductive to personal development. Coakley (2009) refers to this pressured affiliation within the athletics setting as *deviant overconformity*. Engaging in deviant overconformity takes many forms, including participation in bullying practices and hazing rituals (Waldron & Krane, 2005). Deviant overconformity occurs when athletes and coaches uncritically and unquestionably accept the norms associated with the sport ethic. The four tenets of the sport ethic include (a) athletes making sacrifices for the game, (b) athletes striving for distinction, (c) athletes accepting the risks associated with the sport and playing through pain, and (d) athletes accepting no limits in pursuit of success (Coakley, 2009). Deviant overconformity occurs among athletes; this unbridled acceptance of norms will drive athletes to do whatever it takes to gain the power and status associated with being an athlete. A critical factor of deviant overconformity is an athlete's vulnerability to the team's demands coupled with the need to gain or reaffirm group membership (Coakley, 2009).

Coaches who create environments that encourage deviant overconformity in athletes are developing dangerous settings for athletic performance. Athletes who feel the need to constantly affirm their status with their coach will more regularly engage in behaviors aligned with deviant overconformity. Young athletes are willing to subject themselves to humiliating acts, taunting, and in some cases physical harm from teammates and coaches in order to retain membership on the team and gain approval from their coach. Coaches who feel fortunate to have athletes on their team who are willing to "give it all" to the point of deviant overconformity are actually harming their team and program. These types of behaviors may start as isolated incidents; if they are condoned or not dealt with by a coach or athletic administration, they can warp a culture and become extremely difficult to undo.

## The Coach-Athlete Relationship

The relationship between the coach and athlete is integral to the development of players within sports. Coaches serve as role models, mentors, and in some cases, surrogate parents. Coaches are expected to provide guidance both on and off the field, to teach sportsmanship, to foster a competitive fire in each athlete, and to help individuals develop life skills that they can use once their involvement in athletics is complete (Becker, 2009).

As outlined before, there is a power dynamic that exists within the relationship between the coach and the athlete; that is, a coach holds authority over the athletes due to the nature of his or her position (Stirling & Kerr, 2009; Swigonski et al., 2014). Coaches' power over athletes is due to one or more factors, including age, knowledge and expertise in the sport, and previous success (Stirling & Kerr, 2009). Coaches' influence in athlete's lives also extends beyond the playing field or court and into elements of moral, social, and psychological development. Coaches play vital roles in athletes' lives, and they often serve as one of the most influential individuals in their development. This power dynamic is often positive and healthy, with productive growth and development occurring in athletes on and off the field. The dark side of this relationship is manifested when coaches manipulate and abuse athletes via bullying and hazing acts (Bringer, Brackenridge, & Johnston, 2001).

Multiple studies have been conducted analyzing the impact that coaches can have on athletes' understanding and interpretation of bullying in the athletic setting. Steinfeldt et al. (2012) conducted a study involving adolescent football players and found the following results: (a) players who perceived the most influential male adult in their lives did engage or would condone bullying were more likely to judge bullying as an appropriate act, and (b) the more players perceived the most influential adult in their lives supported bullying, the more likely players reported having recently engaged in bullying. These results illustrated two important facts: (a) coaches are often listed as the most influential figure in a young person's life, and (b) that if a coach endorses or condones bullying, the athletes are more likely to accept and endorse bullying as part of the cultural development of the team. Echoing previous research and findings on bullying, coaches can influence personal development and impact the prevalence of bullying in athletics.

Researchers have also been able to learn from athletes what is considered appropriate behavior by coaches in association with bullying in the athletic setting. Kowalski and Waldron (2010) interviewed high school and collegiate athletes to gain insight on how coaches responded to hazing, as well as the role coaches should assume if hazing occurs. Athletes stated that coaches either took a proactive stance against hazing or the coaches accepted hazing. Taking a proactive stance against hazing included a zero tolerance policy for hazing as well as punishment for hazing. Coaches who accepted hazing behavior ignored the actions, allowed hazing if it was under control, and actively encouraged hazing. Athletes' expectations of coaches' roles regarding hazing rituals were wide-ranging, but common themes emerged. Some athletes responded that coaches should prohibit hazing of any kind, while other athletes felt coaches should "look the other way" when hazing occurs. Finally, a few athletes voiced that coaches should have no role in hazing, should or could not know about hazing, and lastly, if they did know, not do anything because they would not be able to curtail it anyway.

The results of the aforementioned studies depict the importance for coaches to establish healthy relationships with their athletes (Bringer et al., 2001; Kowalski & Waldron, 2010; Steinfeldt et al., 2012; Stirling & Kerr, 2009; Swigonski et al., 2014). Coaches wield significant power in their leadership roles and, whether verbally or nonverbally, communicate expectations to athletes regarding the structure and makeup of their athletic teams and program. It is important that positive cultural values are passed on from athletes to coaches; this can occur via strong, healthy relationships between the athletes and the coach.

**Coaches who bully in the athletic setting.** Coaches who exhibit bullying behavior may be guiding athletes based upon myths associated with the coach's role. One of these myths is that negative, belittling, and demeaning language directed at athletes helps prepare them for life, in and out of the athletics context (Kevorkian & D'Antona, 2010). Athletes' confidence and identity is detrimentally impacted if a central figure in their life is consistently putting them down or pointing out their inadequacies. "Coaches can be demanding without being demeaning" (Kevorkian & D'Antona, 2010, p. 40)—this statement highlights that coaches can have high expectations for athletes and hold athletes accountable without being dehumanizing or hurtful.

Examples of coaches' bullying behavior have included throwing objects or equipment at an athlete, belittling and name-calling directed at an athlete in front of teammates, threatening players and forcing them to play through injury, and usage of derogatory language such as homophobic or sexist statements aimed at athletes (Kevorkian & D'Antona, 2010). In some cases, the bullying and abuse inflicted by a coach is sexual in nature. Again, a main reason this type of bullying and abuse occurs is due to the manipulation of the power dynamic that exists between a coach and athlete (Bringer et al., 2001). Coaches may also engage in vicarious bullying through the athletes they coach. Kowalski and Waldron (2010, p. 95) found that coaches would tell athletes on their team to "go get that kid," identifying the athlete on the team to bully. The speculation for this behavior is due to a strict adherence to the sport ethic (as discussed earlier in the chapter) and the social hierarchy associated with the team.

There are numerous challenges that exist when attempting to correct coaching behavior that may be considered bullying. One challenge is the subjective judgment of what behavior is considered "crossing the line" or bullying (Swigonski et al., 2014). Behavior that may be considered bullying in some contexts may not be considered bullying in others; it is based on whether the victim feels intimidated or bullied. There are some actions that regardless of the context or setting are inexcusable, such as name-calling, demeaning or homophobic language, and insults by the coach.

A second challenge associated with correcting bullying behavior is the rationalization or minimization of the coaches' actions. Four different defensive techniques have been noted by Swigonski et al. (2014) in association with rationalizing and minimizing bullying behavior. First, a coach who engages in bullying behavior may try to portray the behavior as socially acceptable. Statements such as "sometimes, a coach may lose it" or "this is how we've done things in the past, and we've continued to win games" invoke the concept that because it is a common action—something that is normally done by coaches once in a while—that action is good. These rationalizations are damaging to the development of athletes, and if perpetuated, then the end result is that bullying becomes a normative behavior between coach and athletes.

A second defensive technique is termed the "backhanded apology" (Swigonski et al., 2014). A backhanded apology is one which is not sincere, and the person deflects responsibility for his or her actions (Bandura, 1978). Coaches who engage in backhanded apologies minimize the harm done by their bullying tactics, as well as put the blame on the athlete for the coaches' behavior. A coach who states that he or she would not have acted in a bullying manner if the individual athlete or team had done what they practiced is placing the burden or responsibility for the actions on the athletes. Again, this is deferring responsibility, and the backhanded apology becomes part of the bullying cycle.

A third defensive technique is associated with advantageous comparisons (Swigonski et al., 2014). When bullying is compared to more heinous or egregious acts, the standard for behavior may shift, allowing a coach's behavior to not seem too severe. Coaches who may verbally bully downplay their actions by stating that "I never push the players around or lay a hand on them" (Swigonski et al., 2014, p. 274). Physical bullying and verbal bullying may be seen as equally wrong, but a coach who makes this statement is saying that physical bullying is much more severe than verbal bullying, therefore shifting the standard for behavior.

A fourth defensive technique is escalation. During escalation, a coach may tell an athlete that if he or she "doesn't like the way things are done on the team, then leave" (Swigonski et al., 2014, p. 274). The bully is escalating the situation and presenting repercussions to the athlete if he or she reports the coach's behavior. A coach is "raising the stakes" and essentially challenging the athlete, potentially forcing a situation to occur that is favorable for the coach.

A coach's past success, as well as the cultural demands that are created by coaches in the athletic environment, may also normalize behaviors such as bullying, which in other environments would not be tolerated (Richardson, Andersen, & Morris, 2008). Athletes may recognize the coach's behavior is abusive, but they also recognize that the coach has achieved a certain level of success, so the abusive behavior by the coach must be what is needed in order to continue to be successful (Stirling & Kerr, 2009). Athletes learn cultural demands for their particular sport via socialization experiences. Over time, these demands become the normative expectations if an athlete participates in the sport (Wiese-Bjornstal, 2010). These norms can lay the foundation for a positive culture within the athletic setting, or they can be the keys to bullying and hazing in the athletic setting.

## The Bystander Effect

Athletes who witness bullying may not be comfortable reporting the behavior due to the concern for retaliation or loss of status within the athletics program (Brendtro, Ness, & Mitchell, 2001). Bystander athletes may also not intervene because they are unaware of what the expectations are associated with intervention on the victim's behalf (Hawkins, Pepler, & Craig, 2001). Often, bystanders who intervene are aggressive in their defensive response for the victim; this may be due to mimicking the behavior of the bully. The aggressive response towards the bully may stop the action and provide short-term relief, but it will not likely eliminate bullying in the long term.

Kevorkian and D'Antona (2010) created three profiles that describe the role of a bystander during a bullying incident. The *disinterested bystander* does not think bullying is a problem and does not want to get involved in rectifying the bullying incident. The *active bystander* wants to help the victim of a bullying incident but does not know the proper steps to do so. The active bystander also fears retaliation from the bullying if he or she intervenes on behalf of the victim. Lastly, the *proactive bystander* knows that bullying is wrong, understands how to effectively intervene, and does take action to stop the bullying and defend the victim.

The goal for coaches and athletic administrators is to create a culture that supports athletes as proactive bystanders, if bullying occurs. Athletes should be educated on how to effectively intervene to reduce and eliminate bullying in athletics, as well as how to support victims of bullying. Praising the efforts of bystanders to proactively intervene if bullying occurs is a positive step towards eliminating bullying from the athletics setting.

## Bullying Prevention and Intervention in the Athletic Setting

There are a number of steps that coaches, as well as athletic administrators and communities, can take to curtail and dissuade bullying behavior. Yet, to dissuade and reduce bullying in athletics, coaches, athletic administrators, and communities need to be aware of the signs and symptoms of bullying behavior—and this has been a challenge. The interpretation of what is considered bullying in athletics is under debate. For example, coaches have differing impressions of bullying behavior, as opposed to aggressive behavior associated with the sport they coach. While monitoring athletes' behaviors both on and off the field has been shown to reduce relational aggression in the school setting (Leadbeater, Banister, Ellis, & Yeung, 2008; Totura et al., 2009), it is important for the coaching body as a whole to learn the signals associated with bullying behavior. At the forefront of this education is the need for coaches, considered as influential adults in athletes' lives, to take a central position regarding prevention and intervention efforts that target bullying (Steinfeldt et al., 2012).

There are a few methods that coaches employ to address bullying in athletics. Some coaches may take a rule-sanction approach (Baar & Wubbels, 2013). The emphasis is on setting rules in place to manage athletes' behavior and including penalties or punishments if the rules are broken. Other coaches may take a problem-solving approach. A problem-solving approach is a collaborative effort to identify solutions to end bullying, inclusive of making bullies aware of victims' feelings (Ellis & Shute, 2007).

A coach's attributions and outcome expectations may also impact the steps taken to prevent bullying from occurring (Baar & Wubbels, 2013).

Coaches may attribute bullying to child-related factors (i.e., obesity) and situational factors (i.e., group dynamics). In studies associated with teachers, attributing bullying to child-related factors tends to reduce the level of sensitivity and need to rectify the bullying among students (Bradshaw, Sawyer, & O'Brennan, 2007; Mavropoulou & Padeliadu, 2002; Novick & Isaacs, 2010).

The beliefs coaches have towards victims of bullying are important in understanding how coaches address bullying (Kochenderfer-Ladd & Pelletier, 2008). Coaches who put an emphasis on victims learning to stand up and defend themselves are engaging in assertive beliefs. Comparatively speaking, if coaches view bullying as a way to learn social norms, they will be less active in helping or aiding victims. These actions are associated with normative beliefs. Lastly, coaches who engage in avoidant beliefs are prone to supporting victims of bullying by preventing the formation of cliques through effective leadership efforts. Coaches with such beliefs help victims of bullying incidents avoid perpetrators and interact or socialize with other individuals.

**Are there impediments to bullying prevention in athletics?** There are a few factors that may impede the identification of bullying behavior, as well as bullying prevention and intervention conducted by coaches. Many coaches may not be aware that bullying is occurring among their athletes (Baar & Wubbels, 2013). Bullying between athletes usually occurs when adults (i.e., coaches, athletic administrators) are not aware of it, or they are not physically present. A coach who is not aware of bullying is not the same as a coach who is not present when bullying occurs. As Johnson and Donnelly (2004) found, some coaches removed themselves from the bullying and hazing process associated with their team. The coaches knew that bullying and hazing rituals were occurring. By removing themselves, the coaches could ignore the actions and also prevent change from occurring—therefore, these abusive acts would still persist. Other coaches may feel that bullying does not exist among the athletes on the team, therefore taking a proactive stance against that type of behavior is not a priority (Caperchione & Holman, 2004).

In researchers' studies examining peer aggression, bullying, and victimization, the results indicated the challenge coaches face in identifying what is considered bullying behavior (Baar & Wubbels, 2013; Coakley, 2009; Endresen & Olweus, 2005; Nucci & Young-Shim, 2005). First, bullying definitions, as stated earlier, highlight intentionality to hurt or harm, repeated actions over time, and an imbalance in a power relationship.

Although a strong body of knowledge exists outlining what is considered bullying in the athletic setting, not all coaches have an exhaustive knowledge of what bullying includes, such as perpetrators' tendencies towards bullying behavior. Second, coaches may mislabel peer aggression or bullying as socially acceptable or assertive behavior due to the competitive nature associated with coaching children in sports. Third, many coaches are volunteers and may not have ample training or education on youth development, bullying, and peer aggression in the sports setting. Their pedagogical training, as well as content knowledge associated with youth work, is limited.

**Creating a respectful athletic culture.** A primary goal within the athletics environment that helps curtail bullying behavior is the development of a healthy culture within a team or program. Coaches emphasized the importance of creating a positive climate within the sports program, which embodied such characteristics as social cohesion, inclusion, and open communication (Baar & Wubbels, 2013). This type of climate included highlighting that bullying would not be tolerated, as well as the harmfulness of bullying. Directive organization, effective pedagogical coaching techniques, clear codes of athlete conduct, and remaining vigilant and alert to possible bullying behavior were also identified as helpful in dissuading bullying.

The construction of a healthy, positive culture begins with the coach and extends to peers. Adult modeling has a significant impact on whether bullying occurs. If adults model positive behaviors, researchers have found that bullying is less likely to occur (Espelage, Bosworth, & Simon, 2000; Fuller et al., 2013). Students who felt support from their peers were less likely to be involved in bullying in any form (Demaray & Malecki, 2001; Espelage & Green, 2007).

Coaches and athletic administrators should also be considering bullying as a larger sociocultural issue (Dominguez, 2013). These leaders should be communicating with athletes and challenging them to consider what type of team the athletes want. Do they want a strong, competitive team of athletes who positively support each other during success and setbacks, or do they want a team of athletes who abuse and harm each other? These questions also have to be considered by the coaches before they communicate a stance to the athletes in the program.

Johnson (2011) noted that bullying and hazing rituals may be replaced by orientation retreats or events. These opportunities facilitate a welcoming, inclusive environment for healthy bonding between athletes. New athletes to the team are able to mingle and interact with current or veteran athletes, potentially developing healthy bonds that feel genuine and are not facilitated out of fear. Coercion, or forceful adherence to principles associated with the team, is replaced with elements of togetherness, cohesion, and positive group growth. As noted, orientations as alternatives to bullying and hazing practices "can replace and in fact surpass the potential of an initiation" (Johnson, 2011, p. 218).

## What Does a Coach Do if an Athlete Reports Bullying?

As Stirling, Bridges, Cruz, and Mountjoy (2011) highlight, there are a number of steps a coach can take if bullying is reported to him or her by an athlete. During the conversation, it is important to actively listen in a careful and calm manner. It might behoove the coach to take notes so that he or she can remember the details of the athlete's report. As the athlete shares his or her thoughts, it is important to not speak poorly about the perpetrator. The athlete who is reporting the bullying may think favorably of the perpetrator, even caring for them, and ill comments directed at the perpetrator may reduce the athlete's comfort in sharing again if subsequent bullying occurs. While the conversation is occurring regarding the bullying experience, a coach should encourage the athlete to share as much as he or she feels comfortable sharing. The primary goal in the conversation should be to make sure the victim gets the best care and support possible, and this can only be achieved if a coach prioritizes the victim. Targeting information by inquiring about specifics regarding the experience may create an awkward and uncomfortable situation, which can slow down the process of addressing the bullying. Unfortunately in bullying scenarios, a culture of silence persists. A coach should praise the athlete for coming forward, being courageous, and sharing his or her experience, and that the experience was not the victim's fault.

Following the report and conversation with the athlete, it is important for a coach to inform all pertinent individuals to keep them abreast of the situation. A similar expectation exists among youth care workers and professionals via certification as a Mandatory Child Abuse Reporter. This certification entails a youth care worker reporting to a child protective services agency, as well as an organization's administration, any suspicion of child abuse. Not all coaches may hold the Mandatory Child Abuse

Reporter certification, but following a similar protocol associated with reporting is paramount for effective guidance of the athlete and anyone else involved in the bullying experience. Lastly, coaches should be aware of their abilities and limitations in their role. An effective coach in this situation should recognize the importance of shepherding the victim to a professional who can counsel the athlete. This type of professional care can help an athlete work through the potential long-term consequences that can arise from victimization associated with bullying.

## Discipline and Bullying in Athletics

As McMullen (2014) discusses, it is important to focus on what the objectives are in conjunction with the punishment or discipline before consideration is given to whether the policy addressing bullying in athletics is appropriate. One goal for punishment may be deterrence—to stop the bullying immediately and prevent future bullying acts. A second goal may be retribution—punishment is levied out so that the perpetrators feel pain, just as the victims did. A third goal may be rehabilitation—the perpetrators should learn from their mistakes and develop alternative ways to interact with teammates.

Disciplinary measures taken once bullying is identified may include immediate intervention coupled with punishment on a case-by-case basis, as well as openly discussing bullying with the whole team or group. There are coaches who tend to engage in avoidant beliefs when dealing with bullying; they believe these beliefs are effective in the athletic setting (Baar & Wubbels, 2013). As mentioned earlier, avoidant beliefs include helping athletes avoid perpetrators of bullying behavior and separating athletes from each other if bullying occurs. The caveat though is that the coach is the "driver" of addressing and discussing bullying and cultural makeup; thought should be given on how much athletes should and can be involved in the process.

If rehabilitation is a goal for perpetrators of bullying, then character education and individual guidance are integral steps in the corrective measures associated with bullying in athletics. The learning opportunity that can result from effective guidance associated with a bullying incident can have a long-lasting impression on a bully. Instead of swift execution of a punishment, a coach can use the bullying actions as an opportunity, with proper administrative support, as a teachable moment for the bully (McMullen, 2014).

**Do zero tolerance policies regarding bullying work?** Currently within the United States, all 50 States as well as the territories of Puerto Rico, Guam, the Virgin Islands, and the Commonwealth of Northern Mariana have either anti-bullying laws or policies in place to help govern identifying bullying and how to respond if bullying occurs ("Policies & Laws," 2015). In several cases, each state's Department of Education is the governing body regulating policies and procedures associated with bullying. At the federal level, there is not a statute addressing bullying or hazing in athletics.

If bullying occurs, there are a number of governing bodies within each state that may be affiliated with handling the action, including school districts, athletic leagues, and conferences. One method that may be used to handle bullying is the creation of a zero tolerance policy. A zero tolerance policy refers to assigning disciplinary action or punishment for undesirable athlete behavior that violates rules regardless of the situation or context (Boccanfuso & Kuhfeld, 2011). The discipline for the perpetrator may include severe consequences, such as suspension or expulsion from school, if the athletics team is school-based. In theory, zero tolerance policies will work and curtail bullying because the discipline and punishment for the offender is so harsh and severe.

Research from a variety of fields on zero tolerance regarding bullying in the academic setting has shown that the severe and harsh punishment for offenders actually has detrimental effects on development. Educational research conducted by Osher, Bear, Sprague, and Doyle (2010) found that suspension from school significantly increases the likelihood of future suspension and expulsion from school, as well as lower academic performance and higher dropout rates. Whitlock (2006) found that students who trust their teachers and view them as respectful, fair individuals are more likely to build bonds with the teachers and perform well in school. Zero tolerance for athletes that includes suspension or expulsion is counterproductive to Whitlock's research. Removing an athlete from school can negate opportunities to building a trusting relationship with staff and faculty, which may detrimentally impact academic performance due to absence from school. Psychological research has also shown that zero tolerance punishments (i.e., suspension, expulsion) further reinforce detrimental behavior by denying students the opportunities to develop healthy social interaction skills and build trusting relationships with adults, some of whom could become mentors and role models in a young person's life (American Psychological Association, 2008). As Christensen (2008) pointed out, "zero tolerance approaches do not prevent bullying—they only place a band-aid on the problem" (p. 14). Zero tolerance policies and approaches to bullying highlight the specific incident and fail to work towards a cultural shift in deterring bullying within the athletics program.

**What are alternatives to zero tolerance policies associated with bullying?** There are a few alternatives to zero tolerance policies associated with bullying in athletics. Character education and social-emotional learning programs are examples of methods that athletics administrators and coaches can take to positively impact the environment and dissuade bullying (Christensen, 2008). Character education programs teach core values and are reinforced through training, practice, and athletes' interaction during their time together. By encouraging core values that are predicated upon healthy character development, the hope is that bullying behavior will be reduced or eliminated. Social-emotional learning programs encourage management of one's emotions, goal-setting, caring and concern for others, the development of positive peer relationships, and the creation of effective decision-making skills (Boccanfuso & Kuhfeld, 2011; Durlak & Weissberg, 2007). Examples of character education and socio-emotional learning programs connected to reducing and eliminating bullying are outlined below.

**The social inclusion approach and restorative justice.** Payne's social inclusion approach (as cited in Christensen, 2008) has also been outlined as a method for addressing bullying. Altering the athletic climate is necessary and can be done by having the team, when together, outline what constitutes bullying. By sharing with each other what are characteristics of bullying behavior, and the detrimental results of bullying, the prevalence is higher for someone to speak out against bullying if the action occurs. The social inclusion approach incorporates restorative justice—if someone bullies, he or she is held accountable, but without the swift punishment or blame that is traditionally associated with zero tolerance. Restorative justice involves bringing all individuals together who may have been involved in the action to discuss the action, the consequences to individuals, and how to move forward in a rehabilitative manner so it does not occur again (Marshall, as cited in Grimes, 2006). If bullying occurred, the perpetrator and the victim would come together with adult leadership to discuss how to move forward and avoid future bullying behaviors. The social inclusion approach involves the bully understanding the deeper impact of his or her actions, and how to make things right replaces shame and punitive discipline. This approach involves a wholesale change with the culture—in this case, the team, the athletic program, and possibly the school if the team is a part of school athletics.

**The teaching personal and social responsibility model (TPSR).** Reactive punishment for engaging in hazing or bullying, such as suspension from matches and practice for the perpetrators, may send an immediate message about the actions. The more effective measure is to create and build a proactive model for team building from the first day of practice (Rees, 2010). An example of a template that helps foster this type of cohesion and positive group dynamics is Hellison's (2003) teaching personal and social responsibility model (TPSR). Using TPSR, athletes learn respect, positive participation in activities with others, self-direction, caring, and ethical behavior. TPSR encourages athletes to develop life skills that will benefit each young person individually, as well as when they work and interact socially with others. Examples of activities that are a part of TPSR include taking on leadership roles within the athletic setting and collaborating with teammates as well as a coach on positive team-building opportunities.

## Conclusion

Bullying behavior does not occur in a bubble; it is perpetuated due to larger, societal issues. As Dominguez (2013) points out, organizations may have spent too much time reacting and focusing on the symptoms of bullying; the target of work should be on the larger problem of how the seed for bullying is planted in youth. Much of the discussion should revolve around how various components of culture support bullying.

Creating a social climate that does not support bullying in athletics in any capacity is crucial for the erosion and potential elimination of this type of behavior in athletics. Change will occur associated with the perception of bullying once changes in the environment happen. Until these environmental changes occur, incidents will continue and more rules will be added on top of the existing procedural methods for addressing bullying.

This chapter has highlighted multiple research studies that point out individual, situational, and organizational factors play a role in whether bullying behaviors occur in the recreation and sport setting. Adherence to the sport ethic and engagement in deviant overconformity may create norms within athletic teams that support bullying and hazing behaviors. Taking bullying seriously and creating a safe environment for youth were initial steps towards developing norms that do not support bullying. These norms also included educating staff on identifying bullying behavior and how to address bullying if it occurs, as well as encouraging youth to build healthy relationships with each other. Coaches who do not acknowledge bullying as an issue are setting themselves up for potentially harmful scenarios. How coaches view bullying, whether it is harmful or part of growing up, and the results of bullying behavior can influence how they intervene if bullying occurs under their watch (Bauman & Del Rio, 2006; Mishna, Pepler, & Wiener, 2006).

In closing, coaches have an incredible amount of responsibility as they work to craft an athletic climate that encourages positive growth within and among athletes on their team. The impact coaches have in curtailing or perpetuating bullying behaviors in the athletic setting is far-reaching. Although winning is paramount in athletics, great coaches are considered "...extraordinary people who left lasting impressions on the lives of those who were fortunate enough to call them coach" (Becker, 2009, p. 112). The goal of creating a positive athletic culture is firmly within a coach's grasp, and their leadership will dictate how that culture is developed and maintained during their tenure with the athletic program.

## References

American Psychological Association Zero Tolerance Task Force. (2008). Are zero tolerance policies effective in the schools? An evidentiary review and recommendations. *American Psychologist, 63*, 852–862. doi:10.1037/0003-066X.63.9.852.

Baar, P., & Wubbels, T. (2013). Peer aggression and victimization: Dutch sports coaches' views and practices. *The Sport Psychologist, 27*, 380–389.

Bandura, A. (1978). Social learning theory of aggression. *Journal of Communication, 28*(3), 12–29.

Barboza, G. E., Schiamberg, L. B., Oehmke, J., Korzeniewski, S. J., Post, L. A., & Heraux, C. G. (2009). Individual characteristics and the multiple contexts of adolescent bullying: An ecological perspective. *Journal of Youth Adolescence, 38*, 101–121.

Bauman, S., & Del Rio, A. (2006). Preservice teachers' responses to bullying scenarios: Comparing physical, verbal, and relational bullying. *Journal of Educational Psychology, 98*, 219–231. doi:10.1177/0143034305059019.

Becker, A. (2009). It's not what they do, it's how they do it: Athlete experiences of great coaching. *International Journal of Sport Science and Coaching, 4*, 93–119.

Boccanfuso, C., & Kuhfeld, M. (2011, March). *Multiple responses, promising results: Evidence-based nonpunitive alternatives to zero tolerance.* (Child Trends Research-to-Results Brief #2011–09).

Bradshaw, C. P., Sawyer, A. L., & O'Brennan, L. M. (2007). Bullying and peer victimization at school: Perceptual differences between students and school staff. *School Psychology Review, 36*, 361–382.

Brendtro, L., Ness, A., & Mitchell, M. (2001). *No disputable kids.* Longmont, CO: Sopris West.

Bringer, J. D., Brackenridge, C. H., & Johnston, L. H. (2001). The name of the game: A review of sexual exploitation of females in sport. *Current Women's Health Reports, 1*, 225–231.

Bronfenbrenner, U. (1979). *The ecology of human development: Experiments in nature and design.* Cambridge, MA: Harvard University Press.

Caperchione, C., & Holman, M. (2004). Gender differences in coaches' perceptions of hazing in intercollegiate athletics. In J. Johnson & M. Holman (Eds.), *Making the team: Inside the world of sport initiations and hazing* (pp. 97–117). Toronto, Ontario, Canada: Canadian Scholars' Press.

Christensen, L. M. (2008). Sticks, stones, and schoolyard bullies: Restorative justice, mediation, and a new approach to conflict resolution in our schools. *Nevada Law Journal, 9*(2), 1–34.

Coakley J. (2009). *Sports in society: Issues and controversies* (10th ed.). Boston, MA: McGraw-Hill.

Demaray, M. K., & Malecki, C. K. (2001). Importance ratings of socially supportive behaviors by children and adolescents. *School Psychology Review, 32*, 108–111.

Dominguez, J. (2013). A fresh approach to peer victimization. *Reclaiming Children and Youth, 22*, 37–40.

Durlak, J. A., & Weissberg, R. P. (2007). *The impact of after-school programs that promote personal and social skills.* Chicago, IL: Collaborative for Academic, Social, and Emotional Learning.

Ellis, A. A., & Shute, R. (2007). Teacher responses to bullying in relation to moral orientation and seriousness of bullying. *The British Journal of Educational Psychology, 77*, 649–663. doi:10.1348/000709906X163405.

Endresen, I. M., & Olweus, D. (2005). Participation in power sports and antisocial involvement in preadolescent and adolescent boys. *Journal of Child Psychology and Psychiatry, and Allied Disciplines, 46*, 468–478.

Espelage, D. L., Bosworth, K., & Simon, T. R. (2000). Examining the social context of bullying behaviors in early adolescence. *Journal of Counseling and Development, 78*, 326–333.

Espelage, D. L., & Green, H. D. (2007). Statistical analysis of friendship patterns and bullying behaviors among youth. *New Directions for Child and Adolescent Development, 118*, 61–75.

Espelage, D. L., & Swearer, S. M. (2010). A social-ecological model for bullying prevention and intervention: Understanding the impact of adult communities children live. In S. R. Jimerson, S. M. Swearer, & D. L. Espelage (Eds.), *The handbook of bullying in schools: An international perspective* (pp. 61–71). New York: Routledge.

Fuller, B., Gulbrandson, K., & Herman-Ukasick, B. (2013). Bullying prevention in the physical education classroom. *Strategies: A Journal for Physical and Sport Education, 26*(6), 3–8. doi:10.1080/08924562.2013.839425.

Garbarino, J., & deLara, E. (2002). *And words can hurt forever: How to protect adolescents from bullying, harassment, and emotional violence.* New York: Free Press.

Grimes, D. L. (2006). Practice what you preach: How restorative justice could solve the judicial problems in clergy sexual abuse cases. *Washington and Lee Law Review, 63*(4), 1693–1741.

Hawkins, D. L., Pepler, D. J., & Craig, W. M. (2001). Naturalistic observations of peer interventions in bullying. *Social Development, 10*(4), 512–527.

Hellison, D. (2003). *Teaching responsibility through physical education* (2nd ed.). Champaign, IL: Human Kinetics.

Horn, T. S. (2008). Coaching effectiveness in the sport domain. In T. S. Horn (Ed.), *Advances in sport psychology* (pp. 239–267). Champaign, IL: Human Kinetics.

Johnson, J. (2011). Through the liminal: A comparative analysis of communitas and rites of passage in sport hazing and initiations. *Canadian Journal of Sociology, 36*(3), 199–226.

Johnson, J., & Donnelly, P. (2004). In their own words: Athletic administrators, coaches, and athletes at two universities discuss hazing policies. In J. Johnson & M. Holman (Eds.), *Making the team: Inside the world of sport initiations and hazing* (pp. 155–175). Toronto, ON: Canadian Scholars' Press.

Kevorkian, M., & D'Antona, R. (2010). *Tackling bullying in athletics: Best practices for modeling appropriate behavior.* Lanham, MD: Rowman & Littlefield Publishers.

Kochenderfer-Ladd, B., & Pelletier, M. E. (2008). Teachers' views and beliefs about bullying: Influences on classroom management strategies and students' coping with peer victimization. *Journal of School Psychology, 46*, 431–453. doi:10.1016/j.jsp.2007.07.005.

Kowalski, C. L., & Waldron, J. J. (2010). Looking the other way: Athletes' perceptions of coaches' responses to hazing. *International Journal of Sports Science and Coaching, 5*, 87–100.

Kreager, D. A. (2007). Unnecessary roughness: School sports, peer networks, and male adolescent violence. *American Sociological Review, 72*, 705–724. doi:10.1177/000312240707200503.

Leadbeater, B. J., Banister, E. M., Ellis, W. E., & Yeung, R. (2008). Victimization and relational aggression in adolescent romantic relationships: The influence of parental and peer behaviors, and individual adjustment. *Journal of Youth and Adolescence*, *37*, 359–372. doi:10.1007/s10964-007-9269-0.

Mavropoulou, S., & Padeliadu, S. (2002). Teachers' causal attributions for behavior problems in relation to perceptions of control. *Educational Psychology*, *22*, 191–202. doi:10.1080/01443410120115256.

McMullen, J. G. (2014). Addressing abusive conduct in youth sports. *Marquette Sports Law Review*, *25*, 181–214.

Mishna, F., Pepler, D., & Wiener, J. (2006). Factors associated with perceptions and responses to bullying situations by children, parents, teachers and principals. *Victims and Offenders*, *1*, 255–288.

Novick, R. M., & Isaacs, J. (2010). Telling is compelling: The impact of student reports of bullying on teacher intervention. *Educational Psychology*, *30*, 283–296. doi:10.1080/01443410903573123.

Nucci, C., & Young-Shim, K. (2005). Improving socialization through sport: An analytic review of literature on aggression and sportsmanship. *Physical Educator*, *62*, 123–130.

Osher, D., Bear, G. G., Sprague, J. R., & Doyle, W. (2010). How can we improve school discipline? *Educational Researcher*, *39*, 48–58. doi:10.3102/0013189X09357618.

Policies & Laws. (2015, May 27). Retrieved from www.stopbullying.gov/laws/

Rees, R. (2010). Bullying and hazing/initiation in schools: How sports and physical education can be part of the problem and part of the solution. *New Zealand Physical Educator*, *43*, 24–27.

Richardson, S. O., Andersen, M. B., & Morris, T. (2008). *Overtraining athletes: Personal journeys in sport*. Champaign, IL: Human Kinetics.

Shannon, C. S. (2013). Bullying in recreation and sport settings: Exploring risk factors, prevention efforts, and intervention strategies. *Journal of Park and Recreation Administration*, *31*, 15–33.

Steinfeldt, J. A., Vaughan, E. L., LaFollette, J. R., & Steinfeldt, M. C. (2012). Bullying among adolescent football players: Role of masculinity and moral atmosphere. *Psychology of Men & Masculinity*, *13*, 340–353. doi:10.1037/a0026645.

Stirling, A. E. (2009). Definition and constituents of maltreatment in sport: Establishing a conceptual framework for research practitioners. *British Journal of Sports Medicine*, *43*, 1091–1099. doi:10.1136/bjsm.2008.051433.

Stirling, A. E., Bridges, E. J., Cruz, E. L., & Mountjoy, M. L. (2011). Canadian academy of sport and exercise medicine position paper: Abuse, harassment, and bullying in sport. *Clinical Journal of Sport Medicine*, *21*, 385–391. doi:10.1097/JSM.0b013e31820f9248.

Stirling, A. E., & Kerr, G. A. (2009). Abused athletes' perceptions of the coach-athlete relationship. *Sport in Society*, *12*(2), 227–239.

Swigonski, N. L., Enneking, B. A., & Hendrix, K. S. (2014). Bullying behavior by athletic coaches. *Pediatrics Perspective, 133*, 273–275. doi:10.1542/peds.2013-3146.

Totura, C. M., MacKinnon-Lewis, C., Gesten, E. L., Gadd, R., Divine, K. P., Dunham, S., & Kamboukos, D. (2009). Bullying and victimization among boys and girls in middle school: The influence of perceived family and school contexts. *The Journal of Early Adolescence, 29*, 571–609.

Waldron, J. J., & Krane, V. (2005). Whatever it takes: Health compromising behaviors in female athletes. *Quest, 57*, 315–329.

Whitlock, J. (2006). Youth perceptions of life at school: Contextual correlates of school connectedness in adolescence. *Applied Developmental Science, 10*, 13–29. doi:10.1207/s1532480xads1001_2.

Wiese-Bjornstal, D. M. (2010). Psychology and socioculture affect injury risk, response, and recovery in high-intensity athletes: A consensus statement. *Scandinavian Journal of Medicine & Sports, 20*, 103–111. doi:10.1111/j.1600-0838.2010.01195.x.

CHAPTER 8

# Drawing Across Perspectives: Implications for Prevention and Intervention

*Lisa H. Rosen, Kathy DeOrnellas, and Shannon R. Scott*

The overarching theme of this book is that considering multiple perspectives provides a more comprehensive understanding of bullying and can lead to more effective prevention and intervention programs. Too often, schools center their efforts only on those identified as bullies or victims, without realizing that bullying is a group process in which bystanders and school staff play important roles (Richard, Schneider, & Mallet, 2012). Expanding the focus to consider how other students, teachers, and school officials can help combat bullying is consistent with the "growing recognition that effective bullying prevention programs should be situated within a social-ecological framework … addressing the characteristics of the individuals involved and the multiple contexts in which they are embedded" (Holt, Raczynskib, Frey, Hymel, & Limber, 2013, p. 239). Indeed, the most successful anti-bullying programs are those that draw on resources across campus (Jimenez Barbero, Ruiz Hernandez, Esteban, & Garcia, 2012). Whole-school approaches to bullying are often effective as collaborative efforts help to shift school culture and bring together those with diverse training and backgrounds to allow for a wider spectrum of support services (Kub & Feldman, 2015).

L.H. Rosen (✉) • K. DeOrnellas • S.R. Scott
Texas Woman's University, Denton, TX, USA



L.H. Rosen et al. (eds.), *Bullying in School*,
DOI 10.1057/978-1-137-59298-9_8

In this concluding chapter, we highlight the ways in which key players can assist with anti-bullying efforts. We point to the importance of examining the perspectives and roles of students, teachers, principals, school resource officers, school psychologists/counselors, nurses, and coaches as outlined in detail in the preceding chapters. Drawing on a social-ecological framework, there are many more perspectives that are worthy of consideration. The previous chapters highlighted the key players in anti-bullying efforts, but in this concluding chapter, we consider an even wider focus by addressing the potential contributions of education support professionals, parents, and community members to anti-bullying efforts. Next, we discuss how multiple players can assist with designing a school-wide anti-bullying program, noting the shared characteristics of many successful programs. We end by outlining potential obstacles to implementation of a whole-school anti-bullying program and offering suggestions for overcoming these challenges.

## Key Players in Anti-bullying Programs

In Chap. 1, Rosen, Scott, and DeOrnellas underscore the importance of designing and implementing effective anti-bullying programs. In so doing, they note that approximately 30% of youth report moderate to frequent involvement in bullying and that negative consequences (e.g., internalizing and externalizing problems) accrue for both bullies and victims. Drawing on research suggesting the vast majority of bullying episodes occur in the school setting, Rosen and colleagues recommend a focus on promoting positive school climate and creating multi-disciplinary teams at schools to combat bullying.

In Chap. 2, Ross and colleagues examine the student perspective and highlights the importance of bystander involvement for anti-bullying programs. Working from the theory of Applied Behavior Analysis, Ross and colleagues describe that behaviors that are reinforced are likely to reoccur, whereas those that are punished are likely to desist. They note that the mere presence of bystanders may reinforce the behavior of bullies who often crave peer attention. In addition, Ross et al. review the multiple roles that bystanders can take including henchmen, active supporters, passive defenders, and active defenders. The goal of prevention and intervention work with bystanders, according to Ross and colleagues, is to create more active defenders who are trained to respond effectively and stop reinforcing bullying behavior. They recommend the optimal way to go about this is by fostering a positive school culture in which students are rewarded for prosocial behavior and taught non-confrontational strategies for responding to bullying.

In Chap. 3, DeOrnellas and Spurgin explore how teachers can best respond to bullying. There is considerable variability in how teachers deal with bullying, which DeOrnellas and Spurgin note is due in large part to differing attitudes; some teachers view bullying as a non-issue at their school, and others view bullying as cause for serious concern. Further, teacher training is emphasized as teachers may fail to intervene if they do not recognize bullying or are unaware of effective strategies for intervention. Focusing on school-wide intervention programs, DeOrnellas and Spurgin suggest teachers can help ensure the success of anti-bullying efforts by creating a classroom climate where all learners feel safe. Teachers can create a safe learning environment in a number of ways including intervening in the moment and not ignoring bullying episodes, consistently enforcing school-wide rules against bullying and disciplining the bully as necessary, fostering positive relationships with students, and serving as a role model to students by making it clear that bullying is never acceptable. As classroom-based curriculum can be an important part of a whole-school approach to bullying, teachers can also educate students about bullying and how to best intervene in bullying situations.

In Chap. 4, Trujillo-Jenks and Jenks describe the central role of principals and school resource officers (SROs) in school-wide anti-bullying efforts. As the heads of school, principals can begin a dialogue about bullying and lead continued discussions on how to best combat bullying on their campuses. Throughout the text, we pointed to importance of seeking multiple perspectives to best design prevention and intervention programs, and principals have the power to invite students, staff from across campus, and community members into these discussions so that they have a voice and a role in anti-bullying efforts. After the planning stage, principals can launch anti-bullying programs on their campus and try to ensure that all key players are aware of their roles and do their parts to appropriately implement the program. Principals can monitor the effectiveness of the program and make modifications as needed. Trujillo-Jenks and Jenks note that the school SRO is often a major partner to the principal in anti-bullying efforts. As trained law enforcement officers, SROs help to enforce the student code of conduct and are the first responders in case of an emergency on the school campus. Moreover, Trujillo-Jenks and Jenks advocate that SROs should play a key educational role as well as be one of the adults on campus with whom students can share reports of bullying.

In Chap. 5, DeOrnellas and Palomares outline the primary ways that school psychologists and school counselors can assist with anti-bullying efforts. Although DeOrnellas and Palomares are careful to delineate differences in these roles, both school psychologists and school counselors are often in the best position as school-based mental health professionals to intervene with bullies as well as victims. This intervention may take the form of individual counseling for bullies and victims as well as support groups for victims. School psychologists and school counselors can work with bullying-involved youth on skill development (e.g., emotion regulation, healthy relationships, and communication skills). At the universal level of intervention, DeOrnellas and Palomares suggest that school psychologists and school counselors can support teachers, administrators, and parents by providing sound strategies for dealing with specific bullying episodes and also offer training and resources for dealing with bullying more broadly.

In Chap. 6, Zinan focuses on the role that school nurses can play in bullying prevention and intervention. Bullies and victims may be frequent visitors to the office of the school nurse either because they are involved in physical altercations or present with health complaints like headaches or stomach aches. Thus, Zinan notes that school nurses can be integral to the identification of youth involved in bullying. Furthermore, nurses can provide a safe haven to victims who present to the nurses office by listening to their concerns and helping them problem-solve ways to best respond.

In Chap. 7, Kowalski provides evidence that bullying is quite common within all levels of athletic environments and offers ways that coaches can help to combat bullying on and off the field. Kowalski notes that coaches are often seen as one of the most influential figures in the lives of young athletes and, as such, serve as powerful role models. Given their position, coaches can contribute to anti-bullying campaigns by modeling positive behaviors, encouraging healthy relationships between athletes, and conveying that bullying is not acceptable. Kowalski suggests that one effective strategy may be for coaches to discuss the potential dangers of bullying and encourage bystander intervention.

Above, we summarized the various roles of key players in school-wide prevention and intervention efforts. As highlighted above as well as in Chap. 4, the principal can help ensure that all of these key players are able to have a voice in designing and implementing their school's anti-bullying program. Additionally, the principal can foster collaborations and encourage all of these key players to actively participate in the school's anti-bullying program. These points are further expanded on below in our discussion of successful programs and suggestions for program implementation.

Given that bullying is best viewed from a social-ecological perspective, there are many potential contributors to anti-bullying campaigns. This text reviewed some commonly overlooked perspectives (e.g., school nurses, coaches), but there are still other potential contributors for which a detailed discussion is beyond the scope of the book. The next section highlights the importance of considering other potential contributors to anti-bullying efforts.

## Widening the Circle: Other Contributors to Anti-bullying Efforts

In addition to students and key school staff members already considered, anti-bullying campaigns can benefit from an even wider range of contributors including education support professionals, parents, and community members. Giving these parties a voice in designing anti-bullying programs brings additional expertise and resources to the planning phase. Further, education support professionals, parents, and community members can be active in the implementation of prevention and intervention programs.

Education support professionals can help to guide the success of anti-bullying campaigns. Paraeducators, food service professionals, clerical/administrative staff, custodians, and bus drivers all fall under the umbrella of education support providers. Education support professionals are often left out of school-wide anti-bullying programs, but there are a number of reasons that their participation should be part of whole-school anti-bullying programs (Bradshaw, Waasdorp, O'Brennan, & Gulemetova, 2011). One such reason is that students sometimes feel more comfortable approaching education support professionals about bullying than they do teachers or someone they perceive in a position of power. Additionally, bullying often takes place in unstructured areas of the school that are often under the supervision of education support professionals (e.g., playground, cafeteria).

There is increasing awareness that the different subgroups of education support professionals can each play a role in anti-bullying campaigns. Bradshaw et al. (2011) stated that "to make intervention and prevention efforts more specific to ESPs' [education support professionals'] job placements, it may help for schools to directly collaborate with ESP subgroups (e.g., school transportation staff, food service staff) on bullying intervention and prevention strategies so that efforts can be streamlined and made more pertinent to staff members' roles" (p. 17). We now briefly detail the roles of the various subgroups, noting the implications for anti-bullying efforts.

Paraeducators, such as teacher aides, assist with instruction and student services working under the guidance of teachers and other professional school staff (NEA, n.d.-b). Of all the categories of education support professionals, paraeducators reported being most likely to observe bullying incidents. In fact, paraeducators may be even more likely than teachers to witness bullying and thus may frequently be in the position to intervene to stop bullying episodes as they are unfolding.

Food service professionals also commonly observe bullying. One food service professional reported that "I have witnessed physical and verbal bullying in the cafeteria, especially when adult presence is low … this usually happens during breakfast when we have a limited staff on duty. Name calling and pushing and shoving are typical things that we deal with" (Leff, Power, Costigan, & Manz, 2003, p. 2). Given the lunchroom is unstructured, students may feel exempt from school rules at meal times when food service workers and paraprofessionals may be in charge, further necessitating training of these individuals in bullying prevention.

School clerical staff including secretaries, administrative assistants, and receptionists often work with bullying-involved youth and their parents. In waiting to see school administrators, students and parents often share reports of bullying with school office staff. The significance of school office staff was conveyed by a NEA (n.d.-a) report that noted "with a shortage of counselors in many schools, clerical service professionals often become the informal counselor to the bully, the target, and their parents at a highly emotional time" (p. 1). Likewise, the school custodial staff may play a role in bullying prevention and intervention efforts. A great deal of bullying may take place in school bathrooms, and custodial staff may be aware of some of these instances of bullying. Similarly, custodial staff may encounter victimized youth who have fled to secluded areas of the school such as a closet (NEA, n.d.-b).

Beyond the immediate school campus, bullying often occurs on buses as students commute to and from school. A survey from the National Association for Pupil Transportation indicated that over 50% of members thought bullying was a serious concern on their buses (Martin, 2011). Despite the problem of bullying on school buses, school policies rarely address the role of the bus driver.

Throughout this text we have advocated for bringing together multiple voices in the design of anti-bullying campaigns, and as outlined above, education support professionals should be included in these conversations. Although 35% of education support professionals reported having been confronted with student bullying concerns within the last month, they also reported feeling less confident in intervening than did teachers (Bradshaw et al., 2011). Even when schools have bullying policies and programs, education support professionals are often not involved and receive much more limited training than do teachers and other school staff (Bradshaw et al., 2011).

In several of the preceding chapters, the role of parents in anti-bullying efforts was mentioned, and we wanted to further highlight their importance here. In terms of bullies, parents can either encourage or discourage aggressive behavior (Espelage & Swearer, 2008). Parents may influence their children's aggressive behavior both directly and indirectly through modeling (Griffin & Gross, 2004; Underwood, 2011). Further, parents can influence bystander behavior by encouraging their children to be active defenders. As Ross noted in Chap. 2, parents can teach their children strategies to stand up for themselves and others. In addition to influencing the behavior of bullies and bystanders, parents can have a tremendous role in the lives of victimized youth. Children may be more comfortable sharing their experiences of peer maltreatment with parents rather than teachers and school staff. Thus, parents can be advocates for children who experience bullying (Lee, 2004).

There is a strong need for collaboration between parents and educational staff. By including parents in anti-bullying campaigns, it is much more likely the skills and lessons centered around bullying that are taught in the school will be reinforced at home. Also, this will allow for parents and educators to work more closely together. A common strategy used by teachers and other school staff is to contact the parents of those involved in bullying incidents (Rigby & Bauman, 2010). In some cases, parents are the ones to contact the school about bullying, and fostering parental involvement in anti-bullying efforts will hopefully garner greater feelings of being supported and heard. When schools fail to consider the role of the parent in anti-bullying efforts, parents often report being unsure of who to contact regarding bullying-related issues and often report teachers and administrators are insensitive to the plight of victimized youth (Lee, 2004). Involving parents in the planning and implementation of anti-bullying campaigns provides an important perspective and has the strong potential to benefit both students and school staff.

Moving beyond the home and school, bullying prevention and intervention programs can benefit from drawing on the expertise and resources of the broader community (Espelage & Swearer, 2008; Gibson, Flaspohler, & Watts, 2015). There are so many potential sources of support from the community, and we just outline a few here. For instance, leaders of extracurricular activities (e.g., Girl Scouts, theater groups) play an important socializing role in children's lives and can help encourage prosocial behavior in youth (Holt et al., 2013). Just as school nurses are important, children's doctors may also be able to identify and guide victimized youth. Schools may also bring in community members such as college athletes to serve as positive role models who emphasize anti-bullying messages. In an extremely innovative way of involving community members, the WITS Rock Solid Primary Program invites police officers into the classroom; students are then ceremoniously appointed to be special officers charged with keeping the school safe and helping peers in need (Holt et al., 2013). From a program evaluation perspective, schools can partner with researchers to assess the efficacy of their existing programs and offer recommendations for improvement.

At the broadest level, governmental support can enhance the probability that bullying prevention and intervention programs will succeed. In the United States, there are no federal laws that directly address school bullying (stopbullying.gov, n.d.). As mentioned in Chap. 4, there is an exception if bullying takes the form of discriminatory harassment based on characteristics such as sex and race. Each state has its own laws for combatting bullying. This is in contrast to countries like Norway and Australia who have integrated national policies for bullying prevention (Cross et al., 2011). Based on the success of such programs, Spiel, Salmivalli, and Smith (2011) conclude that "it turns out that for sustainable violence prevention, national strategies actively supported by the government are needed" (p. 381). These sentiments point to the importance of government support of anti-bullying campaigns and suggest that anti-bullying collaborations could be expanded to include politicians and other government officials.

## Characteristics of Successful Anti-bullying Programs

Although a number of programs that have received empirical support were outlined in the preceding chapters, we offer broad guidelines for program selection and share the common characteristics of successful programs rather than suggesting any specific program. We do so because a number of diverse programs have shown marked reductions of bullying, and as Holt et al. (2013) note there is "no single program or set of strategies that has been found to eliminate bullying" (p. 247). Additionally, programs are more likely to demonstrate decreases in bullying when a school's culture and needs are considered prior to selecting a program. The importance of program fit is reflected in published guidance for schools selecting anti-bullying approaches, in which decision makers are urged to consider "the history, context, and unique needs of the school relative to the context in which the program has proven relatively successful" (Ansary, Elias, Greene, & Green, 2015, p. 28).

In some circumstances, it may be helpful for schools to adapt features of multiple programs. Holt et al. (2013) suggest that "different approaches may address different aspects of the problem suggesting that multiple or combined approaches may be needed" (p. 240). In Chap. 2, Ross presented evidence for a combined approach in which his newly developed Bullying Prevention in Positive Behavior Support was used in conjunction with the well-established school-wide Positive Behavioral Interventions and Supports system to encourage more effective bystander intervention.

While many bullying intervention programs have had positive results, it is important to note that there have been mixed results for the efficacy of anti-bullying programs (Smith, 2011). Not all programs are successful; some have no effects and others even result in an increase in bullying (Vreeman & Carroll, 2007). Given the costs associated with anti-bullying programs, a growing amount of research has sought to identify the characteristics and elements of successful programs. From this research, one of the most consistent findings is that a multi-disciplinary approach to combatting bullying is most effective (Ansary et al., 2015; Vreeman & Carroll, 2007). The value of bringing together different perspectives and resources across campus is the overarching theme of this book, and we have considered many points of view that have been typically neglected in the literature as well as practice (e.g., school nurses, school psychologists, and coaches). Thus, we now focus on other traits of successful programs, noting the role of students, teachers, and other key players in implementation. We also highlight the importance for open channels for communication and collaboration between key players.

An extremely consistent finding in the anti-bullying literature is that successful prevention and intervention programs operate at multiple levels (Ansary et al., 2015; Biggs & Vernberg, 2010). As outlined in Chap. 5, there are three tiers in the intervention spectrum. Universal prevention efforts (Tier 1) are aimed at the entire student body irrespective of risk for bullying involvement. Tier 2 and Tier 3 are more targeted approaches allowing for more intensive intervention efforts (Gest & Davidson, 2011). Selected prevention efforts (Tier 2) are aimed at students who demonstrate one or more risk factors for bullying, whereas indicated prevention efforts (Tier 3) are aimed at those who are already demonstrating bullying behaviors. A multi-level approach is most effective when there is participation across the campus from a multi-disciplinary team.

In terms of planning a bullying prevention program, universal elements may include establishing anti-bullying policies for the school and training students on these as well as providing an anti-bullying-based curriculum (Biggs & Vernberg, 2010). As discussed in Chap. 3, teachers are often responsible for administering classroom-based lessons on bullying. However, school counselors may also be brought in to provide guidance lessons on bullying as noted in Chap. 5. These universal intervention efforts often seek to foster a more positive school culture (Ansary et al., 2015; Biggs & Vernberg, 2010). School counselors and school psychologists are often responsible for administering more targeted intervention efforts. Selected intervention efforts may include social skills training for those at risk of bullying involvement (Biggs & Vernberg, 2010). At the indicated level, school counselors and school psychologists may need to tailor individual interventions based on the characteristics and needs of bullying-involved youth. For example, school counselors may focus on developing emotion regulation skills when working with a child high on reactive aggression who quickly becomes upset and jumps to respond at any perceived wrongdoing. However, a different approach would be needed when working with a child high on instrumental aggression who may appear socially skilled and use aggression to gain status (Biggs & Vernberg, 2010).

Even though multi-level programs are often most effective, principals and school administrators may favor single-level interventions from a cost perspective (Vreeman & Carroll, 2007). Multi-level approaches require more in terms of personnel and resource investment. Teachers can implement classroom curriculum at little cost to the school; however, these limited efforts are unlikely to be successful (Biggs & Vernberg, 2010).

Similarly, program duration and intensity influence the success of anti-bullying programs (Vreeman & Carroll, 2007). In their meta-analytic review of school-based anti-bullying programs, Ttofi and Farrington

(2010) found that programs needed to be of sufficient duration and intensity to be effective. There appears to be a dose-response relationship such that limited efforts have little effect. For example, schools may try to quickly address bullying problems, and some intervention programs have been limited to showing a single film in the classroom or a one-time assembly on bullying, which are not adequate ways of addressing bullying (Strein & Koehler, 2007; Vreeman & Carroll, 2007). The greatest reductions in bullying are evident in programs that include numerous elements that are sustained throughout the academic year (Ttofi & Farrington, 2011).

For a program to succeed, school policies related to all forms of bullying must be in place and enforced (Ansary et al., 2015; Ttofi & Farrington, 2011). If schools are lax in disciplining bullies, bullying is likely to continue. On the other hand, if schools are firm in disciplining bullies, bullying is likely to decrease. For the most effective discipline of bullies, teachers, administrators, and other school staff should share the belief that school bullying is problematic and consistently enforce the school code of conduct (Sullivan, 2011).

Although Ttofi and Farrington (2010) found larger effect sizes were associated with firm discipline, some have called this finding into question. Ttofi and Farrington (2012) clarified that imposing sanctions for bullies does not imply a zero tolerance policy. For instance, one sanction may be simply speaking with the bully about the incident or otherwise encouraging him/her to reflect upon the situation (Ansary et al., 2015). Ttofi and Farrington (2012) acknowledge zero tolerance policies that assign predetermined sanctions (e.g., suspension, expulsion) without considering the situation are often ineffective. Zero tolerance policies may be ineffective because they contribute to an adversarial climate, in which communication is limited and peers may fear reporting bullying due to the consequences (Twemlow & Sacco, 2010). Under such a climate, peers may not report bullying due to fears about the associated punishments. Rather than a zero tolerance policy, Ansary et al. (2015) suggest punishment for bullying behavior should be graduated and reflect the severity of the incident.

In enforcing anti-bullying policies, it is important that schools not ignore unstructured areas such as the cafeteria and playgrounds (Bradshaw et al., 2011). Simply increasing supervision on the playground has been associated with decreased bullying on school campuses (Howe, Haymes, & Tenor, 2006; Ttofi & Farrington, 2011). Students may feel immune from rules in unstructured areas, and increasing supervision may serve as a reminder of the school's anti-bullying policies. Drawing on this research, the KiVa Anti-bullying Program supplies vests to those supervising at recess to increase their visibility and further reinforce the school's stance against bullying (Clarkson et al., 2015). As education support providers often supervise the unstructured school areas as discussed above, it is important to offer support and training to these staff members.

Program awareness and training are also critical factors to consider (Ansary et al., 2015; Ttofi & Farrington, 2011). Survey research has revealed that although schools may have policies against bullying in place, teachers and other school staff may be unaware of their school's particular policies (Bradshaw et al., 2011). Efficacious programs often include training on school policies as well as how to intervene in bullying episodes. If teachers and staff are confident in their abilities to intervene, they are much more likely to do so (Ansary et al., 2015; Bradshaw et al., 2011). Schools should assess the training needs of their teachers and staff as well as provide appropriate resources and in so doing consider the expertise and needs of multiple players at school including nurses, school psychologists, counselors, and coaches.

Certain types of peer intervention can also contribute to the efficacy of school anti-bullying programs. As highlighted in Chap. 2, encouraging bystander intervention is often a successful strategy for discouraging bullying (see also Ansary et al., 2015). However, some forms of peer intervention may be ineffective (Ttofi & Farrington, 2011). For instance, peer mediation is a strategy that should be discouraged as it ignores power differentials in bringing together the bullying and victim (Bauman, Rigby, & Hoppa, 2008; see Chap. 5 for further discussion). Thus, additional research is needed to determine which peer intervention strategies are beneficial (Ttofi & Farrington, 2012).

## Potential Obstacles to Implementing Whole-School Anti-bullying Campaigns

Just as for any program, there are a number of possible impediments to implementing a whole-school anti-bullying campaign. One of the largest challenges may be school- and district-level priorities (O'Connell, Boat, & Warner, 2009). Teachers and school officials may focus on traditional domains of academics such as reading and math and as such may believe that anti-bullying efforts are not directly connected to their school's mission. Indeed, there is a great deal of pressure to center efforts on academic areas due to the No Child Left Behind Act and state testing schedules

(Jaycox et al., 2006; O'Connell et al., 2009). This emphasis on academic development may deter from programs focused on social-emotional development, and there may be limited support for such efforts unless clear connections can be made to improved academic performance. Tension may be experienced as a result of these decisions as revealed in a focus group study in which teachers reported it was critically important to combat school bullying but noted that resources are often focused elsewhere due to testing demands (Rosen, Scott, & DeOrnellas, in press).

Funding is often aligned with school- and district-level priorities. Implementing a multi-level anti-bullying program can be quite costly. Depending on the program adopted, there may be added expenses for materials and technical assistance (O'Connell et al., 2009). If there are not adequate resources available, programs are likely to fail (Biggs & Vernberg, 2010). Lack of resources for training in particular may inhibit program success (O'Connell et al., 2009). As noted in Chap. 5, ineffective interventions such as self-esteem building for bullies or peer mediation may be initiated when school staff members have not been trained in best practices. To help with training and other program needs, schools may turn to community agencies. Additionally, although funding opportunities are limited, schools may pursue grants through private foundations or federal funding to support programs (Biggs & Vernberg, 2010; O'Connell et al., 2009). Albeit challenging, completing a cost-benefit analysis may help schools gain support for their programs (Ttofi & Farrington, 2011).

Another common stumbling block for bullying prevention and intervention programs is a lack of buy-in from school staff (Howe et al., 2006). Support from teachers and staff across the campus is necessary to ensure program adherence as discussed in Chap. 3. Fagan and Mihalic (2003) suggest that "because programs compete with class time and instructional demands, teachers must be convinced of the utility of the program; otherwise, they may fail to fully implement the program or even implement it at all" (p. 238). If not invested in the program, teachers and other school staff may object to any changes in their roles resulting from program implementation (Strein & Koehler, 2007), which may result in the program being ineffective.

Employing a multi-disciplinary approach that incorporates all levels of school staff may also result in challenging issues related to a school's hierarchy, which could impede program success. If teachers and school staff do not believe the program is a priority of the school or do not feel supported by the administration, then they are unlikely to be committed to program implementation (Sullivan, 2011). A lack of communication and collaboration can also be detrimental. In some schools, administrators may ignore important perspectives and select a program on their own without consultation. For instance, in Chap. 5, DeOrnellas and Palomares noted that school psychologists and school counselors are often left out of selecting anti-bullying programs even though they have expertise in student mental health.

Likewise, there may be continued difficulties with communication even after a multi-disciplinary, multi-level program is selected. Sometimes teachers and school staff may be unaware of when a referral is needed. Even when options for referrals are clear, some may be hesitant to refer for fear the student will believe trust has been violated. This sentiment was evident in Maunder and Tattersall's (2010) interviews with teachers in which one commented that she believed it was important to "keep it [reports of bullying] confidential because they come back time and time … to talk to me and I think … if they think they've got your confidentiality … they will talk to you" (p. 121). Teachers were also bothered that they sometimes did not hear what happened after making a referral with one teacher noting that "one of the things we as a school are not very wonderful at is passing information on or back … and sometimes you think so-and-so's had a really rough day, I managed to solve it for him … and I passed the problem on … because that's what we've got to do … what happened? … and sometimes you don't necessarily know what happened to him or her … to put in that amount of effort … should I really get involved and wound up about something and care enough … for me not to get a response?" (Maunder & Tattersall, 2010, p. 121). Thus, there can be a great deal of frustration when either there is a lack of communication about referrals or school staff members are not made aware of their roles and responsibilities in relation to bullying.

## Recommendations for Overcoming Challenges and Implementing a Whole-School Anti-bullying Initiative

Administrators should encourage teachers and staff members' commitment to the school's anti-bullying efforts. Above we noted that a lack of buy-in from staff can have deleterious effects on program efficacy, and Espelage and Swearer (2008) mirror this sentiment in advising that "any program will fail if the adults in the system are not supportive" (p. 348).

However, when teachers and staff members are committed to the program, the chances of success are so much greater.

There are a number of ways that school administrators can help garner support for anti-bullying programs. Principals and other administrators should seek to demonstrate how the program is connected to the school's overall mission as doing so will help to convey the importance of the program (Fagan & Mihalic, 2003). Likewise, it is imperative that administrators communicate their own support for anti-bullying initiatives because teachers and other staff members are unlikely to implement the program if they do not believe it is a priority of the administration (Sullivan, 2011). In addition, giving parties a voice in program development can be critical for gaining their support (Twemlow & Sacco, 2010). Involvement of all key players and stakeholders best begins during the planning phase of the program (Sullivan, 2011). Administrators can seek input from diverse perspectives including students, teachers, school resource officers, school counselors, school psychologists, nurses, coaches, education support professionals, and parents. Members of each of these groups can be invited to join an anti-bullying committee to assist planning and implementation of the program. Considering the viewpoints of diverse parties makes a program stronger and also increases program buy-in.

Moreover, administrators should work to maintain open channels of communication in their schools and encourage diverse collaborations (Fagan & Mihalic, 2003). Teachers and other staff members can become discouraged when communication regarding anti-bullying initiatives is lacking. An important first step is to make teachers and all staff members aware of their roles in the school's anti-bullying initiative (Maunder & Tattersall, 2010). In so doing, it is vital to acknowledge staff at all levels can play an important role in combatting bullying (Maunder & Tattersall, 2010). Throughout this text, we have repeatedly seen that many school staff members can play a critical role in bullying prevention and intervention. Thus, administrators should train all staff in the school's anti-bullying policies and provide resources to help them intervene in bullying episodes (Bradshaw et al., 2011). Teachers and staff members who believe that their school has provided valuable resources are more comfortable intervening when confronted with bullying (O'Brennan et al., 2014).

One key way to open channels of communication is to form collaborative partnerships. Espelage and Swearer (2008) suggest that forming school-home as well as school-community partnerships can be an incredibly valuable asset to anti-bullying efforts. However, it is also important to form these partnerships among school staff. This will help maintain open channels of communication, which is advantageous for sharing concerns about students and discussing ideas for intervention (O'Brennan et al., 2014). Sharing ideas from diverse perspectives can allow for more effective interventions (Maunder & Tattersall, 2010).

Open communication and collaboration help to foster feelings of school connectedness and a positive school climate, which are critical factors for success of any type of anti-bullying initiative. Staff members who feel strong connectedness to the school are much more likely to stand up against bullying (Bradshaw et al., 2011; O'Brennan et al., 2014). School connectedness has been conceptualized as "the belief held by adults in the school that they are valued as individuals and professionals involved in the learning process" (Bradshaw et al., 2011, p. viii). Those who feel a greater sense of belonging at school are more likely to intervene in bullying episodes as are those who believe that other staff members would also intervene in the face of bullying. These findings suggest that school-wide bullying programs would benefit tremendously by focusing on building and maintaining positive relationships between staff members at all levels. Not only will this lead a more proactive stance against bullying, but it will also model positive relationships for students. Therefore, connectedness promoting activities and efforts can be extremely impactful (O'Brennan et al., 2014).

Throughout this text we have highlighted how multiple key players can offer unique insights and different approaches to intervening in bullying. Each staff member at school can play an important role in bullying prevention and intervention. We wanted to end by sharing the sage advice offered by Espelage and Swearer and encourage all school staff to consider that: "if the adults in the school are enthusiastic, positive, and emotionally healthy and have a united focus on doing what is in the best interests of the students ... this environment in itself will help create a prevention-oriented atmosphere and will help prevent problems" (p. 348).

## References

Ansary, N. S., Elias, M. J., Greene, M. B., & Green, S. (2015). Guidance for schools selecting antibullying approaches: Translating evidence-based strategies to contemporary implementation realities. *Educational Researcher*, *44*, 27–36.

Bauman, S., Rigby, K., & Hoppa, K. (2008). US teachers' and school counselors' strategies for handling school bullying incidents. *Educational Psychology, 28*, 837–856. doi:10.1080/01443410802379085.

Biggs, B. K., & Vernberg, E. M. (2010). Preventing and treating bullying and victimization: Best practices and future directions. In E. M. Vernberg & B. K. Biggs (Eds.), *Preventing and treating bullying and victimization*. (pp. 337–355). New York: Oxford University Press.

Bradshaw, C., Waasdorp, T. O'Brennan, L., & Gulemetova, M. (2011). *Findings from the National Education Association's nationwide study of bullying: Teachers' and Education Support Professionals' perspectives on bullying and prevention*. Report prepared for the National Education Association (NEA). Washington, DC. Retrieved from https://www.nea.org/assets/docs/2010_Survey.pdf

Clarkson, S., Axford, N., Berry, V., Edwards, R. T., Bjornstad, G., Wrigley, Z.,... Hutchings, J. (2015). Effectiveness and micro-costing of the KiVa school-based bullying prevention programme in Wales: Study protocol for a pragmatic definitive parallel group cluster randomised controlled trial. *BMC Public Health, 16*. doi:10.1186/s12889-016-2746-1.

Cross, D., Epstein, M., Hearn, L., Slee, P., Shaw, T., & Monks, H. (2011). National safe schools framework: Policy and practice to reduce bullying in Australian schools. *The International Journal of Behavioral Development, 35*, 398–404. doi:10.1177/0165025411407456.

Espelage, D. L., & Swearer, S. M. (2008). Current perspectives on linking school bullying research to effective prevention strategies. In T. W. Miller (Ed.), *School violence and primary prevention* (pp. 335–353). New York: Springer Press.

Fagan, A., & Mihalic, S. (2003). Strategies for enhancing the adoption of school-based prevention programs: Lessons learned from the blueprints for violence prevention replications of the life skills training program. *Journal of Community Psychology, 31*, 235–253.

Gest, S. D., & Davidson, A. J. (2011). A developmental perspective on risk, resilience, and prevention. In M. K. Underwood & L. H. Rosen (Eds.), *Social development: Relationships in infancy, childhood, and adolescence* (pp. 427–454). New York: Guilford Press.

Gibson, J. E., Flaspohler, P. D., & Watts, V. (2015). Engaging youth in bullying prevention through community-based participatory research. *Family and Community Health, 38*, 120–130. doi:10.1097/FCH.0000000000000048.

Griffin, R. S., & Gross, A. M. (2004). Childhood bullying: Current empirical findings and future directions for research. *Aggression and Violent Behavior, 9*, 379–400. doi:10.1016/S1359-1789(03)00033-8.

Holt, M. K., Raczynskib, K., Frey, K. S., Hymel, S., & Limber, S. P. (2013). School and community-based approaches for preventing bullying. *Journal of School Violence, 12*, 238–252. doi:10.1080/15388220.2013.792271.

Howe, E., Haymes, E., & Tenor, T. (2006). Bullying: Best practices for prevention and intervention in schools. In C. Franklin, M. B. Harris, & P. Allen-Meares (Eds.), *The school services source-book: A guide for school-based professionals* (pp. 461–467). Cambridge, MA: Oxford University Press.

Jaycox, L. H., McCaffrey, D. F., Ocampo, B. W., Shelley, G. A., Blake, S. M., Peterson, D. J., … Kub, J. E. (2006). Challenges in the evaluation and implementation of school-based prevention and intervention programs on sensitive topics. *American Journal of Evaluation, 27*, 320–336. doi:10.1177/1098214006291010.

Jimenez Barbero, J. A., Ruiz Hernandez, J. A., Esteban, B. L., & Garcia, M. P. (2012). Effectiveness of antibullying school programmes: A systematic review by evidence levels. *Children and Youth Services Review, 34*, 1646–1658. doi:10.1016/j.childyouth.2012.04.025.

Kub, J., & Feldman, M. A. (2015). Bullying prevention: A call for collaborative efforts between school nurses and school psychologists. *Psychology in the Schools, 52*, 658–671. doi:10.1002/pits.21853.

Lee, C. (2004). *Preventing bullying in schools: A guide for teachers and other professionals.* Thousand Oaks, CA: Sage.

Leff, S., Power, T., Costigan, T., & Manz, P. (2003). *Assessing the climate of the playground and lunchroom: Implications for bullying prevention programming.* Retrieved from http://www.nea.org/assets/docs/ESP_STOP_Bully_Food-final.pdf

Martin, M. (2011). *Summary of bus driver's needs: Recent survey results.* Retrieved from https://safesupportivelearning.ed.gov/events/conferences-learning-events/creating-safe-and-respectful-environment-our-nations-school-buses

Maunder, R., & Tattersall, A. J. (2010). Staff experiences of managing bullying in secondary schools: The importance of internal and external relationships in facilitating intervention. *Educational and Child Psychology, 27*, 116–128.

NEA. (n.d.-a). *Clerical services/administrative ESPs and bullying prevention.* Retrieved from http://www.nea.org/home/63938.htm

NEA. (n.d.-b). *ESP bullying perspectives research.* Retrieved from http://www.nea.org/home/64557.htm

O'Brennan, L. M., Waasdorp, T. E., & Bradshaw, C. P. (2014). Strengthening bullying prevention through school staff connectedness. *Journal of Educational Psychology, 106*, 870–880. doi:10.1037/a0035957.

O'Connell, E., Boat, T., & Warner, K. (Eds.). (2009). *Preventing mental, emotional, and behavioral disorders among young people.* Washington, DC: National Academies Press.

Richard, J. F., Schneider, B. H., & Mallet, P. (2012). Revisiting the whole-school approach to bullying: Really looking at the whole school. *School Psychology International, 33*, 263–284. doi:10.1177/0143034311415906.

Rigby, K., & Bauman, S. (2010). How school personnel tackle cases of bullying. A critical examination. In S. R. Jimerson, S. M. Swearer, & D. L. Espelage (Eds.),

*Handbook of bullying in schools: An international perspective* (pp. 455–467). New York: Routledge.

Smith, P. K. (2011). Why interventions to reduce bullying and violence in schools may (or may not) succeed: Comments on this special section. *International Journal of Behavioral Development, 35*, 419–423. doi:10.1177/0165025411407459.

Spiel, C., Salmivalli, C., & Smith, P. (2011). Translational research: National strategies for violence prevention in school. *International Journal of Behavioral Development, 35*, 381–382. doi:10.1177/0165025411407556.

stopbullying.gov. (n.d.). *Policies and laws.* Retrieved from http://www.stopbullying.gov/laws/

Strein, W., & Koehler, J. (2007). *Best practices in developing prevention strategies for school psychology practice.* Retrieved from http://www.education.umd.edu/Academics/Faculty/Bios/facData/CHSE/strein/BestPracticesforSchoolPsycPrac.pdf

Sullivan, K. (2011). *The anti-bullying handbook.* Thousand Oaks, CA: Sage.

Ttofi, M. M., & Farrington, D. P. (2010). School bullying: Risk factors, theories and interventions. In F. Brookman, M. Maguire, H. Pierpoint, & T. H. Bennett (Eds.), *Handbook of crime* (pp. 427–457). Cullompton, Devon: Willan.

Ttofi, M. M., & Farrington, D. P. (2011). Effectiveness of school-based programs to reduce bullying: A systematic and meta-analytic review. *Journal of Experimental Criminology, 7*, 27–56. doi:10.1007/s11292-010-9109-1.

Ttofi, M. M., & Farrington, D. P. (2012). Bullying prevention programs: The importance of peer intervention, disciplinary methods and age variations. *Journal of Experimental Criminology, 8*, 443–462. doi:10.1007/s11292-012-9161.

Twemlow, S. W., & Sacco, F. (2010). Creating and administering successful policy strategies for school anti-bullying programs. In E. M. Vernberg & B. K. Biggs (Eds.), *Preventing and treating bullying and victimization* (pp. 297–318). New York: Oxford University Press.

Underwood, M. K. (2011). Aggression. In M. K. Underwood & L. H. Rosen (Eds.), *Social development* (pp. 207–234). New York: Guilford.

Vreeman, R. C., & Carroll, A. E. (2007). Do school-based interventions prevent bullying? A systematic review. *Archives of Pediatric and Adolescent Medicine, 161*, 78–88. doi:10.1001/archpedi.161.1.78.

# Index




L.H. Rosen et al. (eds.), *Bullying in School*,
DOI 10.1057/978-1-137-59298-9

Printed by Printforce, the Netherlands